TREND
FOLLOWING
Masters

Also by Michael W. Covel

Trend Following: How to Make a Fortune in Bull, Bear, and Black Swan Markets (5 editions)

The Complete TurtleTrader: How 23 Novice Investors Became Overnight Millionaires (2 editions)

The Little Book of Trading: Trend Following Strategy for Big Winnings

Trend Commandments: Trading for Exceptional Returns

Trend Following Analytics: Performance Proof for the World's Most Controversial & Successful Black Swan Trading Strategy

Trend Following Mindset: The Genius of Legendary Trader Tom Basso

Broke: The New American Dream (Documentary)

Trend Following Radio Podcast

TREND
FOLLOWING

VOLUME ONE

Trading Conversations

MICHAEL W. COVEL

HARRIMAN HOUSE LTD
3 Viceroy Court
Bedford Road
Petersfield
Hampshire
GU32 3LJ
GREAT BRITAIN
Tel: +44 (0)1730 233870

Email: enquiries@harriman-house.com
Website: harriman.house

First published in 2023.
Copyright © Michael W. Covel

Hardback ISBN: 978-0-85719-816-7
eBook ISBN: 978-0-85719-817-4

British Library Cataloguing in Publication Data
A CIP catalogue record for this book can be obtained from the British Library.

*To all those hopeful investors and
traders who think it's possible to
predict tomorrow… please enjoy
this kick in the ass.*

Every owner of a physical copy of this edition of

can download the eBook for free direct from us at Harriman House, in a DRM-free format that can be read on any eReader, tablet or smartphone.

Simply head to:

ebooks.harriman-house.com/trendfollowmasters1

to get your copy now.

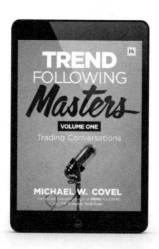

CONTENTS

INTRODUCTION

I'M LUCKY. I get to talk to people. All kinds of interesting, bright, accomplished, and successful people.

Sometimes in person, sometimes on Zoom, sometimes on the phone. It's become my passion, my obsession.

How did this start?

After my first book *Trend Following* (2004), I picked up the phone one day in early 2005 and contacted 15 traders managing collectively around $15 billion. Most agreed to meet with me. On my dime I started flying around the world to talk with trading legends like David Harding, Toby Crabel, and Larry Hite. **Lots of interviews.**

Then my second book, *The Complete Turtle Trader* started. That required getting the secretive Turtle traders to open up and talk. **More interviews.**

Then I started a documentary film project that spanned three years around the world and **100 filmed interviews.**

Then I started a podcast on a lark in 2012. That podcast is now over 1,000 episodes with **hundreds of interviews** and millions of listens, covering topics from trading to psychology, economics to health, and even the CEO of Dunkin' Donuts (one of my favorite interviews). I'm proud to say that I have interviewed so far seven Nobel Prize winners.

But I started with trend following and it's always my core. What follows are some of the most important interviews I've ever conducted about trend following trading. The pages that follow contain the wisdom you need to navigate a chaotic world, and to find the big profits.

That said, if you are looking for candlestick secrets, chart reading nonsense, day trading silliness, or any other get-rich-quick fix, you will be bitterly disappointed—left only to troll me on Twitter.

On the other hand, for you brave souls who want to take a shot at the big time, the pages that follow contain real-world trading wisdom for real people set on achieving real results.

I hope you enjoy the conversation.

Michael Covel
February 2023

Note: If you would like to reach me directly, I can be found here:

www.trendfollowing.com/contact

To receive my free interactive trend following presentation, send a picture of your receipt for this book to **receipt@trendfollowing.com**.

CHAPTER 1

BILL DREISS

Surfing the Waves

BILL DREISS graduated from MIT with a degree in electrical engineering. He then went on to Harvard Business School where he was attracted to Bayesian Decision Theory and operations research. After graduating he went to work for a think tank in California that was doing computer modeling of strategic and tactical warfare, and that introduced him to state-of-the-art modeling. Bill says of his time at the think tank: "We were working under air force contracts and we were exploring different kinds of tactics in missile firing strategies, or ground wars in Europe and that sort of thing. Most of the work was done by young engineers with mathematical backgrounds."

Michael Note

I knew the name Bill Dreiss from the performance tracking services, but I had never talked to him. Niels Kaastrup-Larsen of Top Traders Unplugged connected me. This is how life works—it's all random. Be prepared because life is six degrees of separation. But in the trend following world for me, it's one degree.

Michael Covel: I want to jump in with a philosophical discussion about one of your heroes, if you'd refer to him that way: Benoit Mandelbrot. In 2008, he made a point about efficient market theory proponents. He said they'd like to take the events of 2008 and sweep them under the rug like they're an act of God and forget about them. I'm sure you connect with that. Why don't you tell us where Mandelbrot's going with that comment?

Bill Dreiss: What he's saying is that from a statistical point of view, the markets are not random walks. There's a bias in the markets—a persistence that leads mathematically to what we call fat tails. This is an intrinsic characteristic of the market. It's not an exception or something that's out of the ordinary.

When I was working for Mandelbrot, I applied his idea of fractal dimension to different markets. I did an analysis of all the markets to see if they had, essentially, a fractal dimension that indicated that they were persistent. After analyzing all the markets and finding that to be true, to varying degrees, I formulated what I considered to be a scientific argument for Mandelbrot's conjecture. What he's saying is that the efficient market hype guys got it wrong when they were assuming that the markets were random.

> There's a persistence in the markets that leads to fat tails.

Part of the reason, in my opinion, was that these top economists were unable to beat the market themselves, so they decided that nobody else should beat it either. And so they came up with the idea that the markets were purely random.

What's notable is that Mandelbrot's first paper on fractal geometry dealt with the futures market in cotton. There was a popular book called *The Random Nature of Stock-Market Prices* that was published in 1974. Mandelbrot was the dissenting voice in relation to the random walk theory of the markets at that time. Even now, the random walk seems to be embedded in the academic view.

It's long since been proven, not only by analysis but also by experience, that the random walk is not true, and the idea that the markets do in fact have fat tails is pretty much accepted, certainly among market participants.

That's what provides the basis for trend following. It says that trends persist longer than would be expected if it were a random distribution. It's true that the particular methodology I use is based upon fractal geometry, but the persistence in the markets is what makes any reasonable trend following system operational.

Michael: Let me focus on the word academic for a moment. If someone looks at your background—MIT, Harvard—they're going to see an academic pedigree, but you lean to the more practical side.

In your early career you worked in operations, research, defense contracting, and then you went off in another direction and killed it as an entrepreneur.

But what were you thinking while you were trading? You're making a lot of money over many decades, yet the academic folks are getting all the publicity. The wrong message was spreading. I'm not suggesting you or other trend followers were entirely ignored, but your work was largely anonymous for a long time. What were your private thoughts as you watched these academics going down this one path and here you are actually living it and seeing something entirely different?

> It's long since been proven that the random walk is not true.

Bill: You mentioned my academic pedigree, but I stepped out of that—just in time. I went to work for a think tank in California when I graduated from business school. We were doing state-of-the-art modeling for structure analysis and missile targeting. This was at the height of the Cold War. A lot of the work involved looking at problems from first principles—instead of taking existing tools, we redirected various techniques that led us into much more independent ways of thinking.

One of my early discoveries was that there are a number of topics on which the scientific consensus is not supported. The point is, I think, that to some extent academics are overeducated, in that they learn models in physics that they then try to apply to markets, but these models are not appropriate. Had they started at a more basic level in analyzing these things, they'd arrive at the same place as myself and other traders.

Michael: The freedom to explore different paths is what gave you the advantage.

Bill: That's exactly right. In fact, I've lived my life to maximize that freedom. I've had the opportunity to think about a lot of things independently of a structure that is in some ways fairly restrictive. The pressures of publishing deadlines and other commitments means most academics have a day job that keeps them from spending a lot of time doing creative thinking. I've benefited from not being in that institutionalized environment.

Talking to other CTAs (commodity trading advisors), I find there's a lot of similarity. I know of other CTAs who have been interested in physics and various other topics that had nothing to do with CTAs. They had original ideas on these topics that are not in the textbooks—but they are not crackery, because these are educated, intelligent people. There's another world out there that exists more or less independent of academia.

Michael: Before you devised your early trend following systems, what would've been the first example that you read about or the first person you understood as pioneering trend following—would it have been Donchian?

Bill: My boss at the think tank was a retired Air Force colonel who had come across Donchian, and he got me interested in his ideas. I had access to Air Force computers and I also read Edwards and Magee, the bible of technical analysis, and found it somewhat helpful. Although most of the patterns they used were informative, the only ones that counted for me were things like trend lines, and support and resistance. I set out to design a system that automated that kind of technical trading. That was my first system. My second system, the one that started in 1991, was based upon a more sophisticated analysis of the data that came from Mandelbrot, but generally contained the same features as my original model in terms of trend lines, and support and resistance.

Systems do better because they're more reliable.

Michael: Can I keep you on that early stage? I'm curious. I bring up Donchian and you bring up Edwards and Magee—two different approaches. When you first understood what Donchian was doing, did you go ahead and reverse engineer it and figure it all out for yourself?

Bill: Well, no, I think Donchian was moving average crossovers, if I remember correctly. It was pretty basic stuff. In the early days, simple systems worked well because nobody was using them. You're competing against discretionary traders who had all the impediments of that style of trading. Almost any system would beat the average discretionary trader. That changed over time as more and more people got into the business. But nevertheless, the business is pretty much the same as it was. It's a matter of designing a system and then sticking with it.

Michael: Let's talk more about those early-stage personal philosophies. In preparing to talk with you today, I started to think of isolation—in the sense that here you are, you're figuring out where you want to go. You've got a few pieces of information, a few data points from other people, you weren't necessarily in a collaborative team. You weren't calling up Bill Dunn, John W. Henry, and Ed Seykota— you were doing your own thing.

> **The hardest thing is to stick with your system.**

Bill: That's right. They were doing their own thing, too. We were all discovering the same phenomena. I know Ed Seykota and Marty [Bergin], made the same discovery—or should I say, they confirmed the discovery of Donchian—that a system would generally beat discretionary traders, or most traders in terms of the market.

This has been discussed extensively by Daniel Kahneman in his book *Thinking, Fast and Slow*, in which he talks about comparing clinicians against simple systems. The systems tend to do better, not because they're smarter, but because they're more reliable. They aren't subject to a lot of psychological and other biases that tend to work against the trading. We're born with certain psychological biases, and they're hard to overcome.

Of course, as a systems trader, the hardest thing is to stick with your system. Because you're always looking at the markets and saying, "Oh, gee, maybe it's going somewhere else," or whatever. The most important part, which is understood by all the traders you mentioned and anybody who is successful at trend following, is to stick with your system regardless of what you think the markets are going to do.

Michael: As a trend following trader going back many decades, when you read *Thinking, Fast and Slow* for the first time, wasn't there a side of you that said, "Well, me and some of my peers figured a little bit of this out a long time before it was popular?"

Bill: That's exactly right. But by the same token, Daniel Kahneman was doing his work at about the same time that we were doing our work, though we were operating in different spheres. Maybe we didn't know about him and he didn't know about us, but it wasn't like we scooped Daniel Kahneman—we were applying the knowledge. We were applying his first algorithm to clinical practice back in the '70s. It's a matter of different people working in different fields.

Michael: Let me take you back to where I started this conversation, because I would love you to put on your professorial hat. Let's imagine you've got a room full of doctors, attorneys, young MBAs, all kinds of people, and they don't know about you.

They would say, "Gosh, you did well in 2008." But in the movie *The Big Short*, the one guy who did well did something different: He was in all kinds of markets that were moving. When they hear your track record for that particular year, a lot of people will think, "Oh, he did what *The Big Short* guy did," or "He just shorted the S&P." They won't have this holistic view that it was all of these markets moving. How did that year unfold that enabled you to do so well?

Bill: Well, there's no decision involved in that process. That was the business I was in. I didn't change my trading at all. I might say that this was a banner year for all CTAs who were trend followers, for the simple reason the markets trended strongly. Anybody who was a trend follower was going to capitalize on that.

The difference between me and the guys in *The Big Short* is they actually dug into this stuff and figured out what was going on and had a specific plan to deal with it. Me, I was lucky. It was a market situation, which was amenable to the way that I trade, but I didn't do anything different. I didn't foresee the crash—it happened, and I was in the right place at the right time.

Michael: Your strategy from the ground up was built to take what the markets give you.

Bill: That's right. And that's again where persistence comes in. The markets exhibit persistence and that's what allows me and other trend followers to make money.

Michael: I know you're a fan of surfing. How long have you surfed?

Bill: I caught the bug when I left college. One of the reasons I got into commodities was it was something I could do from wherever I wanted, could live wherever I wanted, and design my life around surfing. Over the last few years I've tapered off a bit because of age, but for a long time surfing defined my life, where I lived, and what I spent my time doing.

Michael: That's an inspirational point to consider in this day and age where so many people don't design their lives. People talk about it on social media and share all these ideas now, and Tim Ferriss has written a book about what you described, but you were doing it a long time before. Did you have anybody in your life who was giving you these freedom ideas to go live that way? Or did you look at it and say, "Okay, this trading thing looks cool. I want to surf, so let's connect the dots here. And this is what I'm going to do."

Bill: It evolved over time. It wasn't necessarily something that came to me all at once. What I remember is that I was working for a company, and I thought, "What about my boss? Do I want his job? Do I want to work 60 hours a week, 80 hours a week, or whatever? Make more money and buy a car, big house? And then what about his boss? Do I want to be his boss?" And then I said, "No, I want to have leisure time. I want to retire when I'm young so that I'm physically and mentally able to do the things I want to do and worry about my old age when I get there."

Michael: Is there anything in the surfing mentality that you've connected to your trading or that you see philosophically in the act of surfing?

Bill: There's a whole sociology behind surfing. It was sort of an *out-bum* mentality—the idea of being free and being able to travel, and being there for the surf. The surf is a jealous companion because when it comes up, you got to be there. It's not like skiing, where there's snow in the mountains and you go to the mountain to ski. The surf comes up at unpredictable times. You have to be available to go surfing when the surf's up—that's the nature of the sport.

A lot of people lived that way; they weren't necessarily commodity traders, they were cab drivers or doctors, anybody who could manage their own lives to the point where they could do what they wanted, more or less when they wanted to. And so, after a while, that became the world I've lived in for most of my life.

The other advantage is that I've been able to think deeply about a lot of different things, not just commodities or surfing, and give free rein to my imagination or my research in other fields. There was also the broader movement of the counterculture and its association with dropping out. But I wasn't dropping out, I was focused more on the moment than on planning for the future, accumulating wealth, or whatever.

Michael: Out of curiosity, did any of your surfing companions ever get an inkling of the career that you were living?

Bill: Nobody knows what it's like to be a trader except another trader. On the other hand, they knew what I did—that I made my money by trading the markets, it didn't take up a lot of time, and I ran a computer program. Some of them were well educated and sophisticated enough to have a general idea of what I did, but the people I surfed with had different professions. They had all worked out a way to live so that they could be free when the surf came up. In my view, I'm not a particularly unique person, I just found a way of making myself available to the surf. Other people had their own ways. In those early days there weren't a lot of people who did that. You pretty much went through all the stages leading to your career. And I stepped off the bus, I guess.

> Nobody knows what it's like to be a trader except another trader.

Michael: Did you always have the even keel that I see right now, even when you were, let's say, 21? Were you always pragmatic and thoughtful?

Bill: I wouldn't call myself even keeled. I was pretty crazy.

Michael: Let's go back to trend following. Back in the day, here's what Donchian's doing, and you look at Edwards and Magee and you got some inclination about where other people were going at that time. And I guess you could have gone the Donchian direction and adopted a fairly simple approach. But in your interview with Niels at Top Traders, you revealed that your approach is a touch more complicated than a typical trend following price action system. It seems like you're getting to the same place, but you're getting there in your own unique way.

Bill: I was taken by the geometrical aspect of traditional technical analysis. My original idea was to take what was valuable in that technical analysis and turn it into a system so that it was not based on judgment. In other words, if you're drawing trend lines and suchlike from a discretionary basis, there are a lot of different possibilities. And if that changes, then you're in a position of relying on your judgment to decide where to put the trend lines, which leads to the inconsistency that I'm trying to avoid. All I did was take what seemed to be fairly straightforward rules and turn them into a system—a computer program.

Michael: Do you think that Edwards and Magee put that work together without the systematic computer approach that you did?

Bill: I put my original system together largely without computers, because I was one of the first people to have a PC back in 1976. Most of my system development and testing was done manually with CRB, chart books, that sort of thing. You don't need a computer to run a system, you have to think like a computer—in other words, do the same thing over and over. Computerizing the strategy was a matter of taking that logic, those procedures, and programming into code.

Michael: The fractal wave algorithm is quite a different approach than if somebody was to explain a breakout price action trading system, but it's aiming for a similar outcome. It's taking what the market gives you. It's trying to get the meat of the trend. How would you describe the fractal wave algorithm to those unfamiliar with it?

Bill: It's based upon the premises of fractal geometry, where you have nested patterns—a pattern within a pattern within a pattern. The most basic pattern is a zigzag: The price goes up, down, and then up. You can use that as the basis for developing a system that incorporates higher and higher levels of detail. The performance of the system is based upon the underlying theory of these distributions that have fat tails. Although it was attractive to design this around the Fractal Wave Algorithm, that's obviously not a necessity.

Michael: It worked for you. You figured it out.

Bill: I was working with a friend of mine. He's the one who came up with the logic behind the Fractal Wave Algorithm. We started off by trying to automate the Elliott Wave, which was popular at the time, but we found out that it was impossible because the Elliott Wave relies too much on discretion to determine where the waves are. What came out of that was a simpler algorithm, which is more like the Dow Theory, in which you have a series of higher highs and higher lows and a series of lower highs. And then those make a larger pattern of higher highs and higher lows, which make a still larger pattern of higher highs and lower lows.

The Fractal Wave Algorithm was essentially the automation of the Dow Theory that provided a substrate for determining where you would put your entry orders and your stop-loss orders, and so on. The fractal wave provided a structure, but it wasn't literally a system. It's a structure that gave you various options as to where to actually place your trades.

Michael: Is your time frame weekly bars?

Bill: My first system was daily, but after a few years it became less effective when I started exploring the fractal wave algorithm. My first idea was to trade the short-term system in the direction of a long-term indicator. What I discovered was that I might as well trade the long-term indicator. In other words, instead of taking pieces out of a trend, I'd try to get as much of the trend as possible. Obviously, that exposes you to a bit more risk, but the risk is mitigated by trading a number of markets. I trade about 40 different markets and it's less onerous to trade off the weekly charts. Also, it seemed to be more in tune with the actual market fundamentals, because, after all, whatever we do in commodities is based upon the cash markets.

I think of myself as a trader who believes in the fundamentals, but I don't trade directly based on those. I trade on the idea. For example, when the price of copper goes up, people start digging new mines, which leads to oversupply, and so on. You have these cycles related to particular commodities that sometimes play out over years. If you're trading longer term, you're more in tune with those longer-term cycles. That's essentially where I ended up. It was partly a matter of convenience, but it seemed to match the market better and avoid a lot of the noise.

Michael: There's no doubt that what you've said should resonate with people who claim to be trend following traders, but when I ask them about their favorite time frame, they tell me it's five minutes.

Bill: They're living in a different universe. I have a good friend who's a high-frequency trader and I know enough about what they do to realize that the dynamics, the theory, the behavior of the markets, all of that is different than long-term trading.

Michael: I would think that if people want to be inspired by you and take a stab at trading, trying to emulate your path makes a lot more sense than trying to emulate the high-frequency path.

Bill: If you look at the people who've been around for a long time, most of them have gravitated toward longer-term trading. It's partly because high-frequency trading's a hard game. There aren't that many people who are successful at it. According to my friend, who's been in it since the beginning, when it started out it was pretty easy because nobody else was doing it. It was the same as when I started out as a systems trader. You had an advantage over the average trader because you had the technology that wasn't being widely applied.

Apparently high-frequency trading is tough these days, and most of the people who are doing it are more market makers than they are traders. If I were thinking about getting into the business now, high-frequency trading would be the last place I'd look.

Michael: There must be some reason that when people first enter this world, they think this short-term stuff is the direction to go in. I'm like you, I think, "Five minutes... what am I doing?" I'm going to be glued to the screen. I'm going to be stressed. It's nothing I'd want to do.

Bill: That's a good point. For instance, one of the things that was popular when I was in my formative years was the Edward Thorpe book, *Beat the Dealer*. It was obviously a trading system, but I asked myself, "Do I want to sit in a smoky casino all day and all night doing this stuff?"

I naturally gravitated toward methodologies that required the least amount of work for the most amount of gain. At that time, the commission rates were unbelievable—the costs you were paying for slippage were high. There were a lot of structural things in the markets that mitigated toward trading longer term. It was too costly to trade short term.

Nowadays, it's a bit different, but nevertheless, you're still having to deal with the noise. And again, it requires a lot of attention, computer power, and you've got to be next to the exchange—all that sort of thing. It's literally another world from the one I live in.

Michael: Let's talk about your personal psychology. You've already talked about surfing and a different lifestyle, about not wanting to be in New York City or Chicago with all the "players." Obviously, you figured out how to do it your way and it's worked well. How did you instinctively know to avoid becoming immersed in the groupthink?

Bill: It was well known then that 95% or so of traders lost money, so the idea was that if you're doing what the vast majority is doing, you're obviously not going to be successful. It was important to try to insulate yourself from being sucked into that logic when you read the commodity news, or whatever, which is always out of date anyway. Plus I didn't want to be a floor trader where I'm coming in every day and yelling and screaming at everybody—I wanted to live a more relaxed lifestyle.

Michael: Were you the first CTA?

Bill: I was one of the first. There was a group that centered around Commodities Corp. on the East Coast. They were sort of independent, following Donchian's lead, but we had a group in San Francisco that was more loosely based. We didn't communicate that much, but there was a handful of us who were getting into the business.

I was in the business before it was regulated by the CFTC—before there was a CFTC. I was in the founding group who, by and large, at least on the West Coast, made independent discoveries through talking to each other. There were a lot of people in the aerospace industry who had mathematical backgrounds, so that appealed to them. It's hard to say who was first.

Michael: When you first wrapped your arms around the idea of trend following and knew that you had a chance to make enough money to do what you wanted for the rest of your life, how did it feel?

Bill: The most important thing for me was to be able to support myself without working too hard, and to provide the time for me to surf and live a life of intellectual freedom. I wasn't focused on the money, because I didn't care about it that much. That's still the case. I was more interested in maximizing my leisure than I was maximizing my income.

Michael: Let me take you back even further to a foundational thought. I talked to the psychologist Alison Gopnik a while back, who has written about Bayesian babies. The idea is that babies learn by seeing one thing and following it, and if it keeps feeling good, they keep going in that direction. I know your early background was in Bayesian Decision Theory. It's not something you learn formally in school, but when one starts to understand this Bayesian thinking, it makes perfect sense.

Bill: The Bayesian Decision Theory that I took was a technical and sophisticated methodology that has not found wide application, at least not in business. You're right—it's more a way of looking at the world and probability theory. It's a thread that's been with me throughout my life. I was convinced early on that probability was epistemological, not ontological, and that's influenced my view of probability. But this is not related to what I'm thinking about in terms of trading. It's a parallel interest that I've had.

Michael: In your trading, were you always of the mindset that your system—the Fractal Wave Algorithm—would be applied uniformly across markets?

Bill: That's right. My original system was not fractal wave, but by the same token involved trend lines, and support and resistance—the basic Edwards and Magee patterns. The idea of it being universal came from the Fractal Wave Algorithm, because it was a way of decomposing data and that applied to any data stream. I've applied it to other markets, such as India and Japan—not that I've traded those markets, but I've tested it—and it pretty much works on everything. Obviously, it works better on some things than others, because the markets have different histories. But if you were to give me a market and say, "Would you trade these without testing?" I'd say, "Yeah, apply the same system, off we go." I have confidence that it would work the way it has for other markets.

Michael: When you're having a good year and you're making a lot of money versus another year where you're losing a lot of money, what emotions do you feel, given those different states of the success, or lack of success, of your system? Do you feel the same during these periods or is there something different internally?

Bill: It's hard to totally insulate yourself from it. To some extent, I feel more comfortable in down markets than I do in up markets.

Michael: To clarify: You feel better when you're losing money than making money?

Bill: Yeah. I have an idea of where it's going and how it's going to end. Whereas when I'm making money, the sky's the limit. The uncertainty is greater when you're making money than it is when you're losing money. In the sense that you're emotionally reacting to uncertainty, then it's sometimes a bit more comfortable when you're losing money. It's because you're being whipsawed, you're being grounded by trades that are getting in and out, in and out, and it's not exciting. And it tries your patience because most of the time the markets are in drawdown; only a relatively small fraction of the time are they making these runs where you're making a lot of money.

We don't make money because we're smart—we make money because the markets give us opportunities and we have the discipline to follow a system.

Michael: I've talked to a lot of your peers, many of whom have been around since you started, but you come at this so differently. When you compare the correlation of performance with other CTAs over time, have you been tightly correlated?

Bill: My performance could be used as an index of CTA performance. And, of course, it's trend following performance. We don't make money because we're smart—we make money because the markets give us those opportunities, and we have the discipline to follow a system. Of course, not all systems are going to work. I've never quite figured out what makes one system better or worse than another. But the people who've been around for a long time have honed in on the same time frame and the same basic strategy. It's a Darwinian process that weeds people out—for instance, most money that's in managed futures is in trend following systems. And that's because the other methodologies haven't survived in competition.

95% of traders lose money and they are mainly discretionary.

You have to wonder who the trend followers are taking the money from. Once again, it comes down to fundamentals—we're selling insurance to people who are producers or consumers, who need the product and are willing to lock in profits. It comes down to a classical arbitrage game in which we're willing to accept risk and take it off the shoulders of the people who don't want it. It's all pretty simple. After all these years, it's gone through a long evolutionary process, and I think it's pretty much stabilized now.

Michael: When I first started researching everything I could find on trend following sometime in the 1990s, one of the most interesting things I observed is it seemed to me that the best traders in the trend following space were 100% systematic. But when I went through all the disclosure documents from the CFTC, there was always, "We're 95% systematic, but 5% discretion." All these trend following traders were saying they were 5% or 10% discretion. And I was thinking, "I don't believe this. This is marketing to appeal to somebody." If you're a systematic trend following trader, you're going to believe in the system, yet they were all saying they were 5% discretionary. I'm curious to know if you've always been 100% systematic?

Bill: The people I know are all 100% systematic. That 5% discretion comment might be a marketing ploy. The number one realization is the need to stick with your system, and to do what it tells you to do.

Michael: Did you ever play with discretion early on, or wonder if it could add some extra value to your system?

Bill: No. I don't know that I was ever interested. I saw clearly that 95% of traders lose money and it was pretty obvious to me that they were mainly discretionary. I had no confidence in my own abilities. I may have tested them out a little bit, but I never had the psychological makeup or even the information to succeed as a discretionary trader.

Michael: The Warren Buffett path didn't intrigue you?

Bill: Warren Buffett does what I do, really. I mean, he's consistent. He sticks with his trades for years. He's a long-term trend follower. One thing that characterizes a so-called discretionary trader is that he's got to have the action, he's got to be in the markets. It's a psychological need that he's satisfying. It's not irrational. A system trader is one way of being a long-term trader and, obviously, the best way to trade the markets is to put your money in an index fund and let it ride.

Michael: We've talked about some of your early stages, but beyond going to school, getting those early jobs, and being exposed to the computers at the Air Force, was there anybody along the way who was influential in the development of your trading?

Bill: The people I worked with at the think tank had a unique way of approaching modeling. We were at the cutting edge. This would be the late '60s and early '70s, the height of The Cold War, there was a lot of money going into these new modeling technologies, and this was the first stage of applying them. We were doing a lot of original work, much of it top secret. There's a limited number of approaches to modeling various phenomena and most of them came into being in that era. I read a book not long ago, *The Physics of Wall Street*, which talks about the various physics models and mathematical models that were being applied. We knew about every one of these models back in the '60s and many of them had been resurrected. For instance, deep learning is like neural nets—it's a continuation of a model that's been around for decades. And this is also true with other models.

These models have become careers and people specialize in the various types of modeling, but we were much more ecumenical than that. We selected the model to fit the task, not selected the task to fit the model—we call that model shopping. And that's what people do nowadays, they're educated to apply certain kinds of models, then they take that model and say, "Okay, I'm going to apply this to commodity trading," or whatever, as opposed to selecting the appropriate model for a specific problem.

Much of what I see today in terms of modeling hasn't changed in years. We're going into probably the second AI winter now. The hype around AI started back in the '80s when everybody thought machines were taking over, and now we're hyping AI. Computing power has expanded so much, but data mining is not thought. Human beings have creativity that computers are incapable of, and that's going to be true for the foreseeable future. If you want to see what AI does, go online, and you'll see all these ads popping up for something you've already bought. Is that intelligence?

Michael: One of my favorite guests on my podcast has been Robert Aumann, who won the Nobel Prize for Game Theory. I was a little petrified to talk to this 90-year-old Israeli game theorist, but what was so great about him was the way he explained things like mutually assured destruction: "Look, we had to have the bombers up there ready to go for 40 years straight. That's what kept the peace." It was one of those lightbulb moments where I thought, "Wow, he took all the math that he has in his head that the average person can't understand," and simplified it in a way that would make sense to anyone.

Bill: That's right. We were doing sophisticated modeling, but by the same token, we understood that in an actual nuclear exchange, most of that stuff wouldn't work, it would be chaos. You had to keep up with that game because the other side was keeping up with the game. That was essentially my understanding—that you were in a situation where you had to do it. And what looked like something that was counterproductive, say, to the public, was actually necessary in terms of the situation at the time.

Michael: As we wind down, I want to look ahead, because one of the favorite topics of the media, about every five years, is that trend following is dead. It's gone, it's over, they're all losing money, it's never going to work again… and then something happens. This is a repeatable pattern. You've been in this industry for decades. If you had to look ahead, how do you see a strategy of trend following unfolding for the next 50 years?

Bill: It'll change in terms of the particulars, I suppose.

Michael: You mean what markets are traded, perhaps?

Bill: I don't know. Obviously, new markets are coming into play, and old markets are going to become inactive. But the basic trend following strategy relies on fundamental characteristics of human psychology and economics. As long as there are markets, there will be trend following strategies. And the same underlying mechanisms that cause those to be viable will persist.

> By and large markets behave the same as they always have.

My current system has been virtually unchanged in over 30 years of trading. I've tweaked it a little bit here and there, but the point is it keeps working. And the reason it works is not because of the system itself, it's because of the existing economic environment.

Let me put it this way. When I look at the market behavior, I don't see anything that I didn't see 50 years ago. In fact, I've seen markets like sugar and cocoa go bananas, seen cotton go up limit two weeks in a row, and then go down limit two weeks in a row. Things that would be astonishing today were not so astonishing back in the '70s, but by and large, the markets behave the same as they always have.

Michael: If you had to look ahead and say, "Well, there's going to be trend following strategies, but there might be changes in the margin," would you also see something like the 40% winners, 60% losers—will that type of philosophical foundation still be a part of trend following? Because we don't have the ability to predict what's going to be the next big trend.

Bill: There are some general parameters that will continue to persist—

that's the sweet spot in the markets. It's almost as if the markets are going to extract maximum pain from traders, and any strategy that capitalizes on that pain is going to continue to make money. In other words, it's back to psychology: Most people are wired to do the wrong thing when they're trading the markets, that's not going to change.

Michael: Are you ever going to retire?

Bill: I've pretty much retired now.

Michael: But you're still trading?

> **People are wired to do the wrong thing when they're trading the markets.**

Bill: For my own proprietary trading, but I'm not holding myself out. I've withdrawn my membership of the NFA and CFTC. I'm not trading for clients; my own money.

Michael: Will you ever stop that?

Bill: Probably. I'm getting close to that. Because even what little I'm doing requires that I stay engaged on a daily basis.

Michael: There must be a part of you that still loves it?

Bill: Less and less. I've got enough money—just put it in an index fund and forget about it.

Michael: I've taken you through all kinds of territory, and I appreciate you giving me some flavor. Consciously, I did not want to take you on a linear path.

Bill: I appreciate that. I was apprehensive about having to tell my story all over again, but I enjoyed this much more than I thought I would.

CHAPTER 2

HAROLD DE BOER

From Farm to
Trend Following

H AROLD DE BOER is the managing director of Transtrend and architect of the Diversified Trend Program, responsible for research and development, portfolio management, and trading. Harold was born and raised on a dairy farm in Drenthe. From a young age, he has been intrigued by linking mathematics to the real world around us. In the final phase of his studies, while working on the project that would later become Transtrend, he became fascinated by the concept of leptokurtosis— or fat tails—in probability distributions, a topic that has inspired him throughout his career.

Michael Note

I'm not sure why it took so long, but after years and years of waiting, Harold finally said yes to an interview. What an amazing story from the Netherlands.

Michael Covel: You have an interesting approach to the markets, best described as a combination of a farmer's common sense and mathematics, while at the same time never losing sight of the underlying fundamentals. People may be thinking, "What kind of strategy is that?" Guess what—it's trend following. You have a consistent track record every month back to the 1980s and you're one of the legends of the industry. Transtrend is now at over $4 billion under management and is absolutely one of the leaders in the trend following world.

I love the phrasing that you use to describe trend following. Here is a quote:

> Our investment strategies are guided by the footprints left by people running after ideas. That is, the prices they set in the market. It's all just an idea. It has no impact if nobody buys it, nobody uses it, nobody votes for it. But every time people do run after an idea, the world changes. Our world is shaped by people running after ideas.

That's a great descriptor of trend following. How did that idea come about?

Harold de Boer: I wrote that when I was asked to explain the idea behind trend following. I like to explain in terms that are not too technical. The fundamental thing behind trend following is there are a lot of people— including economists—who believe in a world reverting to equilibrium. So, prices can be temporarily high, but they will come down again. And prices can be temporarily low, but they will come up again—there is a reversal to a constant state.

But if you look at the world, there has never been a constant state; it's constantly a temporary constant. Look at the big developments of the past. For example, in the Netherlands until 100 years ago, people didn't travel by road. People traveled by water. What if investors had said, "Roads are coming and people are using horses more and more, and carriages, and later on cars, or even trains. But it'll come back to the equilibrium of people mostly using boats."

Of course, that's wrong. It was a normal development. These developments, big developments, are happening constantly. That is the main driver behind trends in markets.

In the last few years, there has been a big move from people driving cars powered by gasoline, toward electric cars. In an electric car there is three times as much copper as in a regular car, so this has a big impact on

Our investment
strategies are
guided by the
footprints left by
people running
after ideas.

the market. It means that there's more demand for copper than there was before and there's more demand for all kinds of other metals.

This is not something that will revert; it's a new development. Maybe in 50 years' time people will not be driving electric cars anymore, but driving something completely different. But there's no way that it will turn back to the cars we had 20 years ago. It's a constant development.

Michael: I like that you describe your work in a hands-on way, so that the average person can approach it. Other people in the industry talk about the statistics behind something—the academic aspects of it. Now don't get me wrong, you guys have your academic and statistical chops as well. You have sophisticated, statistically based strategies; but philosophically, you're clearly comfortable explaining things in everyday terms.

> **Big developments are happening constantly. That is the main driver behind trends in markets.**

Harold: For that I have to thank the professor who guided me through my degree in mathematics with a specialization in statistics. He was an old-school professor whose background was in industry. His experience in industry taught him to see a problem, something that had to be solved, and then identify what kind of statistic would solve it. If that statistic didn't exist already, he would create it. Based on that practical experience, he became what we call in the Netherlands a Doctor of Statistics, and then he became a professor.

My philosophy is: First look at the real world, then choose the techniques, and then apply them. What often happens is that people start with the techniques instead of the real-world situation. There are not many markets where it is reasonable to assume a linear relationship. If you start your research by looking for correlations, you've made a mistake already. You can keep on doing calculations, but the problem is that using a linear correlation measurement such as Pearson's—which is the most commonly used one—already assumes that any relationship will be linear, when there's absolutely no reason to assume that. Those fundamental choices are important.

We often have discussions about whether what we're doing is technical analysis or fundamental analysis. It starts with fundamental analysis:

search, decide which techniques can be used, and only then does it become purely technical. This is somewhat opposite to what other people do. The more traditional financial approach is to start with the technical element and then make the fundamental case.

Michael: You mentioned the statistics professor. Let me take you back in time before that to your early life on the dairy farm. What's the connective tissue between where you are today and growing up on a dairy farm? How did that shape you in terms of your current world?

Harold: There's a lot of connective tissue, because there are many developments going on in the dairy industry too. For example, the Netherlands was a global leader in dairy cows for many years. During the 1950s and 1960s, other countries, including the United States, began importing cows and calves from the Netherlands and breeding from them. The Dutch kept on thinking that their cows were the best in the world, so they were only concerned with the appearance of their animals and other non-relevant issues, while in the United States and some other countries, the stock was being bred for more efficient production and less disease. Then in the 1970s and 1980s, Dutch farmers began to realize, "Hey, we've made a mistake here." My father was among those farmers who started to use the sperm from US bulls to improve their own herds again. That was a development that required a fresh look at genetics and the statistics behind them. My background in statistics started with looking at how we could justify making changes in cow breeding.

Michael: The real-world application of your math background is taking place right there on the family farm?

Harold: I learned statistics from how it applied to cows, and calves, and colors, and all the genes. Then later on, at school, I learned from the statistics books, and they fitted. But that's the way I learned it first.

Michael: You're saying to the younger generation coming up, "Hey, hold on. You might not get exactly the education you need to compete with me at the academic universities. You might need to go to the farm?"

Harold: Not only the farm. It doesn't matter where it is—look around the world. I grew up on a farm surrounded by cows, but you could just as easily get a similar experience in, let's say, a railroad company. Start with looking at the world, see what's happening and what structures are there, and what developments are going on. We have an item on our website that says if you take a picture from 50 years ago, you will recognize it's a picture from 50 years ago. There will never come a time that this picture could be taken again, except for in Hollywood and other places where they can remake history. But aside from that, the world is continuously changing.

Michael: According to the scenario you've described, your math background gave you a real-world view and your farming background introduced you to commodities. When did the transition first happen? We're talking about the 1980s. What was the moment you said to yourself, "Okay, I'm going to go into trading?" There must have been a lightbulb moment when you said, "Okay, there's this trending behavior, that's interesting to me." Explain that story to me.

Harold: My professor said that to finish my degree, it was best to find a real-life problem. This was pre-internet and email, so I had to write letters to all kinds of firms and ask them if they might have some problem which it would be interesting for someone with a mathematics background to study. I got two appealing possibilities. One was with a dairy factory and the other was with a company that traded agricultural commodities. Because of my background, I was thinking, "When I grow up, I'll be working in a dairy factory. So, for now, I'll have a look at this trading firm, because this is something I don't know anything about and it'll be good experience." That's why I chose the trading firm.

The company was a traditional commodity trader that used the commodity futures markets. They had begun to notice that more and more so-called firms were active there. To their astonishment, those firms never took delivery and never did anything in the market, but still made money. They said, "If these people are able to make money in our markets, then we should be able to do that ourselves too on a more technical level." That's where the project started. I came to the project to finish my studies and it proved to be interesting.

We did all kinds of different things. My first research task was looking at the relationship between meats—cattle and ox, or feed cattle as they were known in those days— and grains and feeds—soybean milk, corn, and so on. There are all kinds of interesting relationships between those markets.

From there, we looked at carrying out some kind of arbitrage study, but on further consideration we realized it could be interesting to do that on a more fundamental, semi-fundamental, or semi-technical basis, but it's a big risk, because if you are wrong, it can be a costly error. This

First look at the real world, then choose the techniques, and then systematically apply them.

is, of course, a big disadvantage of arbitrage strategies in general. In the meantime, we were doing all kinds of other analyses, testing strategies that had been written about, as well as traditional technical methods such as trend lines and so on.

Our research revealed that trend following type strategies were interesting, one of the reasons being that many different markets can be traded at the same time, enabling a large diversification. In the case of arbitrage, if you are wrong, the only thing you can do is hang fire because you think the markets will come together. With trend following, it's the opposite way around—if you are wrong, then you get out of your position or go your own way. Trend following is also a much better fit with the idea that relationships between markets can fundamentally change— something that is much harder to account for with arbitrage.

We saw this issue with a trader in Norway that lost a lot of money in a spread between German power and Norwegian power at a time of significant change in the price of emission rights in Europe. Issues such as climate change can seriously undermine an arbitrage strategy, while in trend following it's no problem at all. It's interesting that emission rights are currently [2018] one of the best trends in the markets. By studying these different philosophies and different ways of treating markets, we found out that trend following is good.

The main benefit is that trend following is so great to use in a diversified way. However, we had to solve one issue, because the company we worked within had chosen to only trade commodity markets. You have to realize this idea started just after 1987, which had not been a good year for investing in stocks. They decided, "Whatever we're going to do, we never want to be in financial markets." We said, "With trend following, you can also trade in all these financial markets if you can support diversification certification." We had to explain to them why this made us different from many traditional hedge funds, which typically have a financial background and sometimes fail to see how the same strategies can be applied to commodities. Our experience in commodity trading gave us a completely different view about how markets function. Things such as time structure and old crop/new crop are relevant for commodity markets.

Michael: Let me keep you on that point for a moment. Given that you started in commodity-only markets, when did it occur to you that trend following could apply to other markets? Or did you always know that these techniques could work in the full global suite of markets?

Harold: We didn't realize this could be done for all markets at that time, because there are more markets now than there were then. Let's say stock indices were pretty new. The stock index futures started in 1982, I think SP 500 was the first one.

> Price trends are as inherent to markets as the wind is to the atmosphere.

There were not that many stock market futures and, of course, sector indices and single stock futures didn't exist at all. But currencies and bond markets were being traded, and those were ideally suited for these techniques. Later on, we realized that you could do the same thing, not only with stock indices and single stock futures, but also with emission rights and those kinds of new markets that didn't exist before.

It's relevant to keep active in new markets. I remember, around 1998, we decided that we wanted to trade the Nasdaq futures and our largest client at that time said, "Why would you want to trade such a small market?" We said, "It may be small at this moment, but maybe it'll grow." No one nowadays would call the Nasdaq futures a small market, but at that time it was something new, so was it going to last? Well, it has.

Michael: Rolling forward from events in the 1980s and early 1990s, here we are in 2018, and I gather you now trade for 500-plus markets.

Harold: Yes. But that's not relevant because although there are 500-plus markets, the actual number of different trends is smaller than that. Right now you have an energy trend and you can say, "We trade heating oil and we trade gasoline and we trade oil." But on a day like yesterday, for example, all these markets came down. We used to say the more markets the better—and it's true, you still need diversification—but you also have to realize that real diversification is not measured by the number of markets, but by the number of different underlying trends we can be positioned in.

Michael: Talking about trends, there's another great line that I've seen come from your world: "Price trends are as inherent to markets as the wind is to the atmosphere." I love the way it gets people thinking about trends and movements.

I'm going to ask your opinion about factors. The academic world is trying to make a breakthrough here, but again, strays philosophically from what you've grown up on. What you have done with your firm is to stay grounded and say, "Hey, these big trends exist. They come from sound reasons. We can look at why these things start to happen." But they're unexpected.

What is your view of factors, bearing in mind that academics have claimed that there's a factor for momentum, and there's a factor for value, and you can just isolate it and find it in a back test and apply $100 billion to it?

Harold: There are factors, but those ones you mentioned are not relevant. Relevant factors are if OPEC is doing something that has an impact on the oil price, or on the price of stocks for oil firms, or on the value of the Norwegian Krone, that kind of thing. OPEC is a factor. A central bank policy is a factor. Environmental pollution by governments is a relevant factor. Those are real-world factors as opposed to academic ones. When you talk about investing, you should explain, "We are buying copper now for this and this reason, not because of momentum or because of value, or whatever."

Of course, when many investors are following those factors, it produces a short-term impact. However, that will generate a price movement that does not fit with the underlying markets, because when investors are buying more and more copper for some kind of academic reason, instead of a real-life reason, it doesn't mean that consumers will use more copper, or that there will be less copper produced. Ultimately, it's all about the real-life markets and not about these future switches. When that doesn't work, then those factors are not relevant. The relevant factors are what's happening.

Michael: Does it make you smile, as a man who's been in the markets trading for 30-plus years, when you see some of this new branding coming along? Where everyone, all of a sudden, is talking about factors?

Harold: Yeah, but don't forget branding can become a factor in its own right, which can impact markets. Especially nowadays, you have to understand that markets are being driven in the short term by factors that should not drive them. Prices can go away with a serious force because of investment flows, rather than being driven by what's happening in the underlying markets. People often think that an active investment style, or even a fundamental style, should be able to make more money nowadays because of the large number of passive investors. But that's not true, because the power of all these passive flows is so strong that an active fundamental investor has to be able to withstand that force, which can drive the market in the wrong direction. Sooner or later, it will go in the right direction, but it makes it harder for active investors. This is a problem, because if active traders cannot have a big impact on the market, it's not healthy for the economy as a whole.

Michael: You've explained why many fundamental factors are useful, but do you have moments when your own decision-making is driven by the simple heuristic of price action?

Harold: We have to, because we are not a fundamental trial. It's not that we say, "From a fundamental point of view, the price of cocoa is too low at the moment, so we will buy." No—we will buy if there's an uptrend. But we do realize that there can be a significant uptrend when the market has been too low for a long time, which happened for instance in 2018 in the cocoa market.

This all has to do with to what extent does the market as a whole still function? Market participants play an important role in that. If more and more market participants start to behave in a way that does not match with the underlying markets, they do have big impact. For example, from a fundamental point of view, you could ask why Tesla stock has been rising so much while the company never made a profit for many years. Well, it's because investors are buying it, then they buy more, then it becomes a bigger index and passive investors have to buy even more. Ultimately, it's hard to stop such a thing. Finally, Tesla did make a profit, but this is immaterial; the most important driving factor is getting more and more in indices and as a result the stock will keep on growing. You cannot go short on a company or any other markets as long as there's so much power driving it—even if you fundamentally believe it's being driven the wrong way.

If it's happening, it will impact markets.

Take Brexit, for instance. It doesn't matter whether we think it's a good idea or a bad idea. It's happening, so it will impact markets. We have to take into account that these markets are driven by people who support that idea. If people vote for something because they believe in it—whether it's the president or whether it's a movement like Brexit—it doesn't matter if what they say is true, it's all about whether people are getting behind it. Then it will create trends in markets, which will have an impact on growth as a whole.

Michael: To follow up on your point about Brexit. Yes, you can have a personal opinion, but that opinion is not factored into your decision-making for the funds you are trading.

Harold: No, but it does have a role. We can look at what kind of effect this might have and how our systems work. Are there elements that will not be taken into account by a correlation message, or whatever? Is there any place, any event, that the way we work is not right for? It can be something simple, like are we trading the right markets?

We have to realize that certain events or situations can create trends. We also need to evaluate whether what we have observed fits with the underlying idea. The Brexit referendum was a case in point. In many respects, what we did was exactly what we expected to do and how our system would respond to such a thing. But there were also a few surprises in there and some elements we could have handled better. Based on this experience, we did make some changes to the way we execute business in volatile environments. We profited from that following the outcome of the US election when Trump was chosen, because again, that night, there were some erratic moves in all kinds of markets, which we could better profit from because of changes we made after evaluating what happened after Brexit.

Michael: Before we leave the subject of trends, I want to quote from your world. This is a great short paragraph. I'm going to let you explain it and we can break it apart:

> Trends, in particular those that are most profitable for trend following systems, like those in DTP [a Transtrend program], are comparable in a number of ways to burning haystacks. Once such a fire has broken out, it's often hard to extinguish. The same applies to price trends. But equally important, a haystack normally does not start to burn all of a sudden. The fire is typically preceded by so-called self-heating, a fermentation process whereby the temperature gradually rises, starting at the core of the haystack, eventually leading to spontaneous combustion.

I wish I'd written that in one of my books. I wish I could steal it from you, but I can't because everyone knows it came from you.

Harold: Yes, that's something we worked on when we saw what was happening in the second quarter of 2012, a period in which normally you would expect a trend following strategy to work well. There was a sell-off, especially in emerging market equities, that then also went over to other markets. This was the kind of movement where you would typically think a trend following strategy should be doing well. We made some money there, but we realized, "This is not enough. We should have been doing better in this environment." We tried to figure out what made this period different from previous ones.

Trends are comparable in a number of ways to burning haystacks.

We traced the story back to the Russian situation in the late 1990s. The oil price had been going down for a long time, for obvious reasons to do with the oil industry globally. But for Russia, this was a big problem because its economy was dependent on oil. Until then, most investors in Europe, the US, and further afield were not watching what was happening in Russia, but all of a sudden this Russian crisis impacted all the markets at once. When there is a fire and it is combusting, it's impacting many, many other markets—even markets that should not be affected.

These kinds of movements can create big reverses in some trends. The US stock market could also come down as a result of the crisis in Russia. We normally would not profit from being short the US stock market in that situation, because it was not happening there. Where you can profit is being at the source of the event—to make money, you have to be positioned at the base where the thing is happening.

For instance, at the start of 2018, the Turkish lira had been declining for a long time. This was just a local Turkish issue that had nothing to do with what was happening elsewhere. All of a sudden, one morning, the *Financial Times* published an article about European banks that would have problems because of the situation in Turkey. This sparked a sell-off of stock markets worldwide and of emerging market currencies above all, for instance in South America. The Turkish issue was far from new, but this one story triggered the spread of this fire to all kinds of other markets. At that moment, we held positions in the South African rand and were losing on them because the rand was coming down as a result of Turkey. But to profit from such a situation, we had to be short of Turkey, since we had large short positions in Turkish lira. That's where the fire started and was still going on. That fundamental awareness has been the basis for many changes we've been making to ensure the choice of programs optimizes the chances of high profit. It is likely that we hold sizeable positions in any haystack that could become the next big fire. You have to be in that haystack and not in one that is being impacted, because if the latter, you're probably on the wrong side.

Michael: I like how you describe a gradual start of a price increase or decrease as "self-heating"—the well-informed insiders making moves. When the average person sees a little bit of up or down movement, they're not necessarily drawing much conclusion from that, but a price-based approach such as you employ does lead to a conclusion.

Harold: We have to make sure we do, because that's relevant. If we don't, we're on the wrong foot—and when we're on the wrong foot, we're losing money.

It has to do with a broader change in the world. Let's say until 15 or so years ago, oil traders didn't know everything about oil, but they read everything that was relevant to oil. People trading Canadian bonds were well informed about Canada, Canadian politics, Canadian monetary policy. People trading soybeans, such as our former parent company, knew everything about soybeans, but were not interested in Canadian monetary policy and the like. There were a lot of specialized people and information was held within particular groups.

This was the status quo up to the credit crisis, which started in 2007 in the interest rate markets and infected the stock markets the following year. Now information was being spread in fear, via the internet and social networks, resulting in much more information becoming available to many more people at the same time. You would think, "If people have more information, they can make better decisions." But what happened in practice was that everyone was being exposed to the same information at the same time. For a few days at the start of 2018, many people were only looking at Turkey. The following week, they were looking at something else and forgot about the previous issue. People trading oil maybe should not look too much at Turkey and just keep focusing on what's happening in the oil markets, because that will be more relevant to their business.

If everyone is looking at the same thing at the same time, local self-heating will be less visible because people who should be focused on trading corn are going to be distracted by other factors, while the more relevant factors for the corn trade are not coming into the markets until they become a problem. This is what happened in 2012. All of a sudden there was a drought, but a drought doesn't start overnight—it's something that develops slowly. In well-functioning markets, there are enough informed people who understand the drought is ongoing and as a consequence, the price of corn will rise. If that doesn't happen because people are too preoccupied with storylines that are running in the media at that moment, then the corn market is not developing well. It's hard to recognize trends. This is one of the things that has made trend following more difficult over the last few years. You have to make all kinds of amendments to make it better again.

Michael: I'm getting the impression you don't work under benchmark pressure. How has that unfolded? Listening to you, I can see there's a sound philosophy from the ground up. But investors are often irrational. I'm assuming you've trained your investors well. You've had performance for a long time, which helps a lot. But how have you allowed yourself and your firm to steer clear of benchmarks? Because benchmarks can cause psychological harm, can't they?

Harold: As CTAs we have far fewer problems with benchmark stock investors who are trying to stay close to a benchmark. I wouldn't go as far as to say that benchmarking has had a negative impact, but back in the 1980s, even some of the most successful US CTAs were not recognized by the broader investment community institutions, so they would not invest at the CTAs. Coming into the 1990s and especially the early 2000s, when we had some stock market sell-offs, institutional investors realized that trend following strategies could be okay.

What happened next is that trend following started to be seen as an investment style, as opposed to many different traders doing similar things and all doing well. Rather than going with a name such as John W. Henry or Temple, for example, investors decided to invest in trend following and then had to choose which name to invest in. That didn't ultimately make things any better, because there are essential differences between investment managers, and it's important that investors realize the differences. Trend following became successful in the 1980s and 1990s because all these investment managers were doing maybe similar things, but also a lot of different things. Their variation made them strong together, which is generally true in nature. If you have, let's say, dogs that resemble each other too closely, it isn't healthy for the breed. The same thing happened in the CTA industry, in which it became important to be aware that you constantly had to make the best decision from your point of view, instead of being influenced by an investor demand to follow the trend.

We were successful not because we did what we were expected to do, but because we did what we thought was right. If I go way back in history, when we did the first studies on trend following, we found an article that stated there were three important factors in trend following: 1) you should always be in the market; 2) you should always trade the same size;

3) you should always use stocks. When we did our own research, however, we discovered the reverse: You should not always be in the market; you should not always trade the same size; and you should never use stocks. We accepted everything about trend following except for the three factors being recognized as the basis.

Once I was with one of my colleagues at a conference in Italy. As we were walking to lunch, we overheard the conversation of some potential investors walking in front of us. One said, "Those people behind, they are from Transtrend and they're good."

"Yes," the other one agreed, "they are good." But then the first one replied, "They don't use stocks, though, that's bad." "Yes, that's bad."

Those investors decided not to invest in us because we didn't use stocks. In recent years, there's been a lot of stories about what trend followers are supposed to do and what they're not supposed to do. You see this with independent advisors who resort to box ticking: "Are you doing this? Are you doing this? Are you doing this?" It drives investment managers to take decisions that are not necessarily for the best.

Being selected based on a box-ticking exercise that says a trend following CTA has to use stocks, and if they don't, you won't invest with them, is unhealthy for the industry as a whole. Over the last few years, I've seen some developments in making CTAs more diverse. I think that's important. CTAs should be studying the market and doing their best to make money, but there's no rule they should be using stocks, or crossover strategy, or momentum, or they should be using a value-at-risk measure that is defined in such-and-such a way. Absolutely not.

Michael: Have you always been systematic, going back to the late 1980s?

Harold: Yeah. In the research project we carried out, some things were based on more fundamental strategies. So, the first trades we did in the markets were sizeable, but nowadays we would call them marketable trades in commodity markets. My first research was about developing hogs and the impact of the 1998 drought on the number of pigs and the amount of corn. What kind of price move can you expect then? We decided to take a long position on core hogs and made $1m. From that start, we financed our long-term research. We ended up doing everything systematically, but always keeping in mind the underlying market.

Michael: I'd like to make a point to buttress everything you've said. You lay this foundation of knowing how things work, then use those real-life factors to apply a trend following approach. But some people might not know that you're systematic, which throws another wrinkle into it. You can have strong opinions, but at the end of the day, your system is written down, it's coded, and you're executing in a systematic fashion.

Harold: Indeed. I want to make it clear that our process is not to read about some rules and then apply them. We study the markets and, based on that, we choose techniques, and we systematically apply them. That's different from starting with techniques.

Michael: I guess there's been some change in the last handful of years, but for a long time academic papers, and Nobel Prize winners, were telling you, "Harold, markets are efficient and you can't be doing what you're doing. It doesn't work. And here you are for 30-plus years, scratching your head." I seriously doubt you're scratching your head. You're happy with the direction you've taken, but it must have been interesting to watch this community of folks across academia and Wall Street talking about efficient markets over the course of your career.

Harold: I have turned in a completely different direction to academics. I wouldn't even call many of them academics anymore. Look at the number of articles being published that contain nothing more than theoretical results. If you wanted to publish something like that, say, 20 years ago, the discussion would be about whether you had to take into account 1.0% or 1.5% price impact. The outcome always was, "It may seem like you can make money, but if you take into account the cost and the market impact, there will be no result in practice." Nowadays, you read more and more articles that argue that while markets are efficient, liquidity is large, therefore we don't have to take into account any market impact.

How do markets move if not due to the impact of people trading these markets?

I don't understand the academic reasoning behind that, because how do markets move and how do prices move if not due to the impact of people trading these markets? The role of investors is to be aware that they have market impact, but they're not the ones that make profit out of the markets, and the markets themselves will automatically go in a certain direction. All the participants make the market and all movement creates market impact.

The academic argument that market impact happens automatically doesn't work, because it denies the fact that markets are being moved by what people are doing in them. Take a stock like Apple. People may think that the price of Apple stock rises when many people are buying iPhones, but that's not what happens. They can sell lots and lots of iPhones, but if no one buys the stock, it will not rise. The stock only rises because people are buying it and are willing to pay more for the stock than they were previously. We all hope this is because they expect Apple will sell more iPhones, but if they forget that element, then the price will not move at all—or it will move in another direction. Market impact is the only thing that moves markets, and as an investment community, we have to take that into account. We have to be aware that we should never neglect underlying markets.

Michael: Given the longevity that you've enjoyed in the trend following space, it must be some comfort to have a real-world record that people can look to. Of course, the past is the past and we don't know what's going to happen, but we can draw a little bit of inference from a long track record. It's got to be interesting to some degree to see so many academic folks going straight into fund management with all of these papers and raising a lot of assets on techniques that might not be the best thing in the future.

Harold: I recently gave a presentation about responsible investing in commodities. A lot of investment benefits are derived from long-only positions in commodity futures. Some people present semi-academic arguments why being long in a commodity future would give you some kind of risk premium. These arguments are completely wrong. From day to day, there's a risk premium normally being paid by the ones that are long and not by the ones that are short. There's a fundamental reason for that. So, all these semi-academic stories that say, "Well, you can invest long-only commodities and you can do it like this and you'll get the risk premium," often they refer to claims.

There's one basic rule for anyone who wants to invest in commodities.

If some investor tells you why his strategy works and he refers to claims, you can be sure that he did not read claims and if he did read claims, he did not understand it. Such an investor will surely not make any money on the strategy. The best way to recognize a bad investment manager in commodity markets is someone who refers to claims.

I once came across an investment manager who described claims as a "cost of carry" model. This is based on the idea that you can store a commodity and then sell it at a later date; the price between the futures now and futures in the future is the cost of carry—in other words, the cost to store that commodity. The investment manager illustrated it with reference to feeding cattle. While feeding, the cow has to be, for argument's sake, between three and six months in age. There's no way you can store the costs of this cow for a year, and in a year's time, it's still between three and six months in age. There are some people who would like to believe they could live one year without getting older, but it's completely impossible. Using these kinds of theories and applying them to things that are absolutely not connected is a bad use of academic theory.

Michael: Have you perceived any advantage over the course of your career from being based in Rotterdam or from being Dutch?

Harold: Yes and no. For potential investors, the distance can be a deterrent. What often happens is that potential investors will arrange a trip to London, where they can meet many different investment managers over a couple of days. They will not visit us in the Netherlands, or our colleagues in Sweden or Paris, because we're farther away. However, the ones who make the effort to visit are more motivated, which means we waste less time talking with potential investors who are not serious. It can be an advantage or a disadvantage, depending on how you look at it.

Another difference is with the staff we have. We are not competing for people who can choose to work for another firm around the corner. These people have chosen to work with us and if they wanted to do something completely different, most of them would not even be working in the financial sector. For students from this region, and the Netherlands generally, who want to work for a CTA or a hedge fund, there's not that much choice, and that's an advantage. Something else that helps is because we are different from other CTAs, we're also better at having our own ideas. In London, a lot of people have been working for one CTA and then another and then another, so you find similar ideas within different CTAs. We are a little bit like an isolated desert island where people live completely in their own way.

Michael: You don't want to be tainted by all kinds of bad influences.

Harold: It's not even that we don't want to—it's about being different, and another place helps you to be yourself.

Michael: I've had a chance to speak to so many of your peers. Probably we have mutual friends that we don't know about. One day I'm going to make it to Rotterdam, we'll have to do lunch. It's been a long time since I've even been in Amsterdam.

Harold: Beware, Amsterdam and Rotterdam are not friends.

Michael: They're not friends?

Harold: No.

Michael: You want nothing to do with them? You've drawn the line at Rotterdam, they're not allowed over?

Harold: In football competitions, when Amsterdam plays Rotterdam, the fans from Amsterdam are not even allowed to visit Rotterdam.

CHAPTER 3

JERRY PARKER

The Top Turtle. Period.

JERRY PARKER founded Chesapeake Capital Corporation in 1988. Chesapeake provides investment and portfolio management services to private and institutional investors worldwide. Jerry began his career in 1983 when he was accepted into the Turtle Program, a select investment training program developed by a successful Chicago portfolio manager. When the program ended in 1988, after almost five years of trading proprietary capital, he decided to continue his professional money management career by forming Chesapeake.

Chesapeake's investment portfolios are not biased toward long or short positions and, therefore, can profit in both rising and falling market environments. Chesapeake actively monitors, and has the potential to invest in, over 90 markets worldwide. These can range from tangible assets, such as coffee, crude oil, and gold, to global financial instruments, such as German government bonds, U.S. stock indices, and global currencies.

Michael Note

I never imagined, when I started the Trend Following podcast in 2012, that I would get to 1,000 episodes.

I'm one of the few people in the world where you can take my recorded words, dump them into some kind of AI, and create an artificial intelligence Michael Covel. Take all my books and audio content, throw them into a blender, give the AI a new subject, and the AI mic can keep me going on forever.

So when I was deliberating who to pick as my guest for episode 1,000, I thought about the first trigger of my career. And that trigger was going to a Salomon Brothers interview in 1994. It didn't work out. After, I walked into a Borders bookshop, saw *Financial World's* Top 100 Paid on Wall Street, and read a blurb in there about Jerry Parker. That brief paragraph said something like, "Jerry was in Southern Virginia. He was trained to use a tracking system."

And that was the magic moment for me. I thought, "Well, I don't know this guy, Jerry Parker, but if he could get trained, why the hell can't I?" I just finished my MBA. I thought I had to know balance sheets and Warren Buffett and all that kind of stuff. But here in this one little magazine article was this guy who lived 90 minutes from me, so I got in the car and drove to his office.

He did not agree to meet with me for 18 months. And finally I sent him a fax that said something to the effect of, "The top 10 reasons you must meet with Mike Covel right now." A few minutes later, his assistant called me and said, "You got 30 minutes on this date."

I went down there in December 1995, which was the first moment I met Jerry Parker, one of the legendary trend following traders of the last 40 years, one of the original Turtles, and definitely the most successful.

Michael Covel: In 1983, could you imagine having a conversation with 2021 Jerry? What would that conversation be like?

Jerry Parker: It would pretty much be: You're setting your sights too low. You never know what's going to happen, especially if good things start to happen, incredibly good things. You could always just be so satisfied with what you know, what you expect. Life is usually good, especially for spoiled Americans. Life is good wherever we are, whenever we are happy. We got big plans, big expectations—but in my lifetime, one of the hallmarks has been that it's easy to exceed your expectations because of the way the world has evolved.

Michael: I guess in '83, you had some inkling about trend following, but that was a pretty big change in early '84 for you. Do you ever look back and think, "What a wild ride?"

Jerry: From day one, I understood clearly the opportunity that I had and we all had and how amazing it was, because the biggest takeaway from the Turtles is we were taught by these genius traders who could have probably done well, made a lot of money in a lot of different fields. We started at the top, from the best. We had a pretty good expectation of what we were learning and where this could take us.

> **Part of winning is wanting to be in the game.**

And then all of a sudden you start making 100%, 200% a year. But leaving there and starting your own business, the expansion of the managed futures industry, and CTAs getting lots of assets under management, that was all brand new.

Michael: I know you are humble about these kinds of questions, but I think you're going to win the endurance contest when it comes to the Turtles.

Jerry: Part of winning is wanting to be in the game, even after you've made enough money. And the second part is sticking with the principles. That's where I definitely deserve first prize, because I did stick with the trend following principles. One of the lessons I learned recently was that my mentors were more interested in systematic trading rather than trend following. I got experience in the late '90s when I continued to trade longer term and extend my look-back period. I stuck with the same strategy, hardly any changes. I would do research and come up with changes that I would later say, "Oh, that wasn't a good change. I need to revert back, and not add bells and whistles and unnecessary things to try to prevent drawdowns."

I mean, you want to get rid of those drawdowns, but just stick with those principles and look at the world through the lens of trend following. I would even ask some of the Turtles, "I'm going to start trading single stocks versus indices." Some of their responses would be, "Oh, that's great. Because then you can add in some fundamentals or some other ways of looking at stocks and choosing stocks rather than trend following." And my response was, "No way, I would never do that." I absolutely always refused to give up on those bedrock principles that I learned in December 1983.

Michael: A small group of people get taught by these genius traders. It's a legendary story, but maybe some folks get unfairly positioned into slots. I've had a chance to meet some of your peers, and many of them are highly emotional. What's interesting when you talk about trend following is you're Zen about it. Even though people can execute under the tutelage of Rich Dennis and Bill Eckhardt, maybe when they're out on their own these traders didn't grasp what you just described—the emotional part, the living with it part.

Jerry: You can definitely dig deep into this topic. It can be explained simply. I have children in their 20s and 30s, and let's say they want to trade. Maybe they're not the most skilled in math or they're preoccupied with other things, but I can teach them, "Buy here, buy this breakout, sell that breakout." To some degree, even if they don't understand the math of it at all, they could probably make a nice living. You don't have to get into it much. In some ways, if you don't dig too deep, you do your trades in the morning and then go out and have fun, then maybe you're not tempted as much to try to change it.

> Our main job during these amazing trends is not to do anything.

For me, there is a lot of depth to it and I was uncovering what the principles of trend following meant. Especially as you are faced with opportunities to apply these principles, or not apply them. I've found that a lifetime spent refining your trend following is a perfectly great use of your time. Other CTAs said, "Okay, I got the trend following nailed. I'll add a mean reversion, pattern recognition, carry trade, and all these other things, and I know how to calculate a moving average. So, I'm done with that." I felt like, "No, that's not exactly true." You can dive deep into this and at least learn a lot about what works and what doesn't work.

Michael: January 2020 through August 2021 [and into 2022], has been a stellar trend following period. For a long stretch a lot of people were saying that trend following is dead. You even had some great trend following traders that we both respect who were saying there was a problem with trend following. But you stuck to your knitting. I know you're not running around saying, "I told you so," but the fact is you did tell people so.

Jerry: It's been such a great move in so many of these markets: currencies, commodities, grains, metals, base metals, Bitcoin, lumber—some of these stand out. I was lucky enough to have Tesla in my portfolio. The big lesson we learned last fall is it wasn't our fault. Except, I think it could have been our fault to choose trend following in the first place. You cannot rely upon a method where 5% of the trades are going to make all of your profit. And you've got all this diversification. You need to figure out when the commodities are not going to work, and load up in stocks and bonds. It could have been a mistake to choose trend following and diversification, but I don't believe that. I believe in looking at all the data, not just recent data, and following the rules—not trying to figure out which regime we're in and burden our system, and pollute our performance and our results, with extraneous matters.

It wasn't our fault, because we didn't have big outlier trades, so we weren't doing anything wrong. Apart from, as I said, we shouldn't have chosen trend following to begin with possibly. Now we're all humbled that what pays the bills is these amazing trends and our main job during these trends is not to do anything. Those breakouts in October and November 2020—the markets started skyrocketing. As long as you didn't apply some sort of target or profit objective and just waited for your retracement and your trading stop to be hit—which a lot of them haven't yet—then you were going to do well.

The lesson is, sell your soul, sell out for the outlier, whatever it takes. In the Tesla trade it went up a lot initially, 50 ATRs (average true ranges), it retraced 49, and now it went up 400. Depending upon your look-back period, you could have definitely gotten out a few times if you're looking at the 50-day low or the 75-day low or whatever, which is fine. But if you have some longer-term stuff, that painful drawdown is the price you pay for hundreds and hundreds more ATR profits. It takes guts to do that and not pick up the phone, or your laptop, to dial in and take some profits.

Michael: Let me return to a point you made when you were talking about your two mentors early on, Rich Dennis and Bill Eckhardt—that you would classify them as systematic traders, not necessarily trend following traders. I would classify you as a systematic trend following trader, would I not?

Jerry: Oh, definitely.

Michael: Can you explain what you meant by them being systematic and not necessarily trend following?

Jerry: At some point in time, let's say the late '90s, the shorter-term trend following stuff that we used as the Turtles didn't work well. It hasn't worked well since.

My simple idea was, "If the 20-day low doesn't work, how does the 120-day low work?" And just keep expanding your look-back period so you won't get chopped up and whipsawed out of these large trends. The cost being that when you do have the big trends, your trading stop is going to be far away and you're going to have a bigger drawdown. That's pretty easy.

But it's unacceptable for people who say, "That doesn't feel like a good return-risk trade-off there. I'd rather look at something with a shorter time span, keep that two- or three-week look-back." Your typical outlier might be 20 ATRs versus my typical outlier which might be over 100 ATRs. What they were more committed to is, well, it may not look like trend following that we taught the Turtles, but it will be systematic, rules-based, back tested, and things like that.

From day one of the Turtles, it was pretty well known that Rich Dennis and Bill Eckhardt were skeptical about the future of trend following and the parameters and the way they were teaching us. They were saying, "This may not keep working long," and so I was thinking, "What am I doing here?" Even before the Turtle class was over, there was a pessimism about how long this was going to work.

Trying to evolve away from parameter sets that are too enticing for other people is a good mentality to have. I've settled it all by being so long term and so willing to take ridiculously large drawdowns on profitable trades that my assumption is it's not going to attract many other smart people.

Michael: Even if the parameter sets change, why do the principles stay? It's interesting that even back then, these smart, legendary traders were pessimistic about trend following. But you, one of the students said, "This long-term stuff, I think there's something here." Multiple decades on from then, generations having come and gone, it still seems that if somebody can use the Jerry Parker strategy, they might be okay?

Jerry: Oh definitely. One of the things that happened over the years was trend following started to change from what I would call the classic trend following—one entry rule, one breakout entry, a breakout exit, and a stop loss. As far as the signals go, you hardly beat that too much. Maybe you can throw in one other thing on the entry side.

It started to change from "Let your profits run," to "What's the Sharpe ratio?" and, "We need to be concerned with our daily, weekly, monthly performance rates of return." It's hard to let your profits run if you're going to be concerned about the volatility of your returns. We've got the risk covered, we're taking these small losses. That seemingly is great— that's our money management. We diversify like crazy. We do longs and shorts and then we take small losses. But what changed was we need to pay attention to the volatility of our profitable trades.

And if it's a drawdown on our profitable trade, they've been redefined as losses. How does this happen?

I reject that idea. There's no way to accept that and at the same time keep my philosophical head straight that you got to let your profits run. On profitable trades, you can lose hundreds and hundreds of basis points, whereas on losing trades, you lose 25, 50 basis points max. This was the big change that impacted everyone, almost to a person, except a small group of people like myself who refused to give in to this Sharpe ratio targeting.

Michael: You have talked in the past about European CTAs having trend following plus "other stuff." I think what you're getting at is a lot of big-name traders did add a lot of stuff, and some of that's not worked out exactly right.

Jerry: There's at least two kinds of stuff. One is the ideas that I've mentioned before: pattern recognition, carry trade, short term, mean reversion, maybe AI, machine learning, and things like that, to improve your trend following portfolio. Managed futures is maybe one of the few hedge fund categories that's not good enough to allow allocators to allocate to pure trend—you need to create a portfolio of strategies yourself in order to get assets. I was never interested in that, but I think that's the least offensive part.

The stuff that's more offensive is vault targeting and paying attention to Sharpe. Trend following is the one area where Sharpe has no place—upside risk, downside, it's ridiculous. You're letting those profits run. And your risk is losing trades and how much you're risking per trade.

These guys from the European CTAs that hit it big, they were great at building these great businesses and getting the AUM. I think they figured out that if you want to make a lot of money managing other people's money, you're going to have to take as much of the trend stuff as people can handle and then maybe you add a dash of marketing, "Hey, you can stick around with these traditional trend followers with this big volatility, or we'll manage all of this for you into something that's a little bit more palatable and more scientific, with all of our PhDs, in different commitment to this traditional way of looking at markets, which is Sharpe and volatility of returns."

Of course, it's a great business opportunity for them to say, "Allocate with us, we do it a different way."

There can be periods where having a suboptimal strategy can do well.

When I would go and talk to potential clients, I would say that we're one of the few CTAs that doesn't involve target and we just let the profits run, and we trade single stocks and things like that, so you need to have both in your portfolio. But I guess some of the other CTAs could not resist trashing the Turtles and trying to build a legacy of making things a little more scientific. I would be embarrassed to call my trading science, even if I deserved it. But I think what got me going was the trashing of the Turtles and a simple way of doing things. And now watch us—we're taking it to a new level. In the long run I knew nothing was going to succeed better than the classic approach.

Michael: It's tough for investors to dig through the weeds, define those basic principles, and understand them; to be able to see through the glossy marketing and get the philosophy. Then you get to the rules, the execution. Someone's got to truly understand what you said earlier about the 5% outlier trades. That's tough when there's so many other people out there yelling that they've got the next new thing.

Jerry: There can be periods where doing the wrong thing and having a suboptimal strategy can do well. Especially if you have short-lived trends. There have been many trades over the years where I remember cotton would rally and it would make 15 or 20 ATRs and I would lose it all back. It would just crash the next week. And if you have what I would consider not a great strategy, but take some of those profits, you can have what looks like a better strategy. Clients are weak, and they want to buy into it. If you can convince them that they can

> No one wants to hear, 'Eat more broccoli.'

have what they want and minimize the negativity, they're all over it. No one wants to hear, "Eat more broccoli." And that's pretty much what we were saying the whole time when performance of other CTAs was better.

I'll never convince anyone that Richard Dennis and Bill Eckhardt gave us far superior systems and philosophy, but it's absolutely true. That's what we came from, which was trade for yourself. Maybe you'll have a few clients, but clients will always be tempting you to do the wrong thing. They don't understand. The whole basis of what you do is that it's hard to do, it's counterintuitive, and letting profits run, accepting volatility, is difficult. You need to be aware that whatever lurks out there is not going to brag on you and compliment your trading strategy. It's going to make the most amount of money and be the most robust.

The other guys were coming out of these big trading firms that had marketing departments and were raising lots of assets. They probably had a minimum emphasis on research or trend following in general, moving average crossovers and things like that, and then they're done. Their thought process is, "How do we put together this organization? What will attract people to give us lots of money?" And that's why these big organizations are so much better at raising assets, because that was their main goal.

Michael: I've seen on your Twitter feed, I think you're quoting somebody else, "The big blowups are typically caused by extreme intelligence that causes people to believe their own dangerous stories, that you can predict with accuracy, use leverage because your prediction must be true." I'll let

The whole
basis of trend
following is that
it's hard to do.

you comment on that. But it'll also be interesting to hear your thoughts that given where we are right now (summer 2021) with many markets extended, especially U.S. equities, there's probably a few bubbles lurking out there that could get pierced sometime in the future. They're doing exactly what you're describing, but the leverage is being hidden inside of bull markets.

Jerry: That's a good quote. It gets to the heart of how for some people trend following is so hard because you can add things to it. What makes it so great is that it has one entry rule, one exit rule, one stop loss, and then we're done. And I'm saying, I'm sorry, but you're going to have some drawdowns from your open trades that are going to make you uncomfortable. Because it's our money. We've already spent it.

They even call a drawdown an "open trade loss" now. You take these smart guys with PhDs and you tell them, "Okay, you're finished, now go market or something." And they say, "No, I don't want to be finished. I can always improve, and I need to get rid of these volatile periods, that's what's standing out." It's difficult for smart people to say, "Enough is enough, and I can't improve upon this."

The worst thing going is the back test. I like to look at the trade stats, the average win, the average loss, the win percentage, win/loss ratio, and things like that. People tend to fall in love with the equity curve back test, going back to the '70s and '80s and watching how the markets go up and down, and take away some key clues from all of that. But I don't think there are any clues at all, except that if you're picking up on any risk that you've seen in the past, bank on it looking worse in the future.

Some of these firms put a big emphasis on research, change, and evolving, because this is what clients want to hear, but true trend following is we don't change. The problem is that we are always searching for more and more sample size. And the world has changed a lot since the '80s and '90s. Is it still okay to use all of those trades? This makes people nervous to not evolve and change over time. A lot of the industry, that's their main calling card: "Watch us do our research and watch us evolve and change." And that goes against classic trend following.

Michael: Classic trend following is taking advantage of classic human nature, which doesn't seem to change, does it?

Jerry: I don't think so. It's about looking back over all of that period of time and seeing that you have these outlier trades and you're going to have this volatility and it's fine. It's not good enough for a lot of people for the computer to say, "Hey, if you risk 50 basis points per trade, these parameters are going to make the most amount of money for you." Well, I need to eliminate some of those bad days and months because I'll be getting phone calls and complaints. Deep down I think it bothers traders as much as it does clients. They actually believe that targeting volatility and having special rules, special profits, is something that they should do and want to do.

Michael: Anybody that has heard you talk before thinks to themselves, "He seems like a pretty disciplined guy." I know you're conscious of health, fitness, your weight, and you have been for a long time. I'm curious about the Jerry Parker ethos, because you did not have the same ethos about physical fitness when you were younger.

Jerry: I think practice comes to mind, that's the secret. We all realize that you can practice piano or basketball—all of these disciplines can be practiced as well. I remember when I decided to get in shape. I was 40 and I had never been in shape a day of my life. And so, I had no expectation, but I started to realize that day after day, putting one foot in front of the other, you get better, you practice, and you learn, and you figure out things that you thought were impossible. That's discipline. Once I started seeing results in trading, or in diet and fitness, I ramped it up. I went extreme.

I want to try to make everything as pure and extreme as possible, to get to the core principle, and be the one person who may be able to take it further and deeper than maybe I should. To see if I can push the limits as much as possible. When you first start out, you're not thinking about anything, except let's lose five pounds. And then as it starts coming off, I was getting more and more excited and going, "Okay, we got to go for high school weight." But as you start seeing success in implementing principles and understanding what works and doesn't work, you need to start pushing yourself to extremes that you never thought you could even imagine.

That's what I'm good at. I can get obsessed with things quickly, trading, diet and fitness, but then understanding the basics, learning over time and listening to other people and saying, "Okay, this is something I haven't heard before. It doesn't sound like it fits with my philosophy, but I'm going to think about this and keep it on my list of things to explore. And then maybe I'll get rid of it later or I'll incorporate it into my plan." I was incredibly open-minded about anything people would tell me about trading or dieting and fitness, or any area I was interested in. That's rare these days.

I could print my rules on the front of the paper and people would criticize them.

Rich said many times, "I could print my rules on the front page of the paper, and no one would follow them." He meant they were too hard to follow. Small losses, 40% win rate, let your profits run. But I think now I could print my rules on the front of the paper, and everyone would criticize them. "They're too simple. You don't know what you're talking about. I studied this in college and you're not using Sharpe." The new way of looking at mentors and older people who've learned a lot is to disagree with them. I love a good argument. I try to foment arguments all the time on Twitter, to get someone criticizing my views so that I can learn and hone my responses.

Michael: Interesting what you said about practice and experience. You don't know anything about fitness, you're age 40, you start to lose weight, and then some kind of magical motivation happens because now you are personally experiencing it. That is difficult to share with other people, because it's the magic of experiencing it yourself. All of a sudden it's "Wham bam, thank you, man." It feels so good. You can believe in it, but it's tough to share with other people, isn't it?

Jerry: It's tough. I have had people come up to me and say, "Write down what you did. What do you do?" And I could do that in trading as well. I did that once and I looked at the list and I was shaking my head, because it's not something you want to read upfront. You want to take these baby steps and figure it out for yourself. I had a nasty, competitive streak that I could tap into once I got a glimpse of accomplishments that I had never thought were possible.

It was this same thing with the Turtles. I remember being obsessed with getting to $100m. My friends were like, "What's wrong with you? Why can't you calm down?" I'm like, "No, no, no, 100 million, I got to get to 100 million." I was extremely competitive and not happy if I was in second place. I'm a hugely bad loser. I don't know what made me so competitive.

From day one with the Turtles, I was probably the least disciplined, but thankfully I seldom got rewarded for my lack of discipline. I was chastised, day after day, if I didn't follow my rules or my system. I could immediately see the downside of not following it, because I wasn't getting positive feedback. I righted myself over the years to be better disciplined. But honestly, the amount of money that I've left on the table by not being 100% disciplined, or even close to it, is a sad story. We don't need to get into that.

> To some degree crytpo is the perfect market for trend followers.

Michael: You brought up crypto earlier. Trend following traders would argue, "Crypto is just another market. It can be traded." When did you make the decision, "This passed the smell test for me, I'm in." And I'll let you also comment on crypto itself, because you might be a crypto maven, but that doesn't have anything to do with your trend following trading.

Jerry: The answer to that question is always the same for every market, any market, and that is liquidity and diversification. Obviously crypto is pretty diversified, no one even understands it, which makes it less susceptible to deviating from a rules-based system. To some degree crytpo is the perfect market for trend followers. You have no clue what you should do other than following your system.

What happened with Bitcoin is that all of us older guys who were trying not to be left behind and having been burned so many times for being too skeptical about new ideas, we didn't know how to open up a Coinbase account. And then, all of a sudden, the CME comes up with the futures. I know how to trade futures. I have a lot of them in my account right now. I know where the CME is, and I can put this thing on. Probably one of the reasons that the cash futures spread got out of whack was because all the hedge funds and old guys like me were only interested in doing the futures and we didn't even know how to set up our Coinbase.

I'm skeptical of Bitcoin in the sense that I think it could be a little dangerous in these crazy sell-offs; I'm not happy with that. But that doesn't make it too different from all the other markets I trade, because there's been crazy sell-offs in everything, including lumber and some stocks even. I've been around a long time and I've seen crazy volatility in the bonds and the British pound, for God's sake, so Bitcoin doesn't look any different in that sense. But I do wonder what's going to happen in the long term, because I'm always interested in being able to exit the trade.

Another great thing about the markets since the '80s is the number that are out there. My portfolio is so large now that I can take a lot of small risks in a lot of different markets, Bitcoin being one of them. And Ether pretty soon I think—my friends tell me it's different and it's not 100% correlated to Bitcoin, so I'll probably be adding that as well.

Michael: Bitcoin could be a great trading opportunity, or it could end up being a scam—but a scam that has got a ton of money in it, is liquid, goes up and down, is legally traded on an exchange, and is generally accepted by the public.

Jerry: Anything's possible. I read a lot about it and listen to a lot of podcasts. I know it's not a currency, I don't care about that. It is a great fail-safe for crazy governments and fiat in extreme situations. It has its own personality—it's not gold and it's not a currency. It doesn't need to be to have value.

I grew up in the '70s with Milton Friedman, monetarism, and printing money. None of which matters anymore, I guess. But having that algorithm with a fixed amount of Bitcoin is appealing for a kid from the '70s, because we were taught that what creates massive inflation is the ability to keep printing and printing. So, I hope it stays alive. I hope it does well. And I hope it expands into more and more diverse cryptos that are complementary. We can have a fifth type of asset—currencies, commodities, stocks, bonds, and cryptos. That would be fun, 20% in cryptos.

Michael: Speaking of extreme markets, I want to quote once more from your Twitter feed. And again, I think this is you quoting somebody else. The quote was:

Even if markets are in a bubble, your position should be long until your trend following exit is hit. That's all there is. That's the rule.

Nobody knows what the markets will do and where prices will be tomorrow, next week, next month or next year.

That is a tough thing for people to handle. They might have this extreme intelligence and they have decided, "We are in a massive bubble situation in XYZ equities or whatnot." And they want to apply all that intelligence, but that's not the way it works. There's always going to someone after the fact who predicted the bubble and the burst perfectly. But you can't build a life and a trading strategy around trying to predict the one bubble that's going to happen in your lifetime.

Jerry: It's such a rare thing. And you may have been lucky so you should walk away. Some famous guys made a lot of money in that 2007–2009 period and they ended up starting hedge funds. And from then on, the hedge funds lost money. Maybe all you have in you is that one big trade.

I think we have a bubble in bubbles. There's a quote from my two friends, Moritz and Moritz: "I may have made all my life's fortune in bubbles. So what, who cares? The market goes further than it should. It's crazy. And we rode the trend up. Maybe that's why trend following works. That's fine with me."

Something I've learned over time is you can't predict the markets. Not only that, but today's market has no bearing on tomorrow's. I've been in so many situations where the market closed on an all-time high on Friday and I was making a ton of money. And man, the weekend was so much fun. I felt so awesome about myself. I'm at equity highs. This group of markets that closed on their high, it was a strong close. And of course, it crashed from there. And vice versa.

You think you see these patterns and you think it's so obvious. I cannot believe I'm waiting for the 100-day low to get out of this thing. Why am I doing this? All my friends are taking profits. And then all of a sudden, the market reverses and goes back up. It's on the cards that has to happen to have a two-way market, to have a life where we all know prediction is impossible. You are going to win in some of those situations by just following your strategy, and you're going to win overall. If it wasn't the right thing to do, the computer would tell you. But you get enough of those reversals where it keeps going, it makes new highs. So, I think that's the lesson: put on your trades in the morning, and then don't look at them until the close.

It's so funny to read what other people write about bubbles and the extended stock market. They're so uptight about it and they've been doing it for so many years, and it had been wrong for so long. And I just sit back in my little bubble and just trend follow, and I don't pay much attention.

Today's market has no bearing on tomorrow's.

What gets other people so upset is this idea that, "I need to unlock the secret of these bubbles." But when I was in my 20s, I was like, "I need to unlock the secret of staying on these trends." And it came to me that what I should be concerned with is capturing these outliers and not giving a twit about why they were outliers. I mean, to me it's such a waste of time. But to a lot of people, it means a great deal.

I guess I've been a trend follower at heart before I learned about trend following. That was fertile soil for this incredibly magical experience that we had. I'm in my 60s, and so my memory is not as good as it used to be, but I do have a photographic memory when it comes to things that Rich and Bill said to me, and said to the Turtles.

Michael: Who do you enjoy the most on Twitter? Do you have a couple of names you want throw out?

Jerry: I enjoy Moritz Seibert and his buddy Moritz Heiden—the "Two Quants." And then I enjoy Niels Kaastrup-Larsen of Top Traders Unplugged. Richard Brennan is good. I quote Morgan Housel a lot. Mark Rzepczynski, formerly of John W. Henry's firm. Rob Carver. I have a lot of loyal Twitter followers in Clubhouse, I get a lot from those guys as much as they get from me. Like you said, I'm searching for content out there in the news or quotes from people that I can twist into something that benefits trend following, then I put that out there.

One thing I did want to go back to, is that I think that it would have been a much different experience for the Turtles if we had stayed working for Rich a lot longer. In hindsight, the mentorship that we got was so important, it was more than the rules. I've used this bad analogy of, "Here's a manual, now become a Marine." It's not possible. The manual is necessary, but you're not going to become a Marine without the bootcamp.

Getting that list of rules from Rich and Bill and having those four years is indispensable, but another four or five or 10 years would have been so much better. I think the legacy of the Turtles would have benefited so much in terms of trading, discipline, and business. We would have been much better at our job if we'd had more time with those guys.

The time that we did have was indispensable for our success, not just the rules. And that was with them coming over and talking to us maybe once a month or less, but knowing that they had your back. Navigating the markets in the '80s and the '90s with those guys would have been a big benefit for us for sure.

Michael: You've stood the test of the time from the Turtle experience, but I think there would definitely be some people in the class with you who did well under Rich and Bill's tutelage, but maybe they weren't cut out for it. Or do you think that if everybody had stayed much longer, as you theorized, that would've helped some people who needed more time?

Jerry: Yeah, possibly. Going through the markets and living with the trades, the trends, and the losses, we had four pretty good years where we made a lot of money. Maybe a losing year or two with those guys, maybe changing the environment a little bit, like everyone leaving the office and working from home, and then coming back together once a quarter for an update, maybe that would have been good.

Everyone being in the same room did not always have a hugely positive impact on people's trading. Rich wanted some creativity from the group, and I don't think he got much creativity or new ideas. Going through the tough periods with those guys would have helped everyone.

Note: More on Rich Dennis, Bill Eckhardt, and the Turtles can be found in my book, *The Complete Turtle Trader.*

CHAPTER 4

THOMAS BASSO

Enjoying the Ride

THOMAS BASSO is a retired American hedge fund manager. He was president and founder of Trendstat Capital Management and was originally featured in *New Market Wizards*. He currently runs EnjoyTheRide.world, a website dedicated to trader education. He is also the chairman of the board of Standpoint Funds, located in Scottsdale, Arizona, which specializes in all-weather investing. His publications include *Successful Traders Size Their Positions—Why and How?* and *Panic-Proof Investing: Lessons in Profitable Investing from a Market Wizard*, as well as the self-published *The Frustrated Investor*.

Michael Note

I'm holding in my hands my book, *Trend Following Mindset: The Genius of Legendary Trader Tom Basso*, which was inspired by my many interviews with Tom—arguably the interviews that pushed my podcast to prominence. And if I'm going to have a book about Tom, influenced by Tom, inspired by Tom, including all kinds of work from Tom, you might expect me to talk with Tom again. And you'd be right.

Michael Covel: I saw a tweet where somebody said something to the effect of, "I liked Tom until I heard him say something about politics."

My first thought was, "Okay, what is politics in the modern age?" It seems one side has an open, rational, logical mind, and the other side is pure emotion. Here's somebody who says they liked you before, but they don't like you now because they heard you say something political. And I'm thinking to myself, "What would you expect the engineering mindset guy, Tom Basso, to do? To jump up and down, to scream and yell?" It's not even a political question, it's more about how you operate. I don't know why somebody would expect you to be Mr. Emotion.

Tom Basso: Same thing's true with the Covid-19 pandemic, where I'm downloading spreadsheets of data from the CDC, deriving conclusions of the survivability rates and stuff based on the CDC's own numbers, which I think are a little flawed compared to other studies of how people actually die with comorbidities. I explain this on Twitter and I get all the people who have been watching CNN scared out of their wits' end. They're so frazzled, but I'm simply presenting data.

Michael: Isn't data the first way to analyze anything?

Tom: Exactly. You start with the markets, you get 20 years of data, you run it in a simulation platform, you try not to have any bias except to say, "I'm trying to see where the trend of these prices is going." There's lots of data that looks like it doesn't go anywhere. You're trying to separate the noise from the information. It's a data problem. And mathematically, it's no different from what I did as a chemical engineer. If you're trying to control a reaction and the heat exchanger is getting too cold, the temperature control says, "Open the steam valve, bring in more steam into the heat exchanger, and heat the process up until it hits the right number, and then close down the steam valve because everything's fine now." The markets are the same—it reaches a point we got to do something. It's the exact same math, exact same philosophy.

Michael: If one has this engineering mindset, your first step would be, "Okay, what does the data say?" To take your example of Covid: Who's dying? And is there a similarity between those who are dying? For many

You start with the markets, you get 20 years of data, you run it in a simulation platform, you try not to have any bias.

people in our home country, that might cause a lot of discomfort, but data is not about discomfort—it's just data.

Tom: There's no bias at all. It's just data, numbers. In reality, the group that's the most affected by Covid are older people. Well, older people tend to die more than younger people of natural causes. You can't say that a death is strictly Covid-related when the person was dying from cancer or got hit by a car; comorbidities come into it. The data is just starting to come out now and I will analyze it before the end of 2021 on total U.S. deaths. Usually at some point within a 6–12-month period, they'll be able to tell us how everybody died in the United States in more detail and they'll have it cross-checked. It's going to be interesting to see the total number of deaths versus the population in 2021 versus 2020, when we were at the height of the pandemic. I don't think there's going to be a whole lot of difference in the total deaths.

Michael: Meaning what we did is moved forward deaths.

Tom: Probably shifted the labeling. There might be some lung-related diseases that'll go down and Covid will go up, but total deaths are not going to be significantly different. To look at some of the news in April or May 2020, you thought the world was going to end.

When everything started getting locked down, my life didn't change a lot. I sit at a computer, and my wife and I love to cook. Once a week we'd go out to the grocery store and come home and isolate and it was no big deal. Trading was going well. We had a lot of things to keep us busy. I was totally happy to protect myself and my neighbors, but that gave me a lot of time to start looking at the data. And the data was not supporting closing down what is almost a $20tn economy in the United States and who knows how much globally, just to try to prevent transmission, which it seemed like it didn't prevent anyway. It was foolish. Most people who're in good shape enough to be healthy probably have a 99.7% survival rate even if they get Covid, which is not a guarantee either. Why was everybody warping the entire world for something so ridiculously in your favor of surviving? It doesn't make any sense mathematically.

Michael: Let's go back in time now. It must have been 2012 the first time you came on my podcast. I think it's right to say you took a pause from trading, then restarted?

Tom: When I retired, I took a year off from trading. I was so sick of dealing with clients, the government, auditors, lawyers, and accountants, and spending a hundred grand a year on wasteful nonsense. I stuck my money in a money market fund and relaxed.

Brenda, now my wife, knew I was a money manager, so she comes to me one day and says, "I'm almost embarrassed but I've been doing this thing with this broker. Would you look at it?" And she gave me half an hour of apologies ahead of handing me the sheet of paper. And I looked down it and said, "Why would you be embarrassed at this? You've done an above-average job in my opinion."

I was complimentary—she had done a good job. But Brenda's more of a real estate expert. She does all our real estate. She says, "Sign here, sign here, sign here," and I sign. Then when it comes to trading futures or ETFs or whatever, I'm our guy. I manage her portfolios and she manages my real estate. It's worked out great. I started getting back into trading to manage her money. Then I thought, "Well, as long as I'm doing hers, I might as well do my own." I got all the money out of money markets and I fired everything up. And then I had relatives asking me questions and that started the Facebook stuff.

Michael: So relative connections is how you began to connect with people.

Tom: I was helping relatives because I can put it in a Facebook post. My stepson can see it, my brother in New York can see it, my sister in Wisconsin, Brenda's brother-in-law over in Atlanta. And then some old friends who were traders from the industry saw it and said, "Hey, this is cool." Then all of a sudden, I've got a thousand Facebook friends.

Then people—including Larry Tentarelli, who you know I think, he's a trend follower—are saying, "You should go on Twitter." I said, "Okay. I'll go over there, it's no big deal. I'll put it here and then control C, control V, boom, out on Twitter."

And now I've got 27,000 followers on Twitter. One thing leads to another and you interview me, and it goes viral. My wife and I are at the pool in Malaga and we decide to launch EnjoyTheRide.world as a solution to getting the information from me to the world in the most cost-effective way. Then that goes nuts. We get thousands of people visiting that website every month.

Michael: You spend decades having all this success and learning all these lessons. You've already chosen a path in retirement but then, I guess, this idea of being an educator sucked you back in and started the mind going again and you seem to love that process.

Tom: It's an overused phrase, but I see it as giving back. The industry has been good to me. There were people along the way who threw in their 2 cents to me, helped me through. Larry Hite's chapter in *Market Wizards* resonated with my brain mathematically and helped me develop my volatility controls that Trendstat used successfully

The industry has been good to me.

for a long run—I'm still using them today. People helped me, whether they even knew it or not, by saying something in an interview. I might have read it and it hit my brain the right way—it triggered something and off I went. But at this point in my life, I've only got four accounts I manage for myself and my wife. I don't have to register. I don't have audits. I don't have legal and life's good. I play a lot of golf and I work out.

A gentleman called me from North Carolina about an hour before you and I were due to talk; I've known him for four or five years. He's followed me on Facebook, I guess. I did a Zoom call at his request. I thought it was appropriate to help him at that point in time, so I took an hour. At the end of the call, he thanked me profusely for taking him from completely confused to totally clear on what he needs to do. It's not that hard for me and it's satisfying because I'm helping someone. I could go work in a food kitchen and hand out food to the homeless, but this is an expertise I have that's a little bit more unique.

Michael: People get themselves confused, with all kinds of indicators on their charts, and whatnot. I make the analogy of cleaning the room. Everything's piled up all around the room and you can't even see where the bed is. That's one of the first steps—simplify and remove the clutter.

Where this leads is the timeless aspect your knowledge and of trend following. Young people might be saying, "Okay, Tom's older, he's retired.

What does he know? The markets have changed. There are new markets, there's crypto." What these people don't get is that humans have not changed. You can change the playing field, you can add some new markets, but humans move in herds, and they drive markets up and down. That being the case, your wisdom is going to work long past the time that you and I are on this planet.

Tom: With electronic communications, you have more ability to move the herd quickly with technology and with instant communications than you ever did in the past. In the old days, you had to wait till *The Wall Street Journal* came out the next day to get the fact that "Oh, my God, the markets crashed yesterday," and people started talking about it at the lunch table. And after a couple days, they made a phone call to their broker.

Humans move in herds, and they drive markets up and down.

Today, if Twitter shows the market's down 1%, I'm on my interactive broker's account hitting a sell signal within the next five minutes. The psychology that used to take two years to do a bear market, 50 cents on a dollar in the S&P back in '73, '74, is now accomplished in six months or less. Things happen quicker now, but it's the same psychology, going from euphoria to depression and back to euphoria—that hasn't changed.

Michael: You've got this great phrase: "Enjoy the ride." It's almost Buddhist in the sense that on the surface it looks like just a sentence, but when you have more experience, you realize it offers deep insights into the human condition.

Tom: "Enjoy the ride" came from a certain transaction when I was trying to put an end to a comment about being whipsawed: This is part of trading, enjoy the ride. People jumped on it; it's way beyond me now. People end their tweets: "As @basso_tom always says, enjoy the ride." Now everybody knows what "ETR" means, in the trading world at least. It's crazy.

Michael: Let's tear it apart—ETR is deceptively simple, but complex.

Tom: It means stay in the moment, enjoy the process of trading, and let go of the results. The ups and downs are going to be there, you're going to have whipsaws, you're going to have huge runs.

I've been on lumber for I don't know how long now. I glance over at my unrealized profit on the one contract I now own, because I've sold off the rest, and it's huge. I'm thinking, "This is insane, is the lumber market going to keep going like this?" Maybe, maybe not. I don't know. If I could be in that trade the rest of my life, that'd be okay, but I'm enjoying the moment of where I am today.

There's going to be good periods, there's going to be whipsaws. I'm going to have losing trades and winning trades. And all of that is not worth a whole lot, except to enable me to be right where I am today enjoying talking to you. I'm enjoying seeing what happens to the *Trend Following Mindset* book and enjoying seeing what happens with Standpoint. I'm the chairman of the board, we've got a board meeting tomorrow. The two old guys on the board—me and another guy—call the Standpoint folks "the kids" because they're all a whole lot younger than we are. They call me their surrogate dad. We have a good time, but they're slaying it.

> Market psychology still goes from euphoria to depression and back to euphoria— that hasn't changed.

I'm also consulting with a gentleman who's putting together a trading platform that will do simulations, run trading, and actually execute the trades to the broker. That's been a lot of fun. I'm helping; he's asking questions. I get to use this thing when it's done, that's a nice deal. It's like having somebody customize software for me.

Michael: Let me keep you on ETR because, again, it's deceptively simple, but in reality it's complex. Built into it is how you deal with control. You make decisions on how you run your life every day, but "enjoy the ride" implies that you're giving up control to some degree. A lot of people new to trading—and perhaps the more experienced too—believe that when they look at their systems, they can control the outcome; they can control what's going on day to day. I have people write to me all the time, saying, "Trying to increase my consistency so I make money every day." I reply, "Oh, like Bernie Madoff. Great." Why are you comfortable giving up control?

Tom: When I started out back in the '70s, I'm starting to trade stocks and I'm looking at the New York stock exchange trading billions of dollars a day and here's my piddly little $10,000 or whatever, and I realized that nothing I do in the market's going to amount to anything, I'm an ant compared to elephants.

I've always had this attitude—even in Trendstat days, I was careful to be a fairly small part of whatever market I was in so that I could have liquidity in and out. I never thought that I could control what the markets do because there's so many other players and so many trillions of dollars that go back and forth. I always felt like I was just going along for the ride, and that's where enjoy the ride comes in.

A famous quote from sailing is, you can't control the direction of the wind, but you can adjust your sails. My philosophy is: the market will do what the market will do. I think Brenda might even have stuck that in the foreword of *Trend Following Mindset*, I've told her that so many times.

We'll be watching the morning business show while having breakfast, and somebody will be predicting this and predicting that, and then my wife will say, "Yeah, but Tom says the market will do whatever the market will do." That's my philosophy for the markets. The markets are going to do whatever they do. My job is to go along for the ride and while I'm doing it, I need to manage risk, volatility, margin, the other different things I can control, and enjoy the process.

> You can't control the direction of the wind, but you can adjust your sails.

There's no point in going through life miserable and hating what you're doing. You might as well let the markets do what they're doing and don't agonize over trying to predict—it adds a lot of stress and strain to your body and that's not going to help your process.

Michael: How do you think potentially bright people—maybe they've got a little money, they've had some success in life—can possibly be consistent enough to make money every day or every month?

Tom: I've run into some brilliant minds—people who blow me away mathematically. I'd call them geniuses. I may be a smart guy who did some good things in chemical engineering and adapted it into the markets, but I'm talking true rocket scientist types. They almost can't even pull the trigger on a trade because they are looking at the data and saying, "If I take this data and apply every polynomial regression that I can figure out, I can match exactly what the market's doing and it'll tell me what it's going to do next week, with 100% accuracy in historic simulations, so I'm going to break the bank here."

And of course, it doesn't work. They lose their money, they're shell-shocked, and they start doubting themselves.

They have a tendency to think they can figure out this puzzle that is unsolvable. The markets will always do what the markets will do. And they're so complex. A volcano in Iceland shuts down air traffic for a week across the Atlantic. That's affecting economies, it's affecting stocks in American airlines, and all sorts of stuff. How

The markets will always do what the markets will do.

do you know that volcano's going to blow? There are unexpected sunspots that throw the market off in a direction that none of your algorithms are ever going to predict. You got

to let the market do what it does and realize that it's going to go up, it's going to go down, sometimes it's going to go sideways. And if you can deal with all three of those little scenarios, you're home free. Keep doing it and enjoy the ride.

Michael: Around 20 years ago, the first time I met Ed Seykota, I was doing some homework on him. I came across a high school math paper online, written by his son. His son was a teenager, maybe 14 or 15. This paper was 10 to 20 pages long and it was solid math. I had no idea at all what any of this stuff was about. I drew the conclusion that if his son was this good at math, Ed Seykota would be too. Ed is an MIT grad after all.

Ed Seykota, who understands all that complex math, is the same guy who has the whipsaw music video on YouTube. It's interesting that he has that genius level math and can put it in his holster, so to speak, and then turn around and understand the market psychology like you do, which is to enjoy the ride or the whipsaw song. That's unusual. As you point out, a lot of guys with superstar math ability get frustrated.

Tom: I was going down that path in my 20s. I seriously spent four or five years on a lot of modeling, thinking I could figure it out. And then I realized, somewhere along the way, that letting my profits run and cutting my losses short, simple trend following, made it more robust. As I've mentioned to a lot of traders, there's a difference between perfection and reliability as a trader, versus making money. You're not trying to be perfect; you're trying to produce a profit. Those are two different things. People think being perfect is going to lead to profits. That's not true.

For example, somewhere around two-thirds of the time, I'm wrong; one-third right. I'm okay with that because I don't care about being right all the time, I want to be profitable. And that's something that takes a while for traders to get, but as you mature you finally start figuring out that it's a long-term process and losses are part of it. I think Ed Seykota once said, "Having profits without having losses is like breathing in without breathing out." They're both part of the flow of trading. And when you settle into that, you're okay managing your losses, and letting your profits run.

Michael: I've interviewed you many times, but this is the first chance I've had to interview you on video, and you have this even keel voice and persona. When is the last time you got mad? What causes you to sometimes get off the ETR?

> There's a difference between perfection and making money.

Tom: It's rare, but I can think of maybe some instances where I get mad at myself for not thinking through a reasonable strategy on a golf shot or something. Brenda and I have put together quite the lifestyle. We have our home in the woods for the summertime—up in the mountains at 5,000 ft, it's a lot cooler. I live in Scottsdale during the winter, 330 days of sunshine, 200 golf courses in the metropolitan area— I'm a golf nut. I live in heaven in both places. Our lifestyle is tightly put together and we're both on the same page foodwise; neither of us likes onions, strangely, to give one example.

Michael: Tom Basso does not like onions, that's what makes him mad. We've got to the secret today.

Tom: I published a study of the purchasing power of the U.S. dollar against the U.S. per capita consumption of onions. And as onion consumption has increased every single year in the United States over the last roughly 35,

40 years, the U.S. dollar's purchasing power has gone nowhere but down. My conclusion is we need to stop eating onions if we want to save the dollar. Everybody got a big kick out of that in the trading world. It had a beautiful graph and everything. The joke is that I don't like onions.

Michael: I've gotten frustrated in recent years over the fact that pure data is being ignored. Further, there are powers that be that want data ignored, or they obscure the data, or they lie about it. Then you've got a media system that is pushing agendas. I've come to the conclusion that I can't control it at all, I don't know if anybody can anymore. I have serious doubts as to whether this type of government in the United States will continue well into the future. It's an interesting time right now.

Tom: It is. I seem to be on the receiving end of the negative side of these times. I don't see how quality of life in the United States is improving. There's an economic term that perfectly captures it. It's called utility— the price you pay for what you get. You have something in your life that you've had to pay to put together—for example, you buy a house in the mountains, you get the benefit of the cooler air in the summertime. For me, the ability to play golf in the mountains, to go hiking, to work out, all has a certain benefit and it cost me something to receive that benefit.

When we wrap that all together, that's the utility. If it's a positive utility, it's a good thing. If it's a negative utility, it's not good. Given how I've structured my whole life, my retirement, my trading, and my website, and helping people with simulation packages, that's all a lot of fun. I have a certain amount of utility to my lifestyle. It's on the decline unfortunately, thanks to the U.S. government.

Michael: I look at young people today, they're being bombarded with media messaging and government policy that doesn't make any sense at all, but they don't necessarily have the foundation to be a skeptic, to criticize. I guess everyone's afraid to speak up.

Let's go back to data. If we want to solve a problem, such as crime in the United States, we should start with the data. We should be asking, "Where is the crime? Who commits the crime? When is the crime committed? What cities?" We've reached a point where we're not allowed to ask those questions, which are not intended to be political, because there are people with political agendas who don't want the basic information known. If we were to take all the inputs that you and I are talking about, the actions, the reactions, the media players, the government decisions, and we were to try and model it, the future doesn't look so nice.

Tom: No, it doesn't. It worries me. The utility is going down, sadly. In the condo complex I live in down in the Scottsdale area, I didn't like some of the landscaping. I've taken courses in landscape architecture and pruning and everywhere I go in the world, I always visit the botanical gardens. And I said, "The utility of that landscaping is not good and it's not getting any better because they've left the wrong plants there. There are too many plants. I'm going to convince the board that I'm smarter in landscape architecture than the rest of the residents. I'm going to get their permission to take a whole section of the condo complex and remove every second or third plant selectively, leaving the other ones to grow and be beautiful."

At the end of four days, I had about 20 compliments from residents. The board completely agreed to allow me to create a landscaping plan for the entire condo complex, which I volunteered for and will be happy to do, and it'll be a fun project for me in retirement. What am I doing there? I'm spending some effort, but instead of when I walk the dog, looking at some of this stuff and saying, "Gosh, why would anybody put that plant there?" I'm now going to look at all this beautiful landscaping and say, "Wow, I love living here." I'm increasing my utility.

Michael: You weren't being cocky or overly confident, but you said something interesting about being smarter about the landscaping. I think this is something that's gotten lost in the modern age. You had already given the foundation that you've traveled the world, you've seen the botanical gardens, you have the experience and the passion. You know things that perhaps the average 25-year-old in Scottsdale who might be managing the garden doesn't.

Tom: The ex-board members who used to run the landscaping were a little pissed off at me for taking out a bunch of plants. They came down in a huff in their car two days after I had started the process, and one of the current board members happened to see them out of his window. He watched them for a while, and they'd talk and talk. And then they'd go and look at the plants and then they'd talk some more. They can't even tell what I did. It looks fabulous and they can't figure out what I did because they were going to complain about it. They finally gave up, got in their car and drove back up to the end of the subdivision.

Michael: You've described the United States on almost every issue. You have a certain level of experience on major issues and all these people with inexperience are allowed to make major calls. And there are so many wise people with lots of experience, regardless of political stripe, who are kept out of the power system these days.

Tom: It's true. I find it fascinating that you live in Vietnam and you're a citizen of the world. My Laurens Bensdorp is another one. He's now in Brazil because he chooses to be. He wanted to learn to speak Portuguese.

Michael: It wasn't planned. I came here and there's no welfare system. You immediately see that every last person is hustling. But I enjoy being in a society where people take better care of themselves physically. It says something about the overall direction. All these little things that you don't expect to show up in a country that the United States was once bombing, which seems to be living the American dream better than America.

Tom: The Vietnamese over here in the United States work seven days a week, they hardly ever take a vacation. They send money back home. They strive like crazy to better themselves. That's refreshing to me. There's a certain energy about being in the midst of these people because it makes you want to match their energy. It keeps you alive.

CHAPTER 5

LARRY HITE

Trust the Rule

L ARRY HITE is a hedge fund manager credited as one of the forefathers of system trading. He co-founded Mint Investments in 1981, which by 1990 had become the largest commodity trading advisor (CTA) in the world in terms of assets under management. After forming a partnership with the Man Group in the same year, Larry pioneered the principal protected fund concept, leading to a number of successful structured products and financial engineering innovations. He is the author of *The Rule: How I Beat the Odds in the Markets and in Life—And How You Can Too.*

Michael Note

I first sat down with Larry Hite at his house in Central Park, and he has gone on to become a great, long-time friend. Larry is a trader, first featured in Jack Schwager's *Market Wizards*—one of those voices along with Ed Seykota that you don't forget. I did a foreword for his book, *The Rule*, I've also featured Larry in some of my books, and he was in my film *Broke: The New American Dream*. Every time you meet Larry, there's that nugget, that way he inspires you. Maybe you don't get the same success he's had. Maybe you get close, or maybe you don't get close. It doesn't matter—

it's the wisdom. You take a shot like Larry takes shots, and that's all you can do.

Michael Covel: Let's start today by talking about attitude. You're not 18, I'm not 18, but I talk to a lot of young people on my social media and sometimes I can feel a negative attitude. The way I look at it, if you're alive, you've got a chance to do something. The question I have for you right at the start: Why do you have a good attitude?

Larry Hite: Because my grandmother, my father's mother, had a good attitude, and it came from her to my father to me. And more importantly, the only sensible thing to do is be positive. Because let's

Zero trying, zero result.

say you're so negative you never try, and if you never try, you've got 100% chance of failing. Zero trying, zero result. Even if you are inept, as I was as an athlete for example, when you try you have better than zero chance, and that's the only logical way to go.

Michael: You tell these stories about you not being an athlete. How do I know they're true? You could've been some star New York City track guy. You're making up these stories 60 years later that you weren't a star.

Larry: I was less than a star. Yesterday I talked to a guy who was a major hockey player since he was seven. He was in a car crash where his best friend died and he broke vertebrae in his back. I was interested in what made him come back after that. He had an attitude. He thought if he didn't try, he'd have nothing.

I used to go out at night with my friend Harry. Harry would walk up to good-looking girls and would leave with one, whereas I left alone. I said, "How do you get these beautiful women?" He says, "Oh, every time I see a gorgeous woman, I go up to her and say 'My name's Harry. Let's have coffee.' One out of 10 would say yes."

Now to a 28-year-old horny kid, those were my two favorite subjects: sex and probabilities. I began to understand my grandmother because if you don't try you get zero. If you try, you can do well. That, to me, is not a positive attitude, but a practical attitude.

Michael: So many people think of trying in their head, failing in their head, and do nothing.

Larry: Correct. What does that get you?

Michael: Nothing.

Larry: I actually wanted to talk to you about Amazon. The article that you wrote, where I did an interview, suggested that Jeff Bezos is an across-the-board trader.

Michael: A trend follower.

Larry: I've thought about that, and it's true. I'm 80 next April and I've had maybe two losing years. One of them was because the people at Mann, who I loved and made a lot of money with, wanted to take the leverage up. That was not a good idea. Trend following is great. It's made me who I am.

When I read your article about Amazon and Bezos, I looked at what Bezos has going for him. First of all, he didn't have to put up any money. Michael Dell saw this: the kid who bought the computer from him uses his credit card. Bezos, and Dell, and now almost everybody, gets paid before the delivery. I couldn't figure it out at first. I'm in good company because Warren Buffett, Charlie Munger, and Larry Hite, couldn't figure out what Bezos was doing. He built his infrastructure for speed. He didn't have to put up money. It took me years to figure that out.

Michael: You're making the case that essentially being a good entrepreneur is being a trend follower and being a trend follower is being a good entrepreneur.

> Trend following is great. It's made me who I am.

Larry: Well, who are the richest people around?

Michael: They follow trends. No one gets to be rich to the level of Jeff Bezos unless something big comes from nowhere and goes to the moon.

Larry: Correct. If I may tell you, I work with this incredible guy. He went to Warden; he won all these scholarships both as a football player and as a scholar. He's one of those annoying people. I told him about the 52-week high. He came out to Colorado to visit me and he says, "Hey, it worked." He took the 52-week high and if it dropped down 5%, he got out the first time. If it went back up, he got in. He was wrong 85% of the time. He turned one million dollars into 20 million. Averaged 20% a year. This was pure David Ricardo. Get rid of the office. And that's what I called the rule.

Being a good entrepreneur is being a trend follower.

Michael: For average people, if you've got 85% losers, that's disappointing. If you have average psychology, average understanding of the markets, 85% losses sounds frightening. If they don't have Larry Hite superpowers, it sounds terrible.

Larry: I was lucky enough, I have a computer. My friend did that with a small computer. First of all, he was a multimillionaire to begin with, so he was doing it just to see if what I said works. And he's mathematical. He knows the law of numbers.

Michael: He wanted to test you.

Larry: He's one of these rare people who's a man of action. A real good athlete, scholarships, and where other people talk, he does.

Michael: How do you get around disappointment? How does an average person who doesn't have your lucky experience, as you call it, get around disappointment?

Larry: There's this guy. Billionaire. He invites me to lunch. I'm 30, he could've been my grandfather. He met me through another friend. He's bought telephone companies all over the world and he says to me, "Buying companies, Larry, is not like going to the movies."

Now, obviously, I don't want to be a dummy, but I'm not making the connection between movies and buying companies, so I say, "Harold, I'm a little slow here. Could you wind back and explain this to me?"

He said, "Larry, you go to the movies, you buy a ticket, and then you sit down in the theater and you sit there until the movie ends." He says, "When I buy a company, before I give the money, I have to know what the end's going to be. We can take a computer and we can make a database. We can test."

Before I do something, I've done thousands of counts. This means I don't need courage; I have to know how to add. You don't need great mathematical skill to do trend following. But you've got to add, divide, and know how to do probability. How many guys have you spoken to who use calculus?

Michael: For trend following? None. Surely some of them know how to do it exactly, but it's not relevant to what they're doing with their trading.

Larry: Right. Any 12-year-old kid could do all the math necessary, because it's averages, probability, and most of all risk management.

Michael: That's why you're here today?

Larry: Having been dyslexic, blind in one eye, half blind in the other eye, I'd have been either a broken-down comedian or a floor washer.

Michael: That is a fantastic quote, from one of the best trend followers—a broken-down comedian or a floor washer.

Larry: I'll tell you a test I did. My group was the first across-the-board CTA to reach a billion dollars. Peter, my then partner, said that we have a great system. I said, "No." He said, "Well, what do you mean?"

He was wrong 85% of the time. He turned one million dollars into 20 million.

Alex Greyserman, who I'm still good friends with, we own a lot of real estate together, and I said, "Here's what I want you to do. We do 3,200 trades a year. Set up a number random generator that will pick what to trade, when to get in, but one thing that couldn't be random was when to get out."

Michael: Random trades, random entry, and a hard stop.

Larry: Correct. We ran the random generator and it comes out better than our system. I thought that was interesting.

I have a philosophy called asymmetrical leverage. As an example, when you go in and buy a new high, you put your stop in, or even better than that, you buy a call. You know exactly what you're going to lose. But you don't know how much you're going to make. It's an asymmetrical bet. You could lose two dollars or you could've bought Amazon and gone up 500%.

Michael: Let me keep you on that point. You have Alex put together a random system. It does better than the fund that you are promoting to all these clients that has raised a billion dollars. You're sitting in the office looking at a random system and you know it's better, but because of the way the fund management world works you can't tell your client base, "We've got this random system," because they won't buy it.

I don't need courage; I just have to know how to add.

Larry: Right. But I have learned something better than money. I learned how to bet, and I learned the fallacy of a magic way. The magic way is getting yourself into a position where you can lose a small amount and make a big amount. Every entrepreneur who makes real money gets into such a position. That's the game. It's exactly what Bezos does. If he tries a product and it doesn't work, he gets rid of it.

Michael: Not everybody is going to become the next Bezos. That's not the issue. The issue is that you can do much better in life with his strategy.

Larry: I'll tell you a story. We have these two friends who we met at the Aspen Ideas Festival, which is the only place I've ever been where consistently the audience is as smart or smarter than worldwide experts. He's a doctor—retired surgeon. She runs a big educational company. Surgeons are by nature picky people. You want a surgeon to look carefully at what he's doing.

He builds her a portfolio. It becomes worth a couple of million dollars. She's in a beauty parlor and the women are in a panic over the Covid-19 virus. They're all going to sell their stock. And she sells everything but the gold, so her husband said, "I'm managing your money, I've had years doing this, I made you rich, I am not going to mess with this again." She calls me up, says, "Larry, what do I do with the gold?" I said, "Well, you want to know the real truth? Sell the gold and buy Amazon." Why did I say this? Gold can only do three things: it can go up, it can go down, or it can stand still.

The one thing you can do to increase the power of your money, is to have it go up faster than inflation. With trillions of dollars' worth of debt, the only sensible thing the United States can do to stay as a world leader is not to default on the debt. If you're not defaulting on the debt, what's the most intelligent thing to do? Inflate out. You inflate out, you are still a leader. The whole thing about money is buying power.

Michael: If you're wrong on this economic-political prescription, you've got a stop loss. There's no ego here. If it doesn't unfold the way you expect, you're prepared to go the other way.

Larry: Always. I'm not here to prove I'm a guru through this because I said I'd rather have a thousand debts than one debt. There are many ways for Jeff Bezos to win. There's only one way for the gold to win: that it outpaces inflation. If it keeps up with inflation, you're nowhere.

Michael: How many people in the last, say, 40 years are still influenced by that 1979, 1980 gold move? They always think that exact same thing is going to happen that keeps so many people fixated on gold.

I like numbers because with numbers I can do probabilities.

Larry: I have a good friend who is a good arbitrager. I'm on the phone with him, and silver is high. He says, "You know, it can't go down." I said, "I don't see why it can't go down. Where is that written?" And he gave me 20 facts. I said, "Well, it's dropped below the 30-day low, so clearly it can go down." Because there it was down. That's a fact.

If you fail to make a new high, and the next low is lower than the previous high, that's going down. The market is right there on paper. Failed one, went lower than the next low—I only have one eye, but I can see that. I like numbers because with numbers I can do probabilities.

I'm on the plane in first class, chatting with a fellow passenger. She tells me she lives in New York. She was a Jewish orphan who got adopted by a New York builder after the war. When it was all over, she was worth half

If you don't have people, you don't have a market. And people are herd animals. Like sheep or cattle.

a billion dollars. She says, "I'm putting half of it in gold in Switzerland." I said, "Look, if they start throwing atomic bombs around, how are you going to get to Switzerland?"

Michael: Your point there is to get people to think about the worst-case scenario—things that we never imagine can happen.

Larry: The most fundamental in markets is people. If you don't have people, you don't have a market. And people are herd animals. Like sheep or cattle.

Michael: When you say, "People are herd animals, like sheep or cattle," that's another strike at the ego, isn't it?

Larry: It happens to be true.

Michael: Years ago, when you were in my film, I actually went to a sheep farm to film sheep for this same reason—to watch hundreds of sheep herding together when they were frightened. It didn't translate well to film, but in person it was amazing to watch.

Larry: Crazy things happen. All the good managers in our business are not bold, crazy people. They are good risk takers. I'll tell you a great story. I had a partner who hit a trade. Comes into our lawyer's office and says, "I'm going to tell you something then I'm going to jump out the window." He hit this trade, he was the inside guy, I was the outside guy. I had to go home and tell my wife that we could be bankrupt. But I turned it around.

I was brought up in an immigrant neighborhood and told since I was three years old that it was my job to support my parents and my grandparents. Couldn't argue with that, because my father supported his mother, my mother's mother, and my rich uncle, but everybody in the family chipped in to help us.

My Italian friends all bought a house. Three generations would go in. My father got an apartment for my grandmother, so this was my job—I'm an only child—to support them. Considering I was shitty in school, shitty in sports, I knew I had to be rich. That was my goal. And in Brooklyn, the mafia was considered like the Knights of Columbus.

Michael: The good guys. That's how the world was.

Larry: That's right. If you hauled garbage from a manufacturer, you could only haul it from the guy who works that thing. You didn't get it hauled by them, you would get it dumped back on the stair. The union guys knew my father's business as well as he did. The guy would say, "George, you got a problem. They want to have a strike." And they knew my father's absolute time that he had to be open or otherwise he missed the season. "Better tell you now, George. You're a friend of mine. I always liked you. I think I could get this settled for you for 10,000 dollars." Was my father angry? No. My father said to me, "That's the cost of doing business." And that's the world I grew up with. My father wasn't a criminal, but if he wanted to get something done, he had to do that. I always knew that it was my job to support him no matter what.

Michael: I got to share a union story back to you. In my mid-20s I was assisting at a conference at one of the fancy hotels in downtown Chicago. John W. Henry was speaking. Before the speech, I'm in an empty hall with a couple of organizers and we're setting things up before everybody comes in. Someone said to me, "Mike, walk over there and turn the lights on over on the side of the hall." I start to walk over to turn the lights on. Some guy starts screaming at me, "Don't you dare touch that light switch. Only a union member can turn those lights on." I thought it was stupid, I still think it was stupid, but the reality is even if something's dumb, it can still be real, and if it's the cost of doing business, don't argue with the cost of doing business—just do the damn business, because we can't solve everything in life.

Larry: Exactly. I call my father and I say, "Look, I got a problem. I owe seven million dollars more than I have." And my father says to me, "No, Larry, you don't have the problem. The guy you owe the money to has the problem."

Michael: He framed it in a different way.

Larry: Yeah. I go in to see the guy. He's a bond trader. And he starts to talk tough to me. New Yorkers don't know how to talk any other way. The guy starts to walk toward me. I turn to him and say, "Stop. The best thing you can do is kill me, so I'm not afraid of you at all."

Michael: But he wouldn't have his money if you're dead.

Larry: That's what I explained to him. The only way you get paid is if I can convince these other guys to put more money in. He was a bright guy and when he thought about that, he said, "Yeah, what are we going to do?" His partner walks in and started with the tough guy routine. He turned to his partner and said, "Larry and I did that dance already. I worked it out."

Michael: You're giving a lesson in thinking about how to frame issues, to solve problems. If you can put the emotion to one side, there's a way to get both sides to the best place they can be at that point in time.

Larry: Sometimes emotions work, but under real pressure they might not. When you're an across-the-board trader, you can trade anything. You may be a smart guy, but as good traders we have to control our emotions. There's no better way to control your emotions than to have a method, because then you know what to do.

> There's no better way to control your emotions than to have a method.

I learned about this from Ed Seykota. Do you remember the King Biscuit Flour Hour radio show?

Michael: I do. All the rock bands.

Larry: Right. My cousin put that together. I knew a woman named Mary Alberti. She went to Wharton; she was smart. I was feeling depressed because of my partner and what to do. She said, "Oh, I have a friend you should talk to—Ed Seykota." I call Ed Seykota up. He said, "I could see you two Thursdays from now at one o'clock." I go into the King Biscuit Flour Hour studio. My cousin gives me a studio and mic so I could be clear, and Ed Seykota says to me, "Look, this is a simple business. Decide how much you're willing to lose and go with the trend." I knew that. I've done more than 5,000 simulations, so he was telling me something that I knew, and I felt great.

Michael: He's a magical guy in that kind of a way.

Larry: He's a magical guy in all kinds of ways.

Michael: I think it was 2012, with you, me, Ed, on stage in Chicago. Ed with his banjo. That was fun.

Larry: After talking with Ed, I thought to myself, "It doesn't matter what you do—you could have a 2% stop, 5% stop, whatever—but you've got to keep to the discipline." I'm always thankful to Ed for that. It was certainly an honor to be with him.

Michael: He learned a lot of interesting things from interesting people too, so I guess the fun thing is that he put a lot of work in, but he's also given back to tell other people what he's learned.

Larry: I think of it this way. I'm 80 years old next birthday. I was at a guy's house for lunch who's 99. He's an interesting guy and a billionaire. A mutual friend thought we'd have a good time together and we did. We had a lot of fun. And he had done a lot of interesting stuff, so he invited me back to a club. I could learn a lot from him.

He told me something new about Buffett and Berkshire Hathaway. Do you know why Buffett bought Berkshire Hathaway?

Michael: I assume because he knew that that particular company would make a nice vehicle for other plans that he had, and that ultimately this notion of acquiring insurance businesses would work well in that structure.

Larry: He didn't want to buy a failing textile company, but Berkshire had NOLs on the books—previous, unused losses. The NOLs could be used to offset against taxes. Think about it. The merger gave him these tax-free earnings, so it wasn't a surprise a couple of years later he got fully out of the textile business. He was using the NOLs. I wouldn't have known, I never read it anywhere, but this guy told me the real story.

I'll tell you another quick story. Do you remember Adam Smith?

Michael: The author of *The Wealth of Nations*?

Larry: No, the other Adam Smith. This was a Jewish guy who used Adam

Smith's name because he didn't want to give out his real name. He was on public television introducing Buffett.

I'd been doing well for myself, at my age, but I'm saying to myself, "Why don't I understand a word this guy Buffett's saying? I know he's saying something important, but I don't understand it." I could see he was smart. Maybe this would be a smart thing for me to learn.

I knew I could not get the trades from the partnership, but Berkshire had been in business 20 years buying stocks, so I got a list of every stock Buffett bought and the date. Then I went to Value Line and I bought the page and the date and the print of everything he bought, and I got three guys who were like me and said, "I'm going to find out what he did."

And after a while I was buying his stocks before they were announced because I saw what Buffett was doing. I didn't go any further than that because I figured out I didn't have a use for everything that Buffett knew. I figured if Buffet magically said to me, "Larry, I'm going to give you everything that I know," I came to the conclusion that his knowledge was worth 10 gallons, but I only had a five-gallon pail, so if he gave me all of his knowledge, five gallons are going to go on the floor. So I only took what I thought were the most important things he was doing and I used them.

The way Buffett looked at it was as an equation. An algorithm. He takes the cash flow after tax on top. Takes the price of the stock, plus the debt. What was his after-tax yield? How long did it last? That's exactly what you would do if you were buying a business, and I said, "That's the key to his wealth." It was compounding.

A lot of people who do trends don't trend the right things. I could see his cash flow growing, so that was one of the things that I looked at even more than the price. He was winning, so I stayed.

Then I had too much money in my IRA or whatever, so I bought more Berkshire, the Bs, and I let him keep going. That grew into millions of dollars, but I was trend following all the time. I was not only trend following the price—I was following the cash flow. I say following, but it was an interesting thing that you could take cash flow, break down parts of companies, see how each part was performing, where the money was coming from, and where it was going.

There's a guy I'm teaching for Alex Greyserman once a year. Kids always ask questions. I walked into the room, turned on your podcast of "Jeff Bezos is a Trend Follower," and said, "Sit there. You're going to learn something."

Michael: Do you know how long it would take, if you're a brand new person to my podcast, to listen to the entire series now? Counting up the hours, I think it would take 30 days listening 24/7. I look back on it eight years later, and it's a lot of content.

Larry: You have smart people guests, so it's like getting an MBA. And it's not all finance. In fact, I was on a bike in the gym the other day. I had my cellphone but I didn't have earphones, so I'm playing your podcast out loud and there's a woman behind me. I say to her, "I hope I didn't disturb you." And she said, "Oh, far from it. That's the most interesting bike ride I ever had." She's interested in the guy who's on the podcast talking. And she said, "This is great. I don't get to hear this stuff." Because you do a good job with what you're doing and it's interesting. If somebody went and listened to 800 of those things, they would have a good education about the world because of the diversity of your guests. You have Nobel Prize winners. You have good traders.

I think there are a lot of life lessons that come from having what it takes to be a trader. Self-mastery. Study. And taking action. All of the people you have on know something, and have wisdom and experiences worth sharing.

CHAPTER 6

The DUNN 45-Year
Track Record

Martin Bergin and Bill Dunn

PART 1
MARTIN BERGIN

MARTIN BERGIN is the president and owner of DUNN Capital. He oversees all mission-critical operations of the firm, including research and development efforts, as well as the construction and management of the managed futures portfolios. Martin, who has a deep background in finance and business management, joined DUNN in 1997 as accounting systems manager, and was promoted to vice president and chief financial officer in 2001. He has been the firm's president since 2007. In 2010, a business succession plan was put into place that gave him partial ownership of the firm, with full ownership transferring in 2015.

Michael Note

I loved playing baseball as a teenager. I was pretty good. One of my baseball coaches back in the day age 16? Martin Bergin. Now that is one random piece of trivia.

Michael Covel: You introduced me to DUNN Capital, and the man, Bill Dunn. It's an amazing story that I believe is decades in the making.

Martin Bergin: Almost 45 years. And I don't know if it's all that special. I'm sure there's people throughout the world like Bill who start out with nothing, have an idea, and develop it and create a business. This is the American dream, right?

Bill was originally working as a contractor for the U.S. Government Department of Defense and sat down one day and decided there must be a better way to make a living. He had an idea about using mathematical formulas to develop trading systems, basically trend following, not knowing that there were other people out there who were already doing it.

He had developed this idea on his own and started looking at stocks, but decided that the universe of stocks was too large to do the calculations in a reasonable amount of time. Back in the early '70s, computing ability wasn't what it is today—you had to run things on a mainframe. He ended up learning about futures where the population was much more manageable. At the time there was a handful of futures markets being traded, all in the United States, and that's where he started. He applied his ideas to that market and the rest is history.

Michael: You make this sounds so easy. I'm looking at the DUNN composite performance and you're telling me there's a whole slew of people out there that have performance like this over the last 45 years.

Martin: Not necessarily in our industry, but there's people in different industries throughout the world who have started with nothing and developed things and created things.

Michael: It is an awesome story. Let's jump into some specifics. DUNN's strategies have always featured some volatility. People might look at the performance and they say, "Wow, that performance is awesome. It's incredible." And then they say, "Wow, but I don't know about that volatility or some of those drawdowns." I saw a white paper the other day discussing Warren Buffett's performance in terms of his use of leverage. It talked about his higher volatility standing, and that's not usually associated with Buffett. From your perspective, has there been too much of an unfair focus on the volatility, without necessarily understanding the strategy and why the volatility's been so important to the performance?

Martin: I wouldn't say it's unfair. What people need to understand is to actually do trend following, you have to be able to absorb losses. The whole secret to trend following is being able to ride out small corrections in the marketplace where the trend hasn't actually ended, it's just taken a little vacation. You've got to be able to ride out those bad times to be profitable over the long period. We don't focus on the actual volatility, so much as on what is an acceptable risk to absorb to do what we're doing to make money. Back in the early '70s, Bill decided to stick to a risk target of a 1% chance of losing 20% or more in a one-month period of trading.

> **You have to be able to absorb losses.**

The idea behind that is if you lose 20%, your NAV drops. The second month, you'd lose another 20%, but it's not 20% from the original NAV, it's 20% from the new NAV. We recalibrate this every single day, but you can go for a long time losing this type of money and never run out. You're staying in existence. And that's the whole key to trend following: not to blow up and not to be wiped out. We consider this an acceptable risk, given the profits that'll be made over the long run.

Michael: You mentioned that 20% was a specific target. And you have hit your target consistently, which is only four times essentially, but you did hit that target as Bill planned and desired from early on.

Martin: Right. If history provides you with all the data you need to design these trading systems, if you process that data correctly and design the system correctly, knowing that the future will never be exactly like the past, it's a target. You don't know that you're going to meet it exactly. But in our history, which is 340 months, we've had four experiences of over 20% losses. So, about 1.2% of the time we've lost greater than 20%. That's within the statistical norm. So, we're pretty good at targeting. And when you think back to the early '70s when you're dealing with punch cards and computers that take a lot of time to process, it's quite amazing that you can hit a target like that. In today's world, it's not so amazing. You would expect it from everybody.

> The real trick is to design a portfolio and the management of risk.

Michael: Let's not forget that in 2013 your performance was pretty good too. So, we're not having a historical conversation. You guys are living and breathing it and still cranking it out to this day.

Martin: The secret is to constantly be adapting what we do to the marketplace and to the technology that's available today. The idea of trend following is not sophisticated. Anybody can sit down and develop a system that determines when to be long or short based on the markets. The real trick is to design a portfolio and the management of risk. Those are the key things that separate different managers. And that's where our research has been focused in the last 10 years.

Michael: You're fond of claiming your approach to the markets is 100% systematic, no overrides. Now, I can already see some folks with pitchforks lining up to scream, "Black box. Black box." But the reality is the process that you follow, the systems that you use, were all developed by human beings, and the computers are simply allowing an automation of strategies that were developed internally.

Martin: That's correct. It comes down to how you define a black box. There are programs that we would consider a black box. The data goes in one way, a processing occurs internally, and the data comes out the other side. Or in this case, your orders or whatever you want to do with the market the next day would come out the other side of the box. The difference between what we do and a black box is we know, given the data that goes in, what the outcome's going to be. There's a way to go back and verify that everything did what it was supposed to do. In a black box, there is no way to know when that data goes in, how it's going to come out the other side. That would be like a neural net system, which we have traded in the past. That is truly a black box because given what's put into the system, you are never 100% sure what's going to come out the other side. We do not do that. All our systems are quantitative calculations. We're fully in control of what's happening within the system.

Michael: One of the unique things about DUNN Capital is its location. So many successful fund managers are in the big cities: London, New York, Tokyo, Singapore. And you're in a pretty interesting location that's not expected by most people.

Martin: That's another thing we can credit Bill with. To do what we do, it doesn't require us to be in any special location. All we need is communications and power. As long as we have those two things, we can operate literally anywhere in the world. We collect data on an ongoing basis. We power our computers to do all our processing, and we need communications to communicate back in the orders and do all our trading.

Bill decided that what was important to him was being in a warm climate, so we moved to Stuart, Florida. We're located right on the East Coast. Our offices overlook the St. Lucie River. It's a beautiful location. Our employees like it. It's a nice town. It's quiet. It's got everything you would want. Bill was looking for East Coast. He was looking for warm climate. He was looking for something on the water and close enough to the civilized world that he could go to the opera if he wanted to—we're north of Palm Beach. Stuart has everything that Bill wanted at the time. It's been great for us and we're happy to be here.

Michael: Every time I visit your offices, I always walk away with this sense that everyone's grounded. It's not full of high-flyers jumping up and down and traders screaming. The reality of a successful fund like yours is that's not what goes on.

Martin: We're built for the long term. We're not looking for short-term satisfaction and our employees are the same. One of the interesting things about us is the longevity of our group of employees. People who work here consider it a family, and they honestly enjoy it. They enjoy the area and they become part of the team. It's unusual for us to have somebody come on board and then leave shortly thereafter. We don't advertise either, we hire through experiences. If we run across somebody and we're impressed by them, if we think they would be a good addition to the team, we bring them on board. We figure out the rest of it later.

Michael: You're saying I shouldn't send two million resumés to your office?

Martin: You probably won't get much of a response.

Michael: I'm fairly certain that the core signals in your trend following programs have been consistent going back many decades. However, in the last few years you seem to have taken a lot of different directions. Can you explain that concept of the core still being important, but you have continued to evolve?

Martin: In the early 2000s we had been one of the top performers for years and we had $1.5 billion under management. We were fairly happy and comfortable with the way things were going and we'd dropped back somewhat in our development. We started looking at more exotic things, things that weren't going to be incorporated in trend following, such as neural nets and some other types of programs. We looked at a genetic genomic trading system. In doing that, we lost focus on our core competency and we went a number of years without doing any significant research into trend following, or portfolio development, or even risk management.

In 2004, we refocused and started looking more at risk management. At this point, we had begun a fairly significant drawdown. It took us a few years to implement the research that we had started a while back. In 2006, we actually did implement some things that we had in development, which helped us. From that moment, we've moved consistently forward and the returns have shown that what we are developing has improved our performance.

Proof is in the pudding, right? You can tell everybody in the world that you know what you're doing research wise, but it can't be validated until you can actually prove it in performance, which I think we've done. What this told us is that you got to stay focused and you got to constantly be doing research.

You've got to constantly be looking at what you're doing, why you're doing it. What is your goal? What would you like to accomplish? Is there anything out there that may help you? People get smarter and smarter, and computing ability gets better and better. Problems that we couldn't solve five years ago, we can solve today. So, we've got to keep rehashing what are the issues, what are the problems, what is our goal? And as time passes, we may be able to find the answers.

A perfect example of this is in January 2013, when we implemented a new risk management tool. Previously we had targeted a 1% chance of losing 20% in a month, but we came up with a methodology to change that targeted number on a daily basis. The idea behind it is, you can look at our track record and see the significant number of drawdowns we've had. We had a 60% drawdown over a four-year period, which is something that could scare investors away. At that time, we weren't the only trend follower struggling.

But then 2008 came along and everybody was out of the water and people reconsidered their thoughts about trend following. But how do you decrease the drawdown without decreasing the profitability? A lot of people in the industry would lower the volatility, therefore they don't have the drawdowns, but then again, they don't have the profitability. They've limited both upside and downside.

We want to make as much money as possible given the risk we're taking.

That's not our goal. We want to make as much money as possible given the risk we're taking. How do I mitigate the drawdown without losing the upside? By targeting this risk number and using a proprietary method that looks at the correlations of our positions. We look at the volatilities of markets, which are standard in any kind of risk targeting. But we also have a proprietary calculation that determines whether we think it's a profitable environment versus a non-profitable environment for our trading system.

And that's the key number. When times are tough, we tend to ratchet down that targeted number. It could go down to single digits. Then when

We don't care about people's ideas or philosophies, or politics, or anything else. The only thing we care about is the numbers.

times are good, we ratchet it back up. At no time does it go over the 1% chance of losing 20% or more in a given month. That's the maximum. And our simulations show that we will be at that level going forward about 5% of the time. It's cut the overall volatility of the program from, let's say, 38% to 24% or 25%. Now, the drawdowns aren't as deep as they used to be, yet we will still have the same projected annualized returns that we've had in the past. It's just one number that's changed in our whole process, but it can have a significant effect on performance.

Michael: Let me go a slightly different direction. I had Daniel Kahneman on the Trend Following podcast, who won the Nobel Prize in Economic Sciences for his research into behavioral economics. The way DUNN Capital works seems to be such a fantastic application of the behavioral economics everyone's been talking about over the last decade. When human beings are using these systematic approaches that you're talking about and following a system "religiously," it seems like it is a great application of what the professors have been looking at in the universities. Your systems seem naturally designed to deal with human biases, to put yourself in a position to profit from the trades most people don't want to take.

Martin: Why does it work? I don't know enough about it to give an educated opinion. But what I will tell you is we don't care about people's ideas or people's philosophies, or what's going on out there politically, or anything else. The only thing we care about is the numbers. People always ask me, what happens if there's a recession? I say, I don't know, and I don't care. All that I know is that my system will adjust accordingly and we'll probably profit from it.

The only thing our program needs to work is some type of market movement in a consistent manner. Where we get in trouble is when the markets aren't consistent in one direction or the other, which tends to happen during environments where central banks and governments are trying to manipulate the markets, which is what we've seen in the last three or four years.

Given that particularly poor environment, we're pretty impressed at what we did last year, because we were still able to make a sizeable return. Most of our competitors weren't able to do the same thing. But there'll be times when our competitors will do better than us. So, over the long term, we think we'll do as well as anybody, if not better than most.

Michael: What I find so fascinating about trend following is its adaptive nature. We've been talking about the last 40 years of DUNN Capital. But as you look ahead, as CEO, there's got to be a certain comfort in knowing that the trading strategy will adapt to a future that none of us can foresee. You might take a personal interest in world news, but from a trading standpoint, that doesn't influence your decision-making.

Martin: No, because the markets will absorb that information and it will then be picked up by the price data, which our system will then incorporate. Trend following isn't a predictive system of investing, it's reactive. We're not leading the market anywhere, we're following along, hoping to take advantage of those trends. It's a pretty simple concept. The part that's not simple is being able to do it and survive over a long period of time.

Michael: What's also interesting is the way that your capital in the firm is side by side with investors', transparently.

Martin: That's down to Bill's philosophy. When he was going into this business, it was because he thought there must be a more honest way to make a living. Originally he was what we would call a beltway bandit. The northern Virginia area, outside of DC, has a huge population of people who make money off the government, as consultants. Bill came up with a concept that put him on the same side of the table as a customer. We have an investment business where we are trading exactly the same product as our client, and at the same time. The client only pays us when they've made money—and it has to be new earnings. If we make money for them and then they lose money after we've collected a fee, we got to make up those losses before we can collect another fee. It's a win-win situation.

> **Trend following isn't predictive, it's reactive.**

Managed futures is probably the most honest investment in the world, because you've got 100% transparency, complete liquidity. In a fee structure like ours, you're only paying fees when you've made money. That's not to say there's something wrong with charging a management fee. The only problem is if it's not fully disclosed or it's not clear to the investor what the fee structure is. But otherwise, people can design their business any way they want.

It should be up to the investor to pick and choose where they want to put their money. And the investor has to be educated—there's no question about that. But at every step, we always ask ourselves, if I'm the investor, what would I expect? What's fair? Everything we do is designed to be fair. And we take that view in every aspect of our lives and our business.

PART 2
MARTIN BERGIN

Michael Covel: I was thinking of the New England Patriots. I know a little bit about how Bill Belichick runs the team.

Belichick likes to work internally—his defensive and offensive coordinators come up through the ranks, and I'm sure when he decides to hang up the cleats, it'll be somebody who's been with him forever who will take over the Patriots.

It got me thinking about your situation. You've been with DUNN since, I think, 1997, and I'm sure the first time you met Bill Dunn was years before that.

Martin Bergin: I like the analogy. There are a lot of similarities between building a company and building a sports organization. You're right, I came to work here in September '97, and before that I was a CPA in a firm in Vienna, Virginia, which is the same area where Bill formed DUNN Capital and began trading before he moved down to Florida.

One of the founding partners of the firm I worked for was actually Bill's neighbor, and that firm had been providing services to DUNN Capital and to Bill personally since its inception. The first job I worked on at that firm was going down and auditing DUNN Capital.

Michael: Tell me about meeting Bill and the first time you wrapped your arms around what DUNN Capital was doing as a business.

Martin: Bill can be formidable and intimidating. And when he shakes your hand, he will bring you to your knees. I mean he has big, bear hands and a grip like a vice. I was the lowest-level person on this audit team and there were a couple other players who were higher up in the ranks. There was a certain procedure for the audit that required somebody to sit down with Bill and discuss it, and the other two individuals didn't particularly want to take up his time on something he would consider frivolous, so I got tasked to do it.

That was my first meeting with Bill. I walked into his office, introduced myself, and said, "I need to go over this questionnaire." It was quite intimidating, but it was a good experience and I'll never forget it. I think Bill appreciated it because I didn't act intimidated, although I was, and we made it through the questions. I worked on that audit for seven years, I believe.

Then once I became a partner in the CPA firm, Bill approached me personally to ask whether, if he wanted to hire somebody from our firm, he needed to clear it with me as the partner. I told him that wasn't necessary, but that it would be a great honor for our firm if he wanted to hire one of our people, at which point he said he'd like to hire me.

I had a good thing going at that time and I wasn't sure I wanted to give it up, but his response was, "That's okay, I'm not sure you can even handle it. But why don't you come down and we'll talk about it?" I went down to Florida and it took me about three seconds to say, "Yes." And the rest is history.

Michael: Going back to that early time when you first went down there for the audits, I assume you were unaware of what Bill's business was, but you learned quickly he was running a fund and then you had that lightbulb moment of the type of strategy he was employing. Can you describe that feeling, because even to this day I would still argue, even if it's a smart way to trade, there are relatively few people still employing the methods you do.

Martin: First off, you've got to understand how I operate, because I've always been interested in numbers, finance, investing, and that type of thing. The reason I became an accountant was because numbers were natural to me and this was the easiest way to get through college and get a job. I invested some of my own money and learned all those hard lessons about what you think you know that you don't know, and that there's always people smarter than you out there. I lost enough money to learn

I learned all those hard lessons about what you think you know that you don't know.

those lessons, but it wasn't financially devastating. I was young and I didn't have much money to invest, so there wasn't that much to lose.

You're right, the first time I came down to DUNN Capital I had no idea what they did. But our firm audited a number of CTAs in managed futures, and once I finished the field work, I got more involved. I got a good understanding of what CTAs do with trend following as a strategy—the systematic nature of it.

The aha moment for me with Bill was how client-centric his focus was. It wasn't a marketing ploy to raise money. His belief from the beginning when he founded the firm was, "I want this to be a win-win situation. I want to be on the same side of the table as the investor."

His first investors were all friends, family, and fellow employees at the government who put all their money together and said, "Here, Bill, we believe in what you designed. Go trade it with our money," and that's what he did. He's never charged a management fee and he's always charged incentive fees—in other words, you make money, he makes money. Or if our clients make money, we get a share of it. Then we always reset the high-water mark.

I find this interesting because a lot of equity hedge funds reset it every year. If you lost money all year long and you're down 20%, January rolls around and you make 2% and all of a sudden you're paying a fee, and you ask the guy, "What happened to the 20% I lost last year?" and they go, "Oh, we reset it ever year. We start over." That's kind of convenient.

My aha moment was triggered by Bill's philosophy about investing and taking care of people. And he's the same with his employees. It's like being in a partnership without the responsibilities of being a partner, because everybody shares in the wealth when we do well. Those were the things that attracted me to Bill.

Michael: You have a 0 and 25 fee structure. No management fee and a 25% incentive fee. You have to make money, or you don't get paid.

Martin: Yep.

Michael: Do other firms do this?

Martin: A few. There's a firm in Charlottesville that is, I think, zero and 30. Their strategy is different than ours, it's more short term, but they've done similar things and done well.

Michael: Is there an element that Bill originally set that in motion beyond a good ethical principle? There must've been a certain belief too, strategy-wise, where he said, "You know what? I'm going to do well this way. The extra benefit is that clients are going to do well too."

Martin: I wasn't around when the decision was made, so I can't speak about what was going on in his mind. We never discussed it.

Michael: Well, like you said, it's 40 years ago. So that's a great jumping-off point to get into a little more detail about the impressive performance that DUNN Capital has generated over those four decades. Who else has a track record that long? Warren Buffett is one—anyone else?

Martin: There's not too many of us that have been around this long and have a published track record spanning 30 years. You can see pretty much all the bad things that can happen in those 30 years. There are firms that have been around as long as us, but most of them, if they have a bad moment sometime in their history, reinvent themselves. They roll out a different system, so the bad events of the past disappear because they have a new track record. I wonder how many firms have their primary product with a track record that's over 30 years old.

> Not many trend followers have a published track record spanning 30 years.

Michael: People can learn a lot from looking at your WMA (World Monetary Agriculture program, a DUNN investment fund) monthly performance from 1984 to 2016. Like you said, everything that has happened is embedded in that track record.

Martin: That's exactly right. If you take a 10-year period where trend following has done well and you see no bad events, your belief is it will go on forever, and that's not necessarily true. It's good to see a manager who has weathered the storm and risen from the ashes, or has proven that the strategy has longevity and is just not a process of data mining the history to create the perfect trading model that may or may not work going forward. These pundits who appear on TV or write articles don't know what's going to happen. Nobody knows what's going to happen.

You have to make an educated guess about who you're going to invest with and who you're going to trust with your money. We have such a long track record, and we've invested a lot in research, especially in the last 10 years, to make the system better.

It's how you handle the rough markets that makes the difference.

Technology today is amazing compared to when Bill started. He was using punch cards in his basement and going to the local library and renting time on a mainframe to run his system. Can you imagine that compared to what we have today: instantaneous data, instantaneous feedback, instantaneous risk monitoring. Not utilizing those things to make your system better is ludicrous. We're constantly working to try to improve what we do, improve our track record over time. Either you're in a good trending market or you're not. Anybody makes money in a good trending market; it's how you handle the rough markets that makes the difference.

Michael: For those folks that have memories, 2008 was a fantastic year for your style of trading. October of '08 was a fantastic month. Ben Stein, the movie star and pundit, famously said that if you made money in October of '08 you were doing something wrong. I knew you'd get a laugh out of that.

But there's been this ongoing dialogue saying that since '08 your style of trading has not been good. You had a down year in 2012, but other than that I don't see an issue. Everyone keeps talking about performance being negative since 2008, but your track record doesn't reflect that.

Martin: It's probably because we're doing something different, although I don't know enough about what other managers are doing in our space. I can tell you it's not been an easy environment. The central banks have been controlling the economy since the credit crisis, and it makes for a difficult environment for any systematic trend following strategy. Volatility strategies have done remarkably well because the central banks have caressed the markets and are holding them into a certain range or pattern, but trend following and a lot of systematic managers have struggled. The short-term guys have done well and then not done well, trend following has done well and then not done well. At the end of the day, they're all about flat for this period, and we've done fairly well.

We no longer target exactly the same risk parameters every day. We have this proprietary way of measuring the market environment, and sizing our positions depending on what the market is telling us, if there are opportunities or not.

If we don't see a trending market, we tend to draw back the amount of risk we apply, and then when the markets start to trend again, we accelerate the risk that our system takes. And over the years it decreases our overall volatility without decreasing our upside performance. That's like the Holy Grail, right?

People say, "DUNN is too volatile, too risky. I love their returns but I can't live with the drawdown." That's a fair statement and we're not for everybody. What if we could reduce the drawdown by 25%, reduce the volatility by 25%, and still have the same type of performance? Now people say, "Hey, wait a minute, that interests me." All you're doing is increasing the risk-adjusted return.

There are large managers that have great historical track records, and at one time they traded to a volatility of 25% or more on an annual basis, and over the years they've gradually decreased their volatility to maintain assets. They've become asset gatherers because they're so large, and the management fee becomes much more meaningful to them than the performance fee. So, they can decrease their volatility, thereby removing the risk of outsized losses and drawdowns, then their assets become sticky. But the expected performance has also been greatly reduced, even though they have a track record that shows good performance historically. People have to understand that they're not going to see those historic numbers in the future. That track record has to be adjusted for the volatility that they've adjusted to. What I'm trying to do is the same thing without having to adjust my track record for the volatility. These changes went into effect in January 2013 and we had three outstanding years, especially compared to our peers.

Michael: Even though you've made changes in how you guys deal with volatility or your risk-adjusted changes, as you mentioned, going back to the firm's foundation, there's a commitment there with your trading strategy that's always going to be different. And looking at some of the larger traders today, obviously you're spot on. Nobody could argue with what you said about other track records. Bill set a philosophy in motion that is still different to this day. Even if someone has no interest in making an investment, studying what you guys do is an education, because most firms have evolved to give the client what the client thinks they want, which is what you described as a management fee product.

Martin: Right. Think about what's behind that decision. Over 20% of what we manage is our own money, and the system that we're offering to the public is exactly the same thing we're trading for ourselves. Our positions are being put on at the exact same time their positions are. We share in everything. Everybody gets the same allocation of prices. We make a significant amount of money on our own trading because we're one of the investors who are right along with everybody else.

So, we make 30% on our money, plus we're collecting a fee from our investors, and this allows us to cover our overheads during times when things aren't going well. We can sit here and criticize people who charge management fees, but think about the overheads of some of these huge trend followers—they might have, say, 100 PhDs on staff and then all the associated administrative people to service that. How do you do it without having a guaranteed management fee? They've built themselves into this huge thing that has to be serviced.

It's like all the players that are involved in the financial industry as a whole—brokers, RIAs, banks, trading platforms, exchanges. Each one of those is guaranteed to make money. The way the system is designed, everybody makes money and takes no risk, except for one person in the equation: the investor. DUNN's philosophy is it's already loaded against the investor, so why should we pile on the pressure. I've never had an investor complain about paying me a fee.

Michael: They're making money when they pay you a fee.

Martin: They aren't happy when they're losing money. But they feel better about it when they know I'm not making money either. So if you lose 20% in a year and yet you paid the guy to lose that money for you, that's a pretty tough pill to swallow.

Michael: Let me change the topic a little bit. You guys are 100% systematic—if I was to roll into your office today, I wouldn't find an army of traders with VR helmets on, staring at screens, punching away like they're playing a video game. This discretionary element is not part of your operation.

Martin: Right. We're not 100% systematic in the sense that once we determine the trade, we use a computer algorithm to make it. Everything's traded electronically, but some of our traders use a combination of methods to get the trade done. We calculate our new positions every day and then our trading team is tasked with putting those trades in place before the next day.

Michael: So nobody at your firm is glued to CNBC and if Joe Kernen says something, or some other person says something, you guys are not adjusting positions on the fly, in or out, or adding to positions, reducing positions, or anything of the sort?

Martin: Nope, all emotion has been removed from the equation. Quite a few times when we run our system overnight, it comes up with trades where we want to take a certain position and I can look at that position and go, "Jeez, perfect example." We got long bonds in 2008, and for the whole time from then to the end of 2016, I've been looking at that position going, "This is crazy. How much higher can bonds go? Interest rates are zero, why are we in this trade?" It's probably the place we've made the most money from 2008 onwards. And yet, I've sat on panels in front of huge rooms of people and said, "Who would've thought we would've been long bonds?" And everybody in the room shakes their head. And I say, "I would've sworn it's a terrible trade. But that's where we're making money." Now, we're not long bonds today.

> The system determines whether we're going to be long or short and by how much.

Michael: Obviously we're talking about systematic trend following strategies, but there's no fixed income department there with bond experts that are helping you to do that trade since '08?

Martin: No, it's all done purely on price data. We feed the system the price data every day, and it determines whether we're going to be long or short and by how much. We take a position between what we call plus one and negative one, and it could be anywhere in the middle. Right now we have a slight short position on—that's what the system tells us to do.

Another thing I find interesting is a lot of pundits are saying, "CTAs have only made money because bonds have been in a 30-year bull market," so it's only the carried interest on bonds. That's a fair argument. But what's going to happen when bonds are in a bear market for 30 years and interest rates are going up for the next 10, 20, 30 years?

We're one of the few CTAs that have actually lived through bear markets in bonds and we've made money in those markets. People think it's a carried interest, but all we're looking at is the price of the bond. The carried interest is already in the futures price. The futures price is nothing more than a bet that says, "Three months later I think interest rates are going to be here." Now they're either going to be higher or lower than what people think, and if you're on the short end you sell it, and if interest rates are higher then you make money. And vice versa. It's simple.

Michael: How many folks today getting their Harvard MBA, or their Wharton MBA, wrap their arms around what you're describing? Not only is it a successful client business, a great way to make money, but it's such a cool concept too.

Martin: People overthink things, especially in the financial industry. They've learned how to de-set the marketplace and calculate roll yield, and then they start overthinking the process. You have to get out of the forest, look at the trees, and say, "Wait a minute, all I'm doing is betting on what the price is going to be on the delivery date. And do I think it's going to be higher or lower?" We apply techniques to the data that predict whether it's going to be higher or lower—it's that simple.

Michael: What if you make a mistake? If you're losing money, that tells you something.

Martin: If you're wrong, so what? The system says, "Okay, now you rather be short than long," or vice versa. We've all done it in our own portfolios where we pick a stock we're in love with and it just keeps losing money or doing nothing, and you'd never want to give it up because you have to admit you're wrong. That's a hard thing for a lot of people to do. The system doesn't have any problems admitting it's wrong. It's saying, "Hey, today it's better to be this way. It's better to be long. Yesterday was better to be short."

Michael: Let's talk about another benefit that comes from the return stream that DUNN Capital generates. Everyone's still fixated on what the Dow and the S&P are doing, but when you take a return stream from DUNN Capital and add it to some of these typical indexes, magic happens, doesn't it?

Martin: That's why people invest in managed futures, for the non-correlated revenue stream. For instance, in 2008—when we clearly did something wrong, to quote Ben Stein—it made 50%. It's insurance against your portfolio in general. If you remember, in 2008 hedge funds were huge. Retail investors were investing in hedge funds; everybody wanted to have a hedge fund. The problem was when the credit crisis happened, all of those "alternative" investments in hedge funds became correlated and everybody got crushed. The only strategy that stood out during that time was managed futures and I suspect it's because managed futures can get short as easily as it can get long—it doesn't cost any additional funds to be short a position.

And secondly, it's a much more diverse portfolio, because you're not just betting on stocks going up and down, you're looking at bonds, currencies, and energies—and for our portfolio even commodities, metals, and grains. All of these things create diversity. We trade so many different things that are uncorrelated, we're diverse geographically because we trade throughout the whole world, and then the strategy on its own is also uncorrelated to almost any other investment strategy. There's a slight correlation to bonds, but it's so small that it doesn't matter. There's no correlation to equities whatsoever. People get the idea that no correlation means opposite correlated, but that's incorrect. It doesn't mean that every time stocks go up, we go down, and vice versa.

What I can tell you historically is when there have been black swan effects in equities, managed futures have done well. There's this noncorrelation that occurs throughout the marketplace over time, but an opposite correlation comes into play during bad events, which is where this strategy kicks in as an insurance policy against your portfolio.

Michael: So, for example, if the audience sees the S&P going up 25% in one year, you could go up 30% that year too and still have zero correlation.

Martin: Right, and that's what I call the cost of insurance. It's great to invest in something that makes money when S&P and equities are going down. The problem is you don't want that thing to be losing money when they're going up. Over the last five years the market has steadily climbed, so you would be pretty upset if your investment in managed futures was losing money. Our system has proven historically that even during the good times we can still keep pace or outperform the S&P more than sizably. The chart of our performance since inception, especially plotted with the S&P 500, is one of the most amazing charts in finance, frankly. Everyone looks at that chart and goes, "Where did that come from?"

> The system doesn't have any problems admitting it's wrong.

I'm trying to help people understand that this type of strategy is something that everybody should be participating in. This whole idea that you must have a certain level of capital to avail yourself of strategies like this that can help you make money over time doesn't make any sense to me, but that's another subject.

Michael: It's a subject I wanted to bring up with you, because that is a fairly significant change for DUNN over the years. Offering mutual funds is something relatively new for you, isn't it?

Martin: The reason it didn't happen before is we couldn't find a partner that didn't want to be guaranteed some kind of fee. We had been approached by a number of mutual funds over the years that wanted to represent DUNN. The problem was they wanted us to charge a management fee so that they could share in that fee, and pay their bills, and we always said, "No."

Now we don't have a problem with a fund or a platform charging a fee to cover their costs, but I expect it to be fair and reasonable. We finally partnered with a group in the Baltimore area outside of DC who approached us about taking over a managed futures fund that was already trading. They weren't happy with the performance and thought that we could do a better job for them. We took over responsibility, which opened the door for us to get more involved in the mutual funds space.

Michael: I want to take you back to March of '09. If anybody had to make a prediction about where the S&P was going then, few people would have got it right. You hinted at this earlier, but given central bank policy, given rates at zero, you can't say there's a one-to-one connection, but I seriously doubt the S&P would be where it's at today if we had 6% rates or something to that effect. When you have a run like we've had and you have rates at the level they are today, it's too perfect. It seems like almost anything could break that chain and we could go in an entirely different direction. I guess what I'm saying is, we've had two 50% S&P drawdowns in the last 16 years, why should I not imagine a third?

Martin: I can't speak to that with any intelligence, but I think a lot of people have feelings similar to yours—they're uncomfortable with the run that's happened. Nobody has any basis for that thought process other than the fact it's been good for so long and how can it continue? I mean, it's good for us because I'm seeing a lot of inflow of assets from people that are uncomfortable.

Michael: The S&P could double from here though.

Martin: Right, I could argue exactly that. If you look at the policies that are being put in place in the United States—removing the regulation stranglehold on people and allowing businesses to go back into the free market and do what they do best. You can put people under the worst conditions and they'll figure out how to make money. You can go anywhere in the world and see people who have developed businesses out of their own homes to pay for their daily needs, and when you take the yoke off and allow people to do these things, I could see the S&P doubling. I could also argue that the S&P could collapse. You could make an argument for any theory you want.

Michael: And that brings us back to why you trade price.

Martin: Exactly. Everybody trades information, correct? What has more information in it than price? The accumulation of all information in the marketplace is in that number, and that's all we trade.

Michael: I still think your style of trading is probably one of the best representations that one can find for Kahneman and Tversky's work in prospect theory. For my money, the trading strategies that you guys employ are the best representation of how to trade what we know about behavioral finance. It's like these biases exist and you've built this strategy to keep yourselves going in the right direction.

Martin: Right, and I think you could take the same approach with some other strategies. But we've found the one thing that stands the test of time, as far back as you can research, is trend following. That doesn't mean it's going to be the greatest strategy over a particular period, but over time it's always going to make new highs.

Michael: I've known you for a long time and I think it's a great story that you trained with Bill, learned from Bill, and now are leading the company.

Martin: Bill has been a mentor to me in so many different ways, not just in business, finance, and trend following, but in life in general. He opened my eyes to his views on libertarianism, free markets, and capitalism, and over the years, more and more people have seen the light. I'm not saying that everybody who works at DUNN shares the same views, because we're diverse and all we're interested in is talent. You always look for the best talent, the best quality people, the best individuals, and then you build them into a group all rowing together, with the same goal in mind. We have 22 good people here. Any one of them being removed from the equation would make us a lesser team.

> **What has more information in it than price?**

Michael: I can think back to some early experiences where I had a chance to be around Bill briefly—dinners, meetings, stuff like that—and even though it was from afar, it was still influential. You knew you were in the presence of somebody that was giving you confidence, not in a cocky way but inspirationally. I remember listening to him and going, "Okay, this is how it's done." For me it was a great learning experience.

Martin: He gave you instant comfort, didn't he? And if you were an investor, when you met Bill, within two minutes you were like, "I don't even care what these guys do, I'm in." For me he's still our largest investor.

PART 3

MARTIN BERGIN
AND JAMES DAILEY

J AMES DAILEY is Chief Executive Officer of DUNN. He has responsibilities in the areas of strategic planning, business and product development, client relations, and financial reporting. He joined DUNN in 2003 as a Financial Analyst and was promoted to Vice President of Finance in 2007, CFO in 2008, and CEO in 2016.

Michael Covel: When I look at DUNN Capital, you guys are machine traders going back to the 1970s, yet it's funny how the media makes out that machine trading is novel and wants to blame people in 2018. What are your thoughts when you read in the headlines that the machines are doing dastardly things to the equity markets?

Martin Bergin: The first thing we try to do is differentiate between how you define the machines. We use computers for everything that we do; the fund is completely systematic. The computers are used to crunch data, produce the signals, produce the orders. We aren't actually using the machines to execute the trades as such, but we do use algos as a tool for our traders to help them execute.

> We use computers for everything; the fund is completely systematic. [BERGIN]

What people are talking about when they start complaining about the machines are some of these pre-designed algo trading systems that don't have human intervention, so they're set up to react to price data automatically, and either start selling or buying. I think one of the things that may have contributed to the significant volatility that we saw in equities recently was when equities began to fall, some of these systems started hitting stops and then selling into the fall, and that exacerbated the situation.

Another argument that might be valid is that you have some large trend following funds out there. As the price moves in such a significant number, standard deviation moves every day, say, 4.6 one day over 7 the next. This forced a lot of the trend followers that were holding long equity positions across the board to move contracts, so they were coming in and selling in bulk, which may contribute to these 200, 300, 400, 500-point swings that were occurring every day. But all that's theory, and I couldn't tell you for a fact what created it. The idea that the machines are tearing the stock market apart is nuts—in a way, they probably make the system more efficient.

Machines make the market more efficient. [BERGIN]

Michael: You do a nice job of differentiating, but the idea of machines goes back over 40 years. Perhaps people don't often think about what a machine is doing, for example, in the DUNN Capital world. It's taking the rules that your firm thinks are wise for buying, selling the right percent to bet based on the capital under management, and automating that into a process. A machine, a computer, is pretty good for that. And it's a strange thing that after all these decades, that still can be misrepresented. Even though the machines get blamed, trend following gets blamed in these periods too.

Martin: More importantly, what the machine does is take the emotion out of the decision-making. One of the things I think creates problems for people is they fall in love with a trade. When you see the market turning against you, you tend to want to hold that position. Instead of reacting to what the market's telling you, you wait, wait, and wait, and then it becomes panic selling. And where you start seeing markets drive down is when you hit that panic button. The machines don't have panic buttons. I mean, there's a certain threshold where you start, the volatility increases, the machine wants to reduce the size of its positions because risk has increased. It's a simple calculation of your risk and you reduce your position to get your risk back in line with your expectations.

The second thing that causes it to sell, in this example in an equity market that's been running as a bull market for so long, is when the price starts moving against it to the point where it doesn't want to be long anymore.

The third point that kicks in for us is the way we manage risk, where we adjust our overall risk targets to the market conditions. As we see the end of trends that have played out over a number of years, then we're going to reduce our overall risk. All these are good things that happen because of the machine, which may or may not take place if it's an individual making emotional decisions.

Michael: Can you elaborate on, for example, the headline of a "return to volatility." That's got to be unusual to hear from your perspective, because you guys have got so much data, so many years of performance. You've seen every market climate that can be imagined for 40-plus years.

The machine takes the emotion out of the decision-making.
[BERGIN]

Martin: Let me throw you another phrase. After the credit crisis we entered the "new normal"—remember that? I think we've seen the end of the new normal. It's just the market going back to what it's been in the past, hopefully. Increased volatility is good for the markets, if you are a trend follower.

Michael: When you say back to what it's been in the past, I guess the past is always a little bit different than the future. But in terms of climates in data, you guys have seen every climate under the sun. Sometimes that simple-sounding idea is hard for people to wrap their arms around, that you guys are sitting there right now, fully prepared for whatever climate might unfold.

Martin: That's true to a certain extent, but you have to remember this past year (2017) nobody's ever seen volatility as low as it's been. And it's not only in the equity markets, it was pretty much across the board—to the point that we recognized the risk and changed the way we measured volatility.

In the past we always looked at the current volatility for the short look-back period, which is normal in systematic trading. But we started viewing volatility in two ways. We'd look at long-term volatility versus a short-term volatility, then we always took the riskier of the two, the higher volatility, to calculate our system, because we thought that the current environment was abnormal.

How long would VIX continue to trade under 10 and continue to go down? At some point, there's a price to pay when you're dealing in this type of market environment. It's like a rubber band that kept getting stretched more and more. What we saw in February 2018 was also something more than we've seen in the past. But we've experienced activity like this before with volatility spikes, it's just the degree that's a little different. The systematic programs are set up to adjust and adapt to these environments, but it doesn't happen overnight.

> **Increased volatility is good for the markets.**
> [BERGIN]

Michael: On the flip side, back in October of '87, there were some moves during that period that were off the hook—your firm was able to navigate then as well.

Martin: Right. But it was a similar situation and we're using that period of time to stress test our current portfolio. We have run a stress test over the last six months exactly for this type of market move, and we reacted similarly to what happened in '87. It was a huge return that went down hard and quickly, and came right back within days. It may take weeks, it may take months. It may never come back, it may continue to fall. We don't know, but we know the system will adjust for either environment and we'll be fine.

James Dailey: I get what you're saying though, Michael. This time last year (March 2017) the talk from a lot of the people we meet at conferences and questions from people such as yourself who follow the industry was about how CTAs would perform in a rising interest rate environment. Because it's been a low or a falling interest rate environment for 30 years.

We were actually in existence in trading and doing trend following since 1974, so we have actual, real trading data that we can look at during a rising interest rate environment. So, you're right, we've seen a lot of environments that newer traders have not. I think last week I read that from a prominent S&P peak it was the largest 10-day drawdown since 1985, and we traded for that period in 1985, so we have the data.

Michael: Can you explain what happened in a rising rate environment inside DUNN back at that point in time?

James: We were profitable. There were trends in fixed income and in all the other sectors that could be identified and exploited. Trends will occur in rising and falling interest rate environments alike.

Martin: To put rising interest rates into perspective, most of the time it's all about inflation. Inflation is a trend follower's friend, because that's what we're profiting from. Rising interest rates create trends in other sectors, which we profit from. The other thing that's a misnomer about rising interest rates versus falling interest rates is this whole idea that trend followers make a lot of money off the roll carry in a falling interest rate market. That is true to some extent, but the interest rate in the carriers is calculated in the futures price. People tend to make it a little more complicated than it is; all you're doing is taking a future price and betting whether the interest rate is up as quickly as the marketplace predicts, or vice versa.

> Trends will occur in a rising and a falling interest rate environment alike.
> [DAILEY]

Let's say you're in a rising interest rate environment, but the rate doesn't go up as quickly as the marketplace thought; well, then you're going to be long with those bonds. Even though it's a rising interest rate environment, which would make you think you would be short, but it's a bet on the rates versus market perception of rates. When you're short, it's saying that rates are going to rise faster than the market projects. And we tend to not be as short or as convicted in that trade as we are when we're on the long side of bonds. We make money on that trade, like we do on the long side of bonds historically. And nobody knows what the future holds.

Michael: You are on record as saying DUNN is committed to trend following. It doesn't take much of a leap of faith, even if one is not experienced in trend following, to see a firm that has a track record of

40-plus years with significant gains, and say, "Oh yeah, I can understand why they're committed to trend following." But I still have to ask why?

Martin: It's the only systematic trading method that has stood the test of time. There are white papers that use data that's hundreds of years old to show that trends have occurred since the beginning of time and continue to do so. One thing you would see in the literature prior to 2008 was that trend following was dead, the argument being that computers made information so easily available that the market adjusted immediately to any change or crisis, and therefore there wouldn't be trends, it would always range-bound trading. But processing information just makes the market more efficient, it doesn't mean that trends won't occur: 2008 was a perfect example. Historically, since 2008, we continue to perform well.

> Trends have occurred since the beginning of time and continue to do so. [BERGIN]

I don't hear people talking any more about trends being dead. I think now they appreciate managed futures and trend following for the tail-risk protection and the non-correlated nature of our returns. One of the outcomes of recent volatility, though, is tail-risk protection has always been viewed that when the stock market goes down, managed futures and trend volume will do well. Now we have an environment where the market went down and we also got hurt, because all trend followers were long equities, like the market in general. People perhaps don't understand the difference between a correction, a pullback, and a recession. A pullback or a correction, which is what I feel happened in February 2018, is when trend followers react to that data and reposition their portfolio.

If we continue to see this transition into a bear market, then trend followers will be short equities and other sectors will become profitable and they'll start making money with that given market. Whereas an equity long-only holding investor is always going to be in those equities or cash, so there's no opportunity for them to profit from this market.

Michael: If you look at the total assets in trend following portfolios around the world, it's tiny by comparison to traditional assets. Can you say more about this correlation feature for trend following and compare

If you take two fluently uncorrelated revenue streams and put them together, it's going to increase your risk-adjusted returns.

[BERGIN]

it to traditional assets and explain why it makes sense for everybody to have a piece of a return stream that's not correlated to traditional assets?

Martin: It's simple math. If you take two uncorrelated revenue streams and put them together, it's going to increase your risk-adjusted returns. We view it as a core holding of any portfolio. Because not only is it uncorrelated in a general environment on a day-to-day investment, it also becomes negatively correlated during significant crisis environments. So, 2008 would be the most recent perfect example where the equities are in a bear market and managed futures tend to do well. And it's not just us, but historically across the board all managed futures do well. One of the things that we think we bring to the table that a lot of the other managers don't is that we tend to trade with a higher annualized volatility. We view it from a VAR (value-at-risk) perspective.

The reason we do this is twofold. First, it allows somebody to allocate to a strategy like us for their portfolio. They don't have to allocate as much money to get the same bang for their buck. So, it's all about allocating risk. We will give you twice the amount of risk for the same amount of capital. Secondly, we don't charge management fees, so we're incentivized to make money for our clients. The other thing that helps with that is the fact that it's our own money in the systems with the clients', so we're trading exactly the same strategy that they are. The only difference is they don't charge an incentive fee to ourselves, so, for that reason, the correlation enhances the overall value of the portfolio by having core allocations to these types of strategies.

People have the misconception that they can go into the hedge fund space, long equities, short equities, private equity, real estate, hedge funds, all these different things. But in a crisis environment, they all become correlated in the end. So, even though they're uncorrelated in a normal investment environment, when things go badly, they all become closely correlated, mostly to the downside.

Michael: And the reason you don't have the correlation is because when stocks go down, you're not a long-only stock firm, obviously. You are able to benefit from all these other moves that will happen when the big equity move is on the downside.

Martin: We're able to go short as easy as long, and it doesn't cost a premium to be short. If we wanted to short stocks as a general investment strategy, it actually costs you money, whereas with us, you don't have to pay to short equities. We adjust the futures price; you can either go long or short—it's the same cost for either direction. You pay a commission and you put down a good faith deposit, which says you're going to execute on the contract at the end of the holding period.

Michael: Let me get you to tear apart a couple of things that you brought up in that answer about correlation. You mentioned your two levels of volatility targeting at DUNN. My understanding is this is a relatively new change for the firm—I think going back less than a decade. Why don't you explain how that's unfolded, and the difference?

James: We used to target a static monthly VAR of 20%—we were dialed at that, no matter what the environment. And we did that from our inception all the way through the end of 2012. We had a 1% chance of a 20% or more loss in any rolling one-month period, and that's at the 99% confidence level. We actually achieved that loss, I think, 1.14% of the time.

Michael: One of the most amazing statistics I've ever seen in financial data.

James: It is amazing considering that for a good part of that track record, the computing power was not what it is today. we were good at dialing to that target. We have over 340 months for our WMA program, which is from '84 to now. We had, I think, four penetrations on the downside of that 20% threshold. It intuitively didn't make sense for us to always be dialed to that same risk target when we knew that the market environment wasn't conducive to our style of trading. So, after the debt crisis, there was a period where with all the government intervention in markets there weren't a lot of juicy trends to be had. Markets were pretty range-bound, low-ball, and choppy. Then our signal strengths were pretty low, but we're committed to doing everything systematically and we would never override our program, so we were still dialing to that risk, even though we felt, "Why are we doing this? It's not a great environment for us."

This idea of a dynamic risk target was something we had attacked a few times before in our R&D team, and we finally cracked it toward the end of 2012 and implemented it into the program starting in January 2013. Now we target a VAR that is geared to current market conditions, which can range from monthly VAR of 8% on the low end up to about 20% or 21% on the high end. What we used to dial to everyday, we're now only at our maximum risk 5% of the time. Over time our average value at risk on a monthly basis should be 15%, with the purpose of decreasing the downside volatility and reducing drawdowns, because it seems what investors remember the most are significant bad events.

Of course, nobody likes to have significant bad events. Everybody likes to have the big run-ups. Part of the thought process behind this was that we didn't want to just decrease our volatility for the sake of not having bad events, but because we wanted to still be profitable and productive for our investors. By sizing this the way we have, at 5% of the time, we're at our maximum risk. Looking back, we could go for two or three years without ever getting there, and then we could suddenly be there. For instance, we reached our maximum risk in September 2017, and we stayed there all the way through January 2018. That's a long time to be sitting at the maximum risk, but of course we made a significant amount of money during that period, well over 30%. When you look at that, it makes sense.

There are times when we reduce that bar. The perfect example of that was the first half of 2017. We were at a low bar and we actually lost money six months in a row, but at the end of that period, we were only down around 5.5% or 6.0% for the year. The system works and we have enough data that's statistically significant to show that it's done exactly what we would have expected it to do. And yet we can still have outside performance that we've had in the past. Because of that, our risk-adjusted returns have actually improved dramatically.

Michael: People have a choice though—with you, there's two different ways they can go. There's the institutional direction, which is what we're talking about right now. But then there's still your standard approach, correct?

Martin: Well, no, because we have applied the adaptive risks across the board. We have our standard volatility program, which is what James was describing: the VAR targets. The only difference between that and our institutional product is the institutional product trades at one-half of whatever the standard is. We simply reduce the positions by 50% for institutional versus standard.

James: The standard product has an average VAR of 15, which translates into an annualized volatility over time of 22%. The WMA institutional product, like Marty said, is the same product. The average VAR over time would be about 7.5 and the annualized volatility over time should be about 11%. This has been our methodology since January 2013, so now we have over five years of the actual trading data using this approach.

Michael: If one looks at the backgrounds of DUNN Capital principals, including Bill Dunn, there's what I want to describe as a Joe Friday approach—the feeling that you guys are comfortable with what you do. I still remember the first time I entered your offices—yes, it's a long time ago, but if I was to walk in today, it's not a trading floor of people jumping up and down, screaming, and trying to react to this or that. Give people a feeling for why your approach is so good in this world of 24/7 information overload, when most people are at a heightened state of anxiety all the time. Marty, you mentioned this at the beginning—you seem to be able to keep this desire for constant information in check.

Martin: Yes, there's more information than ever: big data, artificial intelligence, black boxes. People are leveraging all this elaborate computing power to process information. But one thing will never change: People try to get too complicated. Price data incorporates every bit of information that's available in the marketplace. Some people know more than others, but that's all part of the price data. We rely on price. We do research and look at other peripheral data that **Price is the** may help in some way to validate or enhance a signal **most reliable** or give a little leading information or something of **data.** [BERGIN] that nature. But the bottom line is, price is the most reliable piece of data that you can have. And that's why the system relies so heavily on price alone. We look at highs, lows, and closes every day in every market we trade, and we use that information to process our signals.

James: You're right, Michael, our office is quiet. Sometimes prospective clients who come to visit us are a little let down when they go to the trading room and there's one guy sitting in front of a computer monitoring things. Actually most of the execution happens overnight when the volumes are high in markets. Trend following is about discipline, it's not that exciting. The returns can be exciting over time, but day to day it's about discipline. It's about blocking out the noise from the media and everything that's attacking all your senses and focusing on the algorithms and the fact that it's a repeatable process that doesn't give in to emotion. I think most of our investors find that appealing. They get it.

> **Trend following is about discipline, it's not exciting.** [DAILEY]

Martin: The thing is, we're managing money through the long term and not the short term. If you look at all the great investors in history, each one of them was geared to a long-term perspective. The reason that some of them did better than others is clients and investors aren't going to force a successful investor to change their philosophy. Nobody questions Warren Buffett about managing for a 10-year horizon. A newer manager wouldn't be able to get away with that.

But in trend following, everything is geared toward the data, and the data has shown us that the long-term approach is much better than the short term. We've been trying for years to develop some type of shorter-term trend following program to enhance our current program, but we don't see anything that's consistently profitable over 20 or 30 years; it's a nut that we're still trying to crack. It gives us something to do from a research perspective, along with all the other ideas that we come up with, some of which get implemented in the program, some of which are dead ends, so we just move on to the next project or the next idea that somebody comes up with.

Michael: Marty, your statement about price data sounds simple, but boy, there's so much going on there to have an investment belief predicated on that. That can still be tough for people to assimilate.

Martin: It's simple to a point, Mike. When you get into portfolio development and risk management, that's when things start getting complicated. What sets us apart from a lot of other firms is the single driven process is simple, but the package as a whole is not. There are so many different particulars that play into it. Even from our perspective, it would take weeks and weeks to discuss every little nuance. And of course, we wouldn't discuss most of that with people because it's proprietary.

Michael: When I say simple, I don't mean to imply that there's a lack of complexity—more that instead of using some suite of thousands of data sources, you have taken the simple idea of basing your decisions on price data. A lot of people still have a hard time accepting that the complexity behind it is valid.

Martin: The best investment ideas in history have always been simple. Like James said, you have to block out all the noise and get down to the simple calculation that becomes obvious at some point. It's like in *The Big Short*, people look back at what the guy did and think, "Why didn't I think of that?" But he was on the wrong side of the trade, right? He got there too early. But conceptually it made all the sense in the world.

> The best investment ideas in history have always been simple. [BERGIN]

Michael: By the way, where was the trend following component in *The Big Short*? Because all these folks had this one-off trade where they were going to do well—and many of them did. But you guys were right there too at the time and I don't remember seeing you in the film.

James: That's exactly what we were talking about. It's not as exciting as those individual one-off stories.

Michael: Your performance during October 2008 was exiting.

James: Oh, yeah. Trend followers had a huge year in '08 and through the first quarter of '09, but it didn't get a lot of publicity.

Michael: Obviously, with your firm's success and longevity, you see a lot of different things and hear about a lot of different approaches. Are there investing styles out there right now that have received traction in the last decade that people should be concerned about, that go beyond trend following?

Martin: In 2017 we spent time developing a volatility strategy. Part of that was because we purchased a firm in Europe and brought over the principal, Stefan Wintner, who now works for DUNN. One of the things that came to light was concern about these short vol products, especially ETFs, that were prone to blow up, especially in a low vol environment— for example, a move that increased vol by 13 points is not that significant, but could represent over a 100% increase. Or if you're short vol and vol goes up 100%, you've lost 100%. It's a simple calculation.

And I guess it's the greed gene, but some people only see the profits and they chase the dog's tail. This Velocity Shares, for instance, raised a billion dollars in the previous 12 months and it was a fund of over a billion and a half dollars that blew up in one day. People should have known it was coming—but they sit there and say they can't believe it happened, it was a low volatility product, blah, blah, blah. Even in the fund prospectus they told you what could happen. So, you're asking is there anything else on the horizon that I'm aware of that could be troublesome? I don't know that there is.

There are some strategies that are interesting to me. I'm always looking at non-correlated investment products that we may be able to incorporate at some point at DUNN. That's why I was so intrigued by volatility products. Our volatility product is not directional—it's not necessarily short vol or long vol, it more plays off the change in the skew volatility, or the volatility of volatility. That's a second and third component of volatility, which I think is much more interesting than trading the direction of volatility. We did well during the spike, and yet we made a significant amount of money in 2017 too, when there was low or falling volatility. We've proven we can do well in either environment with our vol strategy.

The other thing I'm always looking at is short-term systematic programs that are either trend following derived, or use some other methodology, and are consistently profitable over long periods of time. There's a couple of them out there, but I'm not going to point anybody in any directions.

Michael: Do you guys have any perspective that you would like to share on the advent of the crypto world?

Martin: I never say never. It's pretty funny to see the emotional responses that people give when this is brought up. It's either, "Oh, it's the greatest thing in the world. We're going to trade it next week," or "Are you kidding? I would never trade that in the world, that's the craziest thing." That's ridiculous. If the market matures in such a way that there's volume there to be traded and you have data, why wouldn't you trade it? It's another uncorrelated currency that would do nothing

> **We'll trade any market that is regulated and has adequate volume.** [BERGIN]

but enhance a portfolio. Are we going to trade it tomorrow or even next month? No. But it's something we'll definitely keep on our radar screen if the market continues to grow in the future.

I can remember when the VIX futures were put out there and nobody wanted to trade those right away either, but now it's the largest market in the futures world. There's nothing to say that Bitcoin or one of these other cryptocurrencies couldn't be traded, or maybe they'll make a futures basket of all the cryptocurrencies, who knows?

Michael: You laid out the trend following mantra: "We'll take it as it comes. And if it's something we can trade and it meets our criteria for trading and it's got a trendiness to it, why not?"

Martin: We'll trade any market that is on a regulated exchange and has adequate volume that it can be traded without a problem, and where there's enough data loaded in the system. Even more so if it's uncorrelated to our existing portfolio, because that's what will enhance a portfolio. The more uncorrelated markets you can plug into your portfolio, the better your risk-adjusted returns are going to be.

Michael: Guys, thank you for participating today and giving us a great educational perspective on trend following. I think the first step is for people to understand what's going on, and then they can make decisions about potential business relationships if and when appropriate. I appreciate you guys coming on and giving this college-style lecture that I don't think you could find in too many universities around the world. There's a few professors talking about this, but it's still not regular fare at most universities.

Martin: I agree the biggest key to our industry and the investment world as a whole is education. And you're doing a great job in educating the investment world about trend following managed futures and its value in the marketplace. Keep up the good work.

Michael: I still think one of the most powerful educational exercises that exists in the financial world is to take the month-by-month performance track record of DUNN Capital since its inception, throw it on the table at the beginning of a semester, and spend the whole semester attempting to reverse engineer how that track record came into existence.

James: It certainly tells the story of trend following in a nutshell.

PART 4
JENNY KELLAMS

J ENNY KELLAMS is the Director of Investment Strategy at DUNN Capital. She is primarily responsible for marketing and distribution of DUNN strategies to family offices and financial advisors. Prior to joining DUNN in 2011, she had a 12-year career in the securities industry as a financial advisor, owning her own investment management firm, JK Financial Group.

Michael Note

This interview speaks again to the random nature of life and also to the importance of keeping one eye open to the possibilities and opportunities that might appear at any moment to change your life.

Michael Covel: Take me back to how you broke into Wall Street.

Jenny Kellams: My dad had an accounting and finance background. He came from a farming family in Indiana—both my parents are from Indiana—and he was the first in his family to go to college. He went to Indiana University. I enjoyed math more, but my dad loved investing. He was a controller at a big company in the paper industry, and he would get the daily graphs. He would tell me about investing and using fundamental analysis and technical analysis combined. This is what we did sitting around the dinner table—I talked to my dad about stocks.

Michael: How old were you?

Jenny: Pretty young, probably 10 or under. Dad's best friend Grant was his broker at Merrill Lynch. Grant had also gone to IU, so they were huge Hoosier basketball fans. Me, being the little defiant one, decided I was always going to root for Duke to get them both riled up. Grant would come over to watch basketball games, they would talk about stocks and investing, I'd be rooting for Duke, and I thought Grant was the coolest big brother type you could have. From a very young age, I always wanted to be a stockbroker, which is what you called them back then.

> **Around the dinner table, I talked to my dad about stocks.**

Then we started traveling to money shows. My mom and sister would go out shopping, and I'd go to the conferences with my dad and listen to the speakers. Sam Stovall, for example; I remember seeing Sam speak. I was fascinated seeing all these different people talk about investing. I remember clearly always knowing that's what I wanted to do. It wasn't even a question when I went to college—that was always going to be my path.

Michael: When did you realize it was rare for a woman to have this ambition?

Jenny: When I first decided to try to get into the business, I was living in Gainesville, Florida. Grant, who was my mentor, said, "If you ever get into this business, go work for A. G. Edwards." At the time, they didn't have proprietary or big trading accounts. I was a year out of college, because after I graduated I spent a year trading for my dad.

I went into this little branch in Gainesville and said, "Hi, I'd like to be a financial advisor. Here's my resumé." I was laughed out of the office. I was maybe 22 or 23, and I probably looked 18. They were like, "Who are you and why are you here? No, we only take experienced people, licensed, have a book."

I went home, called Grant and said, "They're not even going to give me an interview." He happened to know this guy's boss's boss or something, so they called me in for an interview, to appease the upper management. I told them what I wanted to do, and again, I think they thought I was a little nuts. "I have a network, and this is how I want to build out my network, and this is my plan."

Over a couple of interviews, I actually got the job. I think they kept thinking, "Oh, well, surely she wants to be an associate or work for whoever," and I was like, "No, no, I want to be my own advisor. This is what I want to do." It was pretty funny, looking back. When you're young and inexperienced, you think you can do anything.

Michael: How long did you have this role?

Jenny: I was with A. G. Edwards for almost three years. Then I was recruited out to be independent for a bunch of different reasons. I had started building my business around the country. My sister was working for Pfizer, actually still does, and many of her colleagues began using me as their advisor on 401(k) plans, stock options, pensions, benefits, etc. I started building a base of clients that was half Pfizer employees, the other half mainly physicians. That was my niche.

From there, I went independent for eight years. I had known Marty Bergin, our president owner here at DUNN, since the late '90s, early 2000s. He was a mentor of mine, and actually was a client too.

Michael: How did you first connect with Marty?

Jenny: Marty moved down in the late '90s to work for Bill. He'd come from the DC area, he was on the audit team and a partner at a CPA firm. Bill hired him away and convinced him to come down to sleepy Stuart, FL. His next-door neighbor was a physician whom my sister knew through her job at Pfizer. This physician said, "Oh, you're new and Marty's new. You two should meet, because there's not many young people who just moved to this area." So, the physician connected them and they became friends. Then my sister introduced me, because I was in finance already, and said, "You might want to talk to this person." I seized the opportunity to get to know somebody with all of this experience, so I would pick Marty's brain. He was a mentor.

Michael: When was the first moment, the lightbulb moment, that you figured out how different what Bill Dunn was doing was?

For me, when I think back, I was doing all this research in the early to mid-90s on trend following traders, and my father was working with Marty. My father was a doctor in the Northern Virginia area and Marty was doing CPA work with their office.

One day, my father said to me, "Hey, Marty's doing CPA work with the best trader in the world." I'm like, "Shut up, dad. That's not true." Then I started to look at the numbers and I thought to myself, "Hold on. Maybe he is the best trader in the world. This guy Bill has done some amazing stuff."

Jenny: My lightbulb moment wasn't until years after I'd actually met Bill. Right out of college, I was trading for my dad in stocks. An old family friend of ours had retired from Publix, where he had been an executive practically since they started. He was trading options on S&P 500 futures. He knew I had graduated with a finance degree and I was doing some trading. He was doing this strategy, and he brought it to me and asked for my help. He wanted to write a book, to hone it. This was early 2000s.

Michael: How did you get in front of Bill?

Jenny: Through Marty. I started doing this options on futures trading around the same time I met Marty. We had been trading it for a couple of years and had an absolutely insane track record—huge returns. I was trying to build out the systematic way to do it. So, of course, I was telling Marty all about it. Marty said, "Why don't you come down and explain your system to Bill? If he likes it and we can do something with it, then we could figure something out." I thought, "Oh, that's cool," not having any clue who Bill Dunn was. Again, I'm a 22-year-old who looks younger, and female.

Michael: Pitching to a PhD guy who's done extremely well.

Jenny: Back then there wasn't Google, so you didn't type in "Bill Dunn" and get your reality check. I didn't have any information other than, "Marty, my mentor in finance, tells me to come down and pitch to his boss. Okay. I'll do that."

I put together my track record, made a little PowerPoint, and drove down to Stuart. I was in the office with Bill, Marty, Pierre, and I think Kurt was in there too. I pitched my idea. I was so proud of it. Bill let me get through the whole thing, then he looked at me and said, "That's the craziest thing I've ever heard. You are insane. I wouldn't touch this with a 10ft pole. Do you understand the type of risk you're taking? How have you not blown up yet? Because if you haven't, you're going to soon."

I took his advice and realized I didn't know what I was doing. So, fortunately we unwound the system and I didn't lose anyone's money.

Michael: When did you first get what Bill was doing, and the scale of it? The weirdest thing about coming to the DUNN office is that you expect a New York city tower—some glass pinnacle steel thing 100 stories tall—and Stuart, Florida, is not like that.

Jenny: Not at all like that. We own this beautiful building right on the water. You come out on the third floor and there's a phone on a table that says, "Push this button." It is pretty funny. There is no reception area.

Michael: It was worse in 1996.

Jenny: I remember that from when I came down in the early 2000s before they redid this building. I would say my aha moment was a couple of years into being an independent advisor and realizing from talking to Marty how amazing their strategy was. But I had no access to it, so I couldn't allocate to it for my clients because it wasn't available for retail. I would have had to advise my clients to take their money, leave my book of business, and go directly to DUNN.

Michael: You said that you saw how amazing their strategy was. When you first heard what these guys were doing, did you know about trend following trading?

Jenny: No, I had no idea.

Michael: For me, discovering trend following was a completely different animal. I remember thinking, "This is unbelievable. How come the world doesn't know about this?" I've got my MBA, but I didn't have a CPA or CFA background. I knew about Warren Buffett's approach with the balance sheets, then to learn about trend following was something totally different. Of course, there's a lot of genius that goes into the trend following systems that you guys employ. I would argue more of the genius is in the discipline to adhere to it.

Jenny: That's exactly what I thought. Trend following is the best kept secret on the planet. Yet, when you do try to tell people about how incredible it is, it's so contrary to the mainstream that it's an uphill battle.

When I first heard about it, I thought, "How do I incorporate this into what I'm doing?" It was totally different than how I was trained. In my training, I learned to buy something that you think is undervalued—you're trying to do prediction. The biggest thing as an advisor is trying to manage people's emotions and help them make the right decision at difficult times. Trend following takes that away, and it's amazing for that. It gives me so much peace because we don't have an emotional aspect to our system. We're not trying to predict. We're just identifying trends going long or short across the markets.

> Trend following is the best-kept secret on the planet.

Michael: With a lot of things that you and I might talk about, we don't think about how they might sound to the average person. If we say "no prediction," a lot of people tune out, because they are completely glued to the idea that there's someone with a crystal ball, or some kind of education, or talent, that enables them to see what the average person can't see. How do you start to work with people to get them away from the notion of predicting tomorrow versus reacting to tomorrow?

Jenny: You're absolutely right. People love things that they can understand, things that are easy, things that are predictable. They love control. They're always looking for that crystal ball, because they want to feel they have some kind of leg up to get ahead. We tell them the only data we need is price data.

Michael: So, the average person thinks, "I've got my *Wall Street Journal*, I've got my IBD, so I'm going to study all of these numbers, all of this data,

We're not trying to predict. We're identifying trends going long or short across the markets.

all of this analysis. Then somehow or another, assuming that I've got the right 1,000 points of data, I can then predict tomorrow." When you say it's all embedded in price, what do you mean?

Jenny: As a trend follower, you're not trying to predict, you're trying to identify and profit from a trend—and more of a medium- to long-term trend. Ultimately, the only data you need is price, because it's already influxed all that information.

I've been to conferences where you'll hear somebody talk about the pigs in China and how the demand for pork is yada, yada, yada. They have all these analysts, all these pundits. I listen to CNBC because I know that's what advisors are listening to and I want to hear what they're hearing, but everything on there is about a story and this person's conviction toward this thing or that asset. What's funny is people will believe somebody's conviction. Yet you have a tried-and-tested system that has been in actual trading since 1984, and they're like, "Well, how do we know that the system works?" It's mind-boggling, because there's a zillion portfolio managers out there who have done well, but no one can predict regularly or routinely correctly all the time. It's impossible, because none of us can see the future.

Michael: You mentioned 1984 and that's for the particular WMA program that you guys are famous for, but the actual DUNN track record goes back to around 10 years before that?

Jenny: Back to 1974, so 45 years.

Michael: That's nuts. How many continuous track records of that length exist in America—and I'm not talking about a buy and hold mutual fund? Warren Buffett is one—he has been at this for a long time. DUNN has also been at this for a long time. I'm sure there are some other names that I'm not aware of, but there are not many at this length, are there?

Jenny: No, there are not.

Michael: Was there a presence about Bill Dunn when you first met him?

Jenny: I have such good memories of a couple of things, and one I think you'll get a big kick out of, because anyone that hears this story thinks it's great, especially if you have any history of understanding that presence you're talking about.

I started in the business in 2000 and I was independent for eight years. Marty had always been a mentor to me, and I'd always stayed in touch with him. I loved being independent, being an entrepreneur, doing my own thing, and I had no intention of ever stepping away from that.

Marty called me in late 2010. I'd come back from an incredible trip to Italy, so I couldn't wait to tell him all about it. He was calling to say, "I've entered into the succession plan with Bill, and I'm going to be buying out the firm, and I wish there was some way you could help us take the business to the next level." I laughed at him, because even though I knew it was a huge deal, I had all this freedom and flexibility and I'd never intended on leaving that kind of career path.

But he planted a seed that a few months later resurfaced, and I called him up and said, "Let's just have a conversation. I need to at least explore it." So I came down to Stuart and met with a lot of people, but not Bill that time. After that, Marty said, "Well, now you need to come back to meet with Bill." At this point, I knew a lot about the company, about Bill, and how he's this legend, so I got nervous. I said, "Marty, what do I do to prepare to meet with Bill? I'm no longer this 23-year-old naive girl who came in with a futures strategy." He said, "Oh, I have no idea. You'll have to figure it out." I racked my brain and I actually built a spreadsheet of a forecast of profitability investing in me instead of his own system.

No one can predict correctly all the time.

My thinking was that Bill invests all of his money in his own system. That's how much he believes in it. So, if I could show him the return on investing in me and how this business could grow, that was the best approach. And that's what I did. I came down here and I was hoping and praying that I did not look like an idiot in front of Bill Dunn. I knew things work out for a reason, so if I didn't get the job, it was okay. But at the same time, I didn't want to embarrass myself.

I came down here, met in Bill's office, and we talked a bit about my background. Then I showed him the spreadsheet. I am obviously not in the research department and I don't have a PhD, but I do know basic

Excel and I am pretty decent at math. I explained the spreadsheet to Bill, and he's like, "No, those numbers aren't correct." I'm thinking in my head, "He has a PhD in Theoretical Physics, how does he not get this? This is simple." Then I walk him through it again, and a second time he says, "Nope, those numbers are wrong." I'm thinking, "This can't be right. I know my spreadsheet's correct." After the third time, he says, "You are correct. You may proceed," and then I knew he just tested me. He wanted to see if I could hold my own, stay convicted to what I had done, and if he could get me to waver.

We finish our meeting, and he says, "Well, let's go to lunch. We're going to go to my favorite place, Conky Joe's." We go down and get in his little two-seater Porsche, and he says, "Listen, we have to start with the conch fritters, and then you have to get conch chowder." I love seafood, but I hate conch. Of course, I had conch fritters and conch chowder, and pretended to like it. But we had a great lunch, and I came back and said to Marty, "Bill was absolutely lovely, but I don't know that this is going to happen. I think it's probably not the time." Then a couple of weeks later, Marty called me up and said Bill came in and told him, "I don't know why we wouldn't hire her."

Michael: I remember being in a conference room at DUNN with some colleagues who were pitching to Bill on how they could expand things and so on. They were using all kinds of jargon, just jargon, jargon, jargon, jargon. I was sizing Bill up and I was thinking, "These guys are screwing up. This man doesn't want to listen to all this jargon." And it got to my turn to speak and I said, "I think one of the biggest problems with this industry is these terms that no one understands, like managed futures." The other guys I was with turned ashen. There was a pause, and then all of a sudden, Bill pounded the table, "I agree. I don't like these terms either." I started laughing to myself.

Jenny: Those moments with Bill are priceless. What's wonderful about having Marty as our president and owner is he had so many years with Bill, and in some ways he's kept a lot of those tried-and-true things in our culture. At the same time, he's taken it to DUNN 2.0, with so much emphasis on research—but a lot of Marty was groomed by Bill.

Michael: If you were talking to someone smart, who didn't know what trend following is, what would you say? I know DUNN has said that it is not a beta shop, but to a lot of people that won't mean a lot. How would you describe what you're doing to those people?

Jenny: One of the most fundamental things about DUNN, one of our core values, is being client-centric. A lot of companies strive to be that, but what's interesting about DUNN is we prove it in the way we do things.

First up, we have never charged a management fee. We are zero and 25. That means we take 25% of net new profit. If you invested money with us and you made money, we would take 25% of your profit, then you'd have to exceed that old high before we would ever take another dollar. Right up front, it's extremely fair. But also, it drives everything we do with the system in order to make sure it's as robust and dynamic as it can be, because that's the only time we make money. The second side of that is, is we eat our own cooking. About 13% of all of the money at DUNN is proprietary, and we trade our money identically. We don't charge ourselves the fee, obviously.

Michael: Could you give us an explanation of beta?

Jenny: Beta, in our sense, means that you can have the basic trend following system that almost turns into an index. We are not striving to be that. We're striving to be best in breed; to actually provide compounded growth. A lot of our peers are trading at lower volatilities, looking for absolute returns. Their systems were set up initially mostly institutional, and then they stuck those large names of firms into package products for individuals. Because of their low wall, they're more of an absolute return. We've gotten it too where a fund of funds comes to us and says, "We'll put you in our fund, but then we want to cut out the fee and give us your beta product." Beta to us is three iterations ago of basic trend following. We don't believe in that.

Michael: In the last few years, there's been all kinds of debates and controversies in the trend following space, and people have said it doesn't work anymore or it's too volatile. Then March 2020 happens and it's the tried-and-true folks that actually make money when a big unexpected event like that happens.

Jenny: I come across advisors, especially in the retail world, who have either used managed features in the past but didn't allocate enough to make a difference, or they invested in something that had too low volatility. So it became kind of a headache to explain to clients why they did this. They've had bad experiences. The vast majority of their AUM may come from institutions that are trading a managed account. They can adjust their exposure however they like. But when you put those low-volatility systems into a package product that has an additional layer of fees, it waters down an already pretty low return stream.

People see that, and then they don't understand the true benefit. They don't realize we've had a compounded growth return that beats the S&P since '84. If you showed people our annual returns, you'd be hard pressed to find anybody who would say, "Oh, no, I don't want any of that." But then if you show them the monthly returns, you might have a few people that are unconvinced. It's a lack of understanding of what drives a trend. We have a lumpy return distribution.

Michael: Even if people have no earthly idea about finance, trading, and investing, lumpy returns are still against human nature.

Jenny: Absolutely. That is one of the most difficult things, because if you look at the overall compound return, especially as a complement to a traditional portfolio, if you look at a stock-bond cash portfolio, maybe even some real estate, and then you add trend following and DUNN in particular, you would be hard pressed to find a portfolio that would not benefit on a risk-adjusted return, because it provides such a different return stream. Most advisors understand that there's virtually no correlation to stocks, but they have a harder time getting their clients to stay convicted to it.

Everyone has such a short time frame in judging things. They should be seeing this as, "Okay, we have this portfolio for the next 10, 15, 20 years, and look how it could improve your risk-adjusted return and look how it could smooth out the ride overall and be additive."

It's like anything. We live here in Florida, right in the middle of where hurricanes crop up. If a hurricane gets named in the Atlantic and it's heading toward the southeast coast and I don't have hurricane insurance, I can't call up the insurance company and say, "Oh, by the way, now I want some insurance because I see this storm coming." I try to tell advisors all the time and other people who say, "Yes, this would be great, but I only want to own it when I need it." Well, you're never going to know when you need it. Again, it goes back to prediction: "I only want to be in this when it's good." Well, I only want to play golf when it's 75 degrees and no humidity and not a cloud in the sky, but it doesn't always work out that way.

Michael: I mentioned some of the controversy over trend following in the last couple of years. But if you look at this year, 2020, it's interesting. We had this March 2020 thing happen. I could feel the anxiety building, even though I'm not running a fund. Then the Fed does some hocus pocus, they elevate stocks and people go, "Oh, forget it. I need buy and hold." Whereas this year, if you look at it through a different lens, you should be saying to yourself, "If there was ever a year that said, 'I need something more than buy and hold,' it's right now," regardless of the fact that they were able to hocus pocus and elevate stocks again.

Jenny: Absolutely. You and I are passionate about trend following. I've been here almost 10 years, it's what I think about and what I talk about for most of my day. But looking back to the 1980s, the star fund was the Fidelity Magellan fund run by Peter Lynch. I think the average annual return for a huge period of time was 30% or something crazy. They did a study of the returns of the people invested in the fund, and what do you think they made?

Trend following takes the emotion out.

Michael: They got killed on fees?

Jenny: No, they actually lost money, because they would chase either fear or greed. The market starts going down, they sell at the wrong time. It starts running back up, they buy back in because of their fear of missing out. What's wonderful about trend following and DUNN's system is that we've taken emotion out. We stay true to the system and to the rules, and as a complement to your traditional assets, you can see how much it will impact your overall portfolio strategy. It's getting people to actually do that.

Michael: We're talking about a complex strategy reduced to rules that anyone can understand. Now, if I was to contrast that with the example you brought up, the thing I remember about Peter Lynch is that some of his stock picks he would get from his teen daughters, who would tell him what was hot at the mall. That was the strategy. You and I both know, that's not a strategy, that's the '80s throwing money around, and he happened to be the guy sitting there for that 10-year stretch, and then it was all over.

Jenny: This is pretty funny, but my dad used to say the same thing to me. I don't know if he got it from Peter Lynch, but he used to say, "You know, Jen, if you see something at school that is up and coming hot, tell me what it is." I always thought it was his way of trying to get me interested in investing. Actually, when I first entered high school in the early '90s, I told him to invest in Tommy Hilfiger. To this day, I don't know how much he made on it, but when I got my first car, he said, "Well, you helped pay for this because of your stock pick." That helped get me hooked on investing, because I thought, "Ooh, if I can just have an idea I can make some money—I like this." It's part of the reason that I got into this industry.

Michael: Do you think your path to where you are today is down to luck? How do you see yourself in terms of being open to opportunity? Even though you described yourself as being a little nervous, you still showed up to DUNN Capital.

Jenny: I think how you meet people always plays a part, but it's the whole age-old saying that luck is when preparation meets opportunity.

I'm passionate about investing in education because I realize how much it's needed. But I'm also passionate about DUNN and our system because I know we care about people and we want them to have a good experience and make money. Potential investors have a qualification call with Marty. It's rare that you actually speak with the owner of the firm and he'll tell you, "These are things you can expect." That's so important, because money is personal to people. They look at their future or they look at their goals. You want to set the expectation of what you could possibly go through over time and make sure that they're prepared for that. As for me, I've always been committed to education and consulting. I love working with people. I cover the United States, and getting to meet so many different people, advisors, institutions, foundations, and so on, is fascinating.

Anybody that knows me knows I'm absolutely passionate about golf. I've been fortunate enough to play all over the world. When I had only been at DUNN for a year or so, I got the opportunity to go to New Zealand to play the famous courses at Cape Kidnappers and Kauri Cliffs, which are both owned by Julian Robertson of Tiger Management, the original long-short legend. Right before I left for New Zealand, I happened to run into Bill. I said, "Oh, Bill, I'm going to New Zealand to play golf, and I'm going to have breakfast with Julian Robertson." He stopped in his tracks, looked at me in the eye, and said, "You realize he's a legend, right?"

When I get to New Zealand, I get to play golf, I have breakfast with Julian. My friend who I was there with was interviewing him for an article, and we met some of his grandkids at the hotel, and it was casual. He happened to ask what I did, and I told him. I was struck by the fact that he didn't know anything about trend following. Here is a legend in an alternative strategy who has no idea about this other legend that is Bill. I realized trend following was not mainstream. We're committed here to making it mainstream. We believe it should not just be for the elite, it should be for everyone.

Michael: I think a lot of people learned about trend following based on stuff that I've done, but I do shake my head. It's a tough egg to crack, isn't it?

Jenny: It is. It's kind of fun, though. Every new meeting or call is a challenge of engaging with people's expectations and helping to educate. It's almost like an aha moment. When people get it, they're like, "Wow, I've found something that I wish I had found a long time ago." You see how much it can impact people, and that's what makes me passionate, not just about the whole industry, but also about DUNN in particular.

PART 5
NIELS KAASTRUP-LARSEN

N IELS KAASTRUP-LARSEN is Managing Director of DUNN Capital (Europe). Niels has been in the managed futures business since 1990, holding management positions at several leading CTAs: GNI Fund Management, Chesapeake, Beach Capital, and Rho Asset Management, the last two of which he co-founded. He is also the founder and host of one of the world's leading podcasts within the hedge fund and CTA community.

Michael Note

Niels Kaastrup-Larsen runs a podcast called Top Traders Unplugged that happens to feature many of the traders that have been included in my books over the years, including Jerry Parker, David Harding, Martin Lueck, Alex Greyserman, Richard Dennis, and more. A who's who of trend following pioneers and trend following excellence.

Michael Covel: I've gotten on this hook of doing many interviews with non-traders, because it's fun and I get to talk to a lot of interesting people. And frankly, their mindset is almost the same as the philosophy of the trading process that we talk about. Many psychologists and economists have come to the same understanding that you've got to take risks, you've got to give it a shot, and you're going to get a lot of small losses. That's the only way you're going to find the big home run.

Niels Kaastrup-Larsen: It's so true. That's why you have such a big audience, because when you stick to a small niche like I do, there is a limit to how many people want to listen every week. But I think your range of guests is amazing. Sometimes it's a Nobel Prize winner and other times it's an author or a trader.

Michael: You're approaching 30 years in the hedge fund space, going back to the late '80s?

Niels: I actually started as a bond trader in 1987. I started in September and I think there's some truth in the fact that early experiences stay with you. Clearly the events of October '87 made me somewhat of a cautious person when it comes to investing. That was an interesting time. And then '91 was when I first got introduced to managed futures trend following.

Michael: How did that happen?

Niels: I came from a cash bond trading background. Growing up and living in Denmark at the time, I was trading government bonds for one of the larger banks there. What I saw back then was that institutional investors, when they wanted to speculate, were using cash bonds, but, of course, they were expensive and they were not super liquid. What we did as market makers back then was every time we got hit with a large position from a client, we would hedge that in German Bund futures in London. We realized how liquid and how inexpensive they were to trade.

> The events of October '87 made me somewhat cautious when it comes to investing.

I guess also I had an entrepreneurial gene inside of me. Myself and a colleague broke out and started our own little firm. We teamed up with the largest futures broker on the Life Exchange, but our business plan was to go to Danish institutional investors and say, "Why don't you use the German Bund futures to do your speculation in instead of Danish bonds?" We went around Denmark talking about the wonders of futures, the wonders of being in London and its cheapness. But of course, nobody wanted to move their money to London. Nobody wanted to trade futures. Futures had a bad reputation back then.

Around 1991, I had to go back to this firm and tell them that we weren't succeeding, we couldn't move any business to them. Then they said, "Listen, we understand it's difficult, but we have this little group in the corner down here, probably 25 or 30 people in total, and they do something called managed futures where there is a track record from managing money using futures. And maybe it would be easier for you to talk to investors about that, so you have something to show them."

That's how I got into managed futures. Of course, I had to read up on the subject and came across the Turtles. I've never looked back; I've never done anything else other than managed futures and trend following. And you're right, it's been almost 30 years now.

Michael: Can you still recall the feeling you had when you first understood what the Turtles, AHL, Richard Dennis, Bill Dunn, and John W. Henry were doing?

Niels: It took some time for me to fully realize and appreciate the value. Coming from a trading background, I was brought up with the philosophy that you should buy low and sell high. Once I started looking at what these guys were doing and what trend following is—how you define rules, buy breakouts, and sell breakdowns—I saw that this was the complete opposite. It took me some time to fully understand that this was better than buying low and selling high.

But seeing the returns that they produced had an immediate impact on me—I think the best way often is to look at the evidence. When you looked at the track records, these were firms that delivered spectacular returns, but were not necessarily more risky than being invested in the stock market. Starting out in this industry in September 1987 then seeing the crash on October 19, 1987 certainly gave me some level of appreciation for risk, yet I was seeing returns that were significant but didn't seem any more risky.

Then I started looking into what they were doing to minimize the risk yet unleash the upside potential. It was a process for me to fully understand and appreciate that these guys were doing something different, but it made a lot of sense. And of course, once you then get into the nitty gritty details and the appreciation of diversification—trading markets that are uncorrelated, the risk management, and not relying on one single market or one single sector to do the heavy lifting for you—it all fell into place.

As I said, I find what we do makes so much sense compared to a long-only strategy, which is also why it's frustrating to me why still so few people embrace the strategy and the concept, because what evidence do they have to support the idea that you shouldn't include it in your portfolio to some extent?

Michael: I think the strategy has been positioned as controversial by people that perhaps have other agendas.

I still remember going down that initial path of discovery. I see the Turtles, and what they're doing, and that's interesting. Then John W. Henry, I see what he's doing, that's interesting. And then I remember the first time I started to look at DUNN Capital. I was thinking, "What's this? Who is this? What's going on here? Hold on, they seem to be in the same head-space as these other guys that I'm looking at, but the returns are even more dramatic on the upside." It was an amazing feeling, like being an investigative journalist.

Back in those days, trend following wasn't a topic that you could find a lot of insights on. It was touched on at conferences and in the back pages of magazines, but there wasn't a tremendous amount of explanation. I had to do a lot of digging.

Niels: By the early '90s we had the MAR reports (Managed Account Reports). They were trying to track the industry and you could see the rankings and the league tables, which gave you some flavor that this could be the beginning of something—even though back then, I think there was less than $10 billion under management in total. I'm pretty sure most of these pioneers didn't have a lot of contact with each other, so they were doing it on their own—an incredibly courageous decision to apply new techniques to markets and not being able to find a lot of validation anywhere until much later.

Michael: The common ancestor would have been Richard Donchian. At some stage of the game, they must have all picked up an old copy of *Stocks and Commodities* magazine and read about him.

Niels: They definitely got their inspiration somewhere. And Donchian would be a good choice.

Michael: We're talking about a particular philosophy of trading that goes back decades, yet I still get these emails from people saying, "Hey, Mike, I saw a headline in Bloomberg and trend following is dead. It doesn't work anymore."

Niels: I see a lot of investors all over Europe and Asia. We have a 45-year track record, yet people will still question, does this work? This is why I'm still frustrated that people don't accept the evidence, yet they are willing to listen to people who they know deep down are making an educated guess or a forecast about what they think is going to happen, when instead they have the opportunity to invest with managers who have delivered on their promise for all these decades. Maybe people are not willing to invest in an uncomfortable strategy, but over time, it's still a lot better than an 8% average return in stock markets with 50% plus drawdowns.

Michael: Everyone in the trend following world is going to have their own version of the special sauce and everyone's going to think their flavor is the best. That's human nature. But if we stay with the bigger picture of trend following, how does it make you feel when you read some of the inconsistent statements coming from people trading in entirely different ways—or even from those trading the same way? It can be confusing for the average person, can't it?

Niels: It can be, that's a great point. The phrase that we often hear, "this time is different," is at the root of the problem, because people want to believe that somehow markets have changed to a point where strategies that have been around for a long time shouldn't work anymore. They forget that markets are the result of human behavior.

We have periods where some people prefer to sell at a certain level and some people prefer to buy at the same level and markets are relatively calm. Then, from time to time, we get new information that pushes more people to be buyers than sellers. And we get these shifts in price or momentum or trends—or however people want to phrase it—and that creates these opportunities. It would be weird if suddenly that behavior were to stop.

Why would we always interpret information to a point where markets would be in balance? We wouldn't. There's no evidence of that. But I do think we've made it a little bit difficult for ourselves to promote trend following as a strategy. On one hand, we're honest by saying that it's a hard strategy to own, because it is. It's fine to be transparent about that. But on the other hand, we've always said that trend following is not difficult to do. It's relatively simple.

We have done ourselves a disservice by using that narrative around the strategy. If I look at how trend following was done 20, 30, 40 years ago, and how we do it on our side today, there's a world of difference. It's much more sophisticated in how we apply the techniques. The basic rules might still be simple. Putting them together is not simple and it's certainly not easy. On top of that, you have all the challenges of implementation. I'm not saying that we as an industry are not at fault, I think we can take some of the responsibility, but deep-down human nature always wants to question things and there is a tendency to believe the markets have changed.

There were some articles in 2019, after the last major drawdown for the industry, saying that because of the way Donald Trump tweets, suddenly markets were moving too quickly for trend followers. And at the time we were at the beginning of one of the strongest performance periods ever. In fact, only once in 45 years have we had eight months in a row with positive performance and this year we had seven months in a row. Again, look at the evidence. Why are you suggesting that Donald Trump's tweets make it impossible for trend followers to make money? It's silly, but people choose to print these stories every so often.

> **There is a tendency to believe the markets have changed.**

Michael: People sometimes don't think about the game inside the game. First off, this is all click-bait for these publications. It's all designed to get you to click and they make money from you clicking. If the headline says, "Trend following is a strategy designed by aliens located in an underground bunker in Zurich," people click on that and then send me an email. We also need to ask whether the quote comes from someone with authority on the subject.

Back in the day, if I wanted to reach out to an authority on the subject of trend following, I could contact Jerry Parker, Bill Dunn, or John W. Henry—people who had been around. What people sometimes forget with today's media coverage is to check who the author is and look at their bio. They could possibly know what's going on, but when you click a little further, the last 10 articles they've written are all unrelated. It's literally somebody writing copy to get you to click. That's tough for investors, because it often looks serious: "Oh my gosh. It's a headline on Bloomberg, this must mean something." No, it doesn't.

Niels: I completely agree. I have from time to time looked up the people who write these stories and they often have little experience of what we do, but have strong opinions about it. As trend followers, we can only do so much. We continue to tell the story, showcase the evidence, talk about it, and educate people in a slightly different way.

Michael: I'm thinking of Jerry Parker. I would argue that when it comes to participation on Twitter, he would take the lead out of anybody involved in the trend following space. What's the big inspiration you take from Jerry Parker?

Niels: I'm fortunate enough to have a long relationship with Jerry, because I used to work for him back in the mid-90s. I completely agree with you that Jerry does a great job of educating people and making these points on social media. What's interesting about it is that back in the '90s, Jerry was much more guarded about sharing information, because there was still a lot of mystery around the Turtles, the rules, and the secret sauce, yet today he is incredibly generous in sharing and helping, not just investors but also a lot of young traders.

One of the most important things he took away from the Turtle project was the mentorship he got from Richard Dennis—the fact that losing money is okay as long as you follow your system, and you should be celebrated for following your rules. Even mediocre rules are better than intuition when it comes to trading. Jerry's doing a great job in passing on those key concepts. And I'm fortunate to having seen it up close, but also having been able to observe how he's continued to build his track record for so many years.

Michael: In full disclosure, when I was doing my TurtleTrader book, which came out in 2007, I had spoken with Jerry in person many times before that project went into motion. For the book, I could not get him to talk. I got about half the crowd to talk to me, and the other half of the crowd wanted to take me to court. You're right, Jerry was more silent, but deadly. Now, when I want to read something smart about trend following, I go to Jerry on Twitter. I don't know another trend following trader that's participating as much as he is.

Niels: I agree. I wish there were more. On that note, I saw that Larry Hite published a book, *The Rule*. It's incredibly important that some of these pioneers leave a legacy—so that we can be reminded about those early days, and those timeless early teachings. It also reminds me a little bit of Ray Dalio, because he was also careful how he interacted with the press until he retired, since when he has been a wealth of information. If people don't take advantage of some of this information, they're losing out.

Michael: Back in 2012, Larry and I were talking about cowriting a book. And then I decided to take a sojourn to Asia. And so poor Larry got delayed. But ultimately I think he's much happier to have done the book as a solo project and not with a co-author, because his experience, his name, and everything he's done should have been only authored by Larry Hite. That's what he delivered. I think he did a great effort.

Niels: I listened to your conversation with Larry and he's a class act. There's so much great information in what he says. Also the way he says things. I'm going to butcher this, but one of his quotes is something along the lines that there is little magic in trend following, but what it does is magical, or something along those lines. How great is that? It captures the essence in a few words.

Michael: Let me open up a little debate. I wrote these names down today: managed futures, CTA, quant, systematic trend following. Why can't we settle on one name? Why is there a definitional issue with this style of trading?

Niels: It doesn't help. Some of it is based on how the regulators classify the strategy. That's where the CTA definition came from: *commodity trading advisor* tells people what we do. It's confusing, but we have to live with it. I remember back in the early '90s, which was a tough time for the CTA and trend following crowd, a lot of managers started to call themselves hedge funds as they thought that was more acceptable to investors. But later on, they went back to the CTA managed futures classification. I don't know what the answer is, but it certainly seems to be confusing to many people.

Michael: You mentioned Jerry Parker's mentorship from Richard Dennis. I'm the only person that has, literally, a copy of every place he has ever been quoted. Every interview he gave in the '70s, '80s, and '90s contained these one- or two-line parables where he was taking a complicated subject and breaking it down in a way everyone could understand. When you go back and you look at his public statements over the years, they're consistent and eye-opening.

> It's been proven many, many times that a complex problem needs a simple solution.

Niels: One of the strengths of the trend following approach is that we try to make things as simple as possible, but not too simple. This comes from behavioral finance. It's been proven many, many times that a complex problem needs a simple solution and few things are more complex than the financial markets and how they interact on a daily basis.

Even though I said earlier that the way we apply trend following today is more sophisticated, the basic rules are still relatively simple. Richard Dennis is a master of that in the way he expresses himself. What he did back then is super important, not only in terms of sharing his information with the group of 20 Turtles, but also because it created this narrative that our industry to some extent is lacking.

He once told me, "I knew that I was using two-thirds rules in my trading and maybe one-third was intuition." He was curious to find out whether it could all be rules-based and whether he could prove it. And he went on to do that through the experiment, keeping it pretty simple.

Michael: He may not take credit for it, but there's some brilliant marketing there. When you look at the mystery, the word Turtle, and how that famous *Wall Street Journal* article unfolded, it's got to be one of the most famous Wall Street stories. I would think among people that know about trading, the Turtle story is right up there.

Niels: Richard Dennis came across to me as an incredibly humble man, not looking for fame in any way unlike many other people who are associated with Wall Street. There's a lot of great things to be said about him and we should be grateful for having someone like that do what he did.

Michael: Let me take you to something that's near and dear to you personally right now. I'll set it up. Around 1983 or 1984, I was 16 years old, playing baseball. My coach's name was Marty. And Marty (Bergin) is the guy who owns and runs DUNN Capital today. Started by Bill Dunn, being run by Marty now. What an amazing confluence of events. Why don't you share a couple of experiences or thoughts?

Niels: If we start with Bill, there's a lot of commonalities with some of the other great legends from back then. They all had a lot of courage to do what they did. They obviously had commitment, consistency, and clear thinking about what they were trying to achieve. And they were certainly not shy of implementing this with conviction. Once they felt comfortable that they would never go out of business even if they had volatile returns, they stuck with that.

But maybe some things that are not so often described about these people when you come close to them is that there's a lot of humbleness as well. They can be humble to the outside world, but also to the markets, knowing that from time to time they would be taught lessons. And that's why they all diversified their investments quite a lot.

It's a mix of different characteristics. I think a lot of the legends, including Bill, shared that. You would never sense from someone like Bill Dunn whether it was an up 10% day or a down 10% day. There's no emotional association with the daily or the monthly performance swings.

It shows you a lot about the character when you meet people who can do that, because back when they started out, there was a lot less computer power. But Bill and his son, Daniel—who is still with our firm today—literally started out going to the library every day. They had one of these punch machines that they could queue up their run, so to speak, and it would give them the buy and sell calculations for the day. It was not until the late '70s that they got a computer.

Bill created an enormously important, valuable platform and track record that Marty has done an amazing job in taking forward. With Bill, you had the virtues of discipline and being fair to clients. Our unusual fee structure, where we only charge our clients when they make money, was something that Bill instilled back in 1974.

Marty has kept the focus on trend following and not swayed away from that. He has kept those traditions, while at the same time creating an environment where people can innovate and improve, which means that what we do today is a bit more sophisticated. We have more of a statistical approach to trend following, trying to deliver a package that more investors would be willing to take into their portfolio, because we know that it's such a hard strategy to hold on to. If we can deliver that with a slightly higher risk-adjusted profile, then that's a good thing as long as we keep all the benefits that trend following offers.

One thing that stays clear for me is something that Bill would always say in the office: the best time to invest in trend following is at the bottom of a drawdown, the second-best time is today. That is a simple, timeless description of how you should view the strategies—similar to some of the great lines from Larry Hite.

Michael: An interesting tangent about Jerry Parker and Marty Bergin is that they both have an accounting background. Anybody thinking that *The Wolf of Wall Street* is the archetype for how one makes money might need to reassess when we're talking about Marty Bergin and Jerry Parker. If you sit down with either of these men in their office, they are not going to give off anything remotely close to DiCaprio in *The Wolf of Wall Street*. For a lot of people that's still hard to believe, because that DiCaprio imagery is what many people do think of being how you make money on Wall Street.

The best time to invest in trend following is at the bottom of a drawdown, the second-best time is today.

Niels: I remember that in one of your books you referenced your first visit to DUNN's offices being this weird moment where you come in and it feels like being in an accountant's office. Through all the firms that I've worked with, you get that same feeling when you go into the office. It's different to what people see on television and in the movies. It's a very organized process. We try to take all the emotions out by following strict rules and processes. That's why we can be calm and collected even if the markets are volatile.

Michael: Here's another name for you. There was a little firm back in the day called AHL, started by Martin Lueck, David Harding, and Michael Adam, which went on to have great success and spawned two further ventures, Aspect Capital and Winton Capital. They were all absolute pioneers in the trend following space. I still remember my first conversation with David Harding in his office and finding him remarkably blunt and direct. It is interesting, though, that right now there's a little bit of controversy around these pioneers who were side by side for a long time and made their fortunes in trend following. What do you think about that?

Niels: These three people are amazing individuals. Like you, most of my conversations on my podcast are done remotely, but when I had to interview Michael, David, and Marty for their 30th anniversary, we decided to do it in person—at Abbey Road Studios. It was interesting to observe the chemistry between these three people with so much shared history, but also a legacy of competing a little bit against each other. I learned a lot from that two-and-a-half hours, for sure.

Regarding the controversy you mentioned, I think trend following can be done up to a certain size. Once you get into the double-digit billions of dollars, something like that, I think you lose some ability to take the best out of trend following. You have to slow your systems down, not to get too much trading cost. Maybe the most important thing is you lose a lot of the commodity markets because they are too small, so you lose the diversification benefit. Because of his success in building Winton into what it is today, I think David has found that maybe there are other things he can be doing that yield him a better return than just trend following. When you look at it that way, he's probably right that in his situation, doing $20 billion or $25 billion-worth of trend following probably doesn't yield him the returns that he and his investors are looking for. With Aspect, DUNN, or Chesapeake there are no issues like that because the size is different.

I don't think David is saying trend following doesn't work; he's saying there are other things that he can maybe get to work better. I also questioned him a little bit about the whole concept of lowering his volatility. His explanation was that he didn't want to experience an October 19, 1987 for his clients, even though, of course, we know that diversified portfolio equities is one small part of that. Who's to say that because equities have a bad run, that's a bad thing for trend following? I don't think it is.

You learn a lot listening to the stories from these three guys. What I find fascinating is that even after so many years, you can feel they're still hungry for learning, they're still hungry for improving—there is a quest for continuous improvement. It's clear—never rest on your laurels.

It's fine that there is a bit of debate, but of course the journalists are having a field day, because the unfortunate thing about David de-emphasizing trend in his portfolio is that a lot of people take that as a sign of trend following suddenly not working.

Michael: In the last decade (2010s) David Harding's funds under management soared to around $30 billion. It's dropped now. And then the other large trend following traders, maybe one or two billion. You are correct to point out that investors need to look with a wide set of eyeglasses to understand what's going on, because if you have one trader who has $30 billion under management and another with $1 billion, that's a different game.

Niels: The problem is that investors often want the big names. In the last 20 years or so, we've certainly seen a lot more institutional participation in the industry. That has caused everyone to say, "Okay, well, in order to get these types of investors in, we should lower our volatility." The whole industry has de-levered their returns, which makes it look like it's not working as well. That's by design. It's not because trend following doesn't work. On our side, we've actually seen the opposite. Our returns for the last six years are stronger, better, than they have been in the last 35 years.

Currently there is this quest to look average and a reluctance to take risk. Just going off on a tangent a little bit here, we mentioned earlier about conviction and how even within our own industry, we've seen certain managers talk about how trend following doesn't work so well, because we have been relying on interest rates as the big return driver in the last 35 years. And it is true that trend following as a strategy has made a lot of money from being long bonds over long periods of time. To me, that's because the strategy is designed to have conviction where the trends are. It says nothing about where the trends and the best returns will be in the next 30 years.

Michael: It's interesting that you talk about wanting to be average. I can still recall the first time meeting Bill Dunn—one of the most intimidating handshakes that I've ever had. When you meet a guy like that when he's tearing it up, you walk away inspired. You don't walk away from meeting Bill Dunn in his prime and go, "Oh yeah, I want to go back and get the T-rate. What's my money market account?" You walk away going, "I could do anything. He did it. He's inspired me." That's the attitude you take from those people. It doesn't mean some high-risk mentality, or that people are trying to go for broke by any stretch of the imagination. But with this particular strategy, you will get volatile returns if you are doing it a certain way.

You're right when you point out that with so many institutional investors, the game changes a little, because you're not dealing with the same mindset. These are the kinds of things that investors need to take into account. Again—back to the headlines—you got to do a little homework, you can't accept blindly what you read in the media.

Niels: When you go and meet investors, there's definitely this fear that if they allocate too much to one asset class or too little, they will look different from the average. So, there's a strong force about being in line with everyone else, which is not what we are trying to do as individual firms. I see a lot of that from an investor's point of view, which is a shame.

But also going back to this thing about not taking on the volatility of the strategy, it reminds me of a conversation with Bill Dreiss—another legend, in my opinion. Bill was talking about how a lot of the strategies that people seek in order to give investors this smooth return end up warehousing risk until, as we saw with Long-Term Capital Management, it all blows up. What we as trend followers are doing is recognizing the risk every day.

Michael: Real-time recognizing of risk.

Niels: Exactly. We are realizing it on an ongoing basis, so it's completely different. Private equity is one of those strategies, at least for a long period of time where you didn't have to market your positions and you could create this false impression that it was a safe type of investment with little volatility.

Michael: You're making a great point, because people want to look at private equity, or venture capital, yet nobody has any idea what's going on behind the scenes. It's the Wizard of Oz behind the curtain.

Niels: But there are parts, certainly from venture capital, that you can transfer directly to what trend followers are doing, namely taking a lot of bets and waiting for the five winners of that year to pay for all the losers. It's funny how people tend to pick certain things that work for them. We know why, it's human behavior, it's how we are wired. So, there's no surprise, but it's interesting to observe how you can pick and choose whatever you feel best about, and ignore other parts of the evidence.

Michael: Nobody criticizes the strategy of venture capital openly as something bad or negative compared to trend following, although it's essentially the same mentality. When you start the year off at DUNN Capital, you don't know what's going to happen in terms of where the trend might appear from, you're going to take whatever appears. It is interesting that the same mentality gets praised on one side and criticized on the other.

Niels: Yeah, that's fascinating. Human nature, as you say.

Michael: There's another guy I find fascinating too. There's some great NPR interviews and audio stories about it. Jason Blum, of Blumhouse Productions, a Hollywood production firm, has the same mentality. He did the paranormal activity on a lot of these horror films. He's says, "Look, I'm going to allocate a million bucks to each film. And I know nine of them are going to fail and one of them is going to make me $200 million." Boom, it's the same mentality.

Niels: Completely. Thinking back to Larry Hite again, when you go back to the root of trend following, it all starts with cutting your losses. The winners will take care of themselves. If you have the strength and the discipline to make sure you don't let those losses run out of proportion, that in itself is a great first rule.

The edge of trend following is knowing what you don't know.

Another example of keeping things incredibly simple comes from Alex Greyserman, who worked with Larry Hite at Mint for many years. He told me about going for an interview at Mint and trying to find out from Larry what was the real edge of that firm. Alex was an academic expecting something fancy, so imagine his disappointment when Larry replied, "Knowing what you don't know."

If you ask Alex today what is the edge of trend following, it's exactly that: knowing what you don't know. That's not a sexy story to try and get across to investors compared to some discretionary global macro manager who has a great thesis about why the dollar is going to go up or down. Knowing what you don't know doesn't quite cut it, but it's so powerful.

CHAPTER 7

ERIC CRITTENDEN

The All-Weather
Approach

ERIC CRITTENDEN is a Chief Investment Officer at Standpoint Asset Management LLC. He has over 20 years' experience designing and managing investment strategies, with an expertise in systematic trading in both mutual funds and hedge funds. Aside from creating sound investment strategies, his ability to simplify and communicate complex topics is what sets him apart from other investment managers. Eric's experience and research have shown that his all-weather approach helps to diversify across asset classes and investment styles to protect investors from the risks of concentration while also providing strong returns.

Michael Note

Eric Crittenden is a trend following trader. He has two-plus decades' experience. He's been around the block. He's seen all kinds of environments, and he has a great perspective. Eric also has a fund that happens to have Tom Basso as its chairman.

Michael Covel: I jotted this down and posted it on Facebook the other day. I don't know where it came from, but I was getting tired of watching nonstop emotional thinking. You can pick what you like or don't like, and we can run with it:

> This is my process. Number one, to critically think. Number two, to expose logical fallacies. Number three, to obliterate hypocrisy. Number four, to destroy sacred cows. Number five, to laugh at team or partisan views. Number six, to rip histrionics. Number seven, to nail emotional persuaders. And number eight, to firebomb identity politics.

I didn't think those were necessarily controversial, I thought they were getting us to the point of *thinking*. Have we lost something in the last bunch of years, where thinking is not in vogue anymore?

Eric Crittenden: A safe place to take that would be to talk about why. Why do all those things?

Michael: Did you like them?

Eric: Yes, absolutely. But they're hot-button things. People, when they hear that, they hear accusations. They hear criticism. And they immediately go into defensive mode, and they dig in and entrench, and they're ready for war.

But if you skip all that, and you go to the why part, you start presenting a vision of getting stuff done. And then you tie those things to an outcome that most people would like. You can tell someone they have bad breath in a way that gets you punched in the face, or you can tell someone they have bad breath in a way that makes you a friend for a life. It's the same information. Why do you get such different outcomes?

Michael: It's a real challenge today, though. Whether you're in business, or whether you want to persuade a friend, because sometimes if you make it too weak-kneed, so to speak, maybe you don't get the point across. There's a fine line between going too far or not going far enough.

The sales cycle for changing someone's mind goes through predictable stages that hinge upon trust, credibility, and outcomes.

Eric: I call it a sales process, but it's a consensus process. Regardless of whether we want it to be this way or not, it happens in stages. Meaning, you can't meet someone, have one conversation and change their mind, unless they're impressionable. It's unfortunate, but the sales cycle for changing someone's mind or getting them to see things a different way goes through predictable stages that hinge upon trust, credibility, and outcomes. You can't get it done in one conversation.

That's a little bit of an answer to your question: what's changed? We're in a cycle where everything is supposed to be instant. That's what social media does. Social media is junk food for the mind. It brings out the worst in everyone, and it doesn't allow for what I am suggesting is necessary for true communication.

Michael: What would you say to people about critical thinking? How would you explain it? Why is it important to you?

Eric: When you say critical thinking, I actually don't know what you mean. I'm not sure what your definition of thinking critically is in this context. If I'm a defensive person, or if I have something to lose, or if I'm skeptical of you, my connotation around that is going to start off being negative. And if you combine that with the social media instant gratification environment, we naturally go down the wrong path.

To answer your question, though, showing people what you mean rather than saying it has a chance of working. And again, we're back to the sales cycle where it requires trust, credibility, and multiple conversations, unfortunately.

Michael: Are you implying that I might want to throw in a firebomb at the beginning of the conversation to get people riled up?

Eric: It's worked for you in the past. It's not a bad thing. It can be a good thing, because like you said before, you've got to get people's attention at some point. And we all have to please our base at some point if we want to be influential. The question is, what are you trying to get out of the conversation?

Michael: For me, I want to break things down. To critically think about an issue, I start by reducing things to some level, to where we can look at the component parts, and there's no emotion around the component parts. But I find, if people are scared, you ultimately have a hard time getting down to that level.

Eric: It depends on your audience and your motivation. If I'm facing a hostile audience, I tend to invert things, start with the ending and go backwards. That throws them for a loop and forces them, for a period of time, to be objective and open-minded. You can get your points across in the stealth manner that evades their defenses, until the smartest ones start to catch on. That's pretty effective. I call it inverting. Charlie Munger at Berkshire Hathaway is a master at doing that, always inverting, starting from the end and working from right to left, rather than left to right. Because if you go left to right, they see you coming from a mile away.

Michael: Let's use trend following managed futures as an example. You've got the hostile audience in front of you. Let's say they're pretty bright. They've been exposed to markets and investing. But they're hearing you for the first time, and they're not familiar with managed futures or trend following, and you need to start the outcome as you said. How do you walk them back? Once they hear that you can take an all-stocks portfolio and an investment stream that can increase the return, and also reduce the risk, they like the sound of that. But taking them back to get to how it all works is tricky, isn't it?

Eric: Trend following is a good example. You outlined a group of people that don't know what it is, but even more difficult is a group of people that know what it is and have already decided that they don't like it or don't want it.

I recently put a video out on YouTube called *The Blind Taste Test*. That's one of my favorite tools for getting through to people who don't like managed futures, and it's real simple. All I do is anonymize a bunch of different asset classes, strip the title away, and give them color codes. Stocks might be red, bonds might be yellow, managed features might be pink. A combination of bonds and stocks might be blue, and then a combination of managed features and stocks might be orange. Don't tell them what it is, though, and have them go through the calendar year returns, total return, volatility, number of down years, drawdown, and whatnot. Just ask them to indicate to you which one they gravitate toward, and which ones they gravitate away from. Let them make their choice in an objective manner. It's the like the old blind taste test between Pepsi and Coke.

Of course, I already know what the answer is because I've done this hundreds of times. Overwhelmingly, people choose the blend that includes managed futures and stocks together. And when I ask them to eliminate an asset class, not knowing what they are, overwhelmingly, people choose to eliminate stocks on a standalone basis, because they've got the highest drawdowns and volatility.

Then, later on, when I reveal to them what they chose, there's a lot of surprise. Some people are incredulous. They can't believe it. Some people get a little bit upset, but they cannot overlook the fact that when they were objective, they chose 50% trend following managed futures. Then I've got a foothold, and it's amazing. Even people that are in the business of writing articles that are critical of managed futures are now, to some degree, open-minded and curious about why, when they were forced to be objective, they chose managed futures. Now, that's more than you would ever get if you walked in and said, "Hey, I'm a managed futures guy," started talking about alpha, cointegration, covariance, diversification, and all that stuff. You would get zero out of that.

Michael: As you use that example, I have to go back in time to share something with you. Seventh grade, for me, I won the science fair at my school.

When we set up for the science fair, I was right next to a friend of mine. He went on to become an ER surgeon. Everyone knew he was going to be a surgeon when he was in seventh grade. He was a smart guy, and everyone knew he was going down that path. He did this whole blind taste test thing. Everyone was like, "Wow, he's going to win."

Now, I had a father who was a dentist. And I was seeing all these fantastic pictures of periodontal disease, people's gums rotting away. I sat down and made this great presentation about periodontal disease, and I had pictures that no one else in seventh grade had. I won the science fair. In some ways, it almost dovetails with what you're talking about. You do all the research, and you can show all the blind taste tests. But then the guy standing over there with all the crazy pictures and the crazy story gets the attention, and gets all the adulation.

Eric: Lures work. Shock value works. You're meeting some unmet need in the marketplace, and it was probably entertainment for your audience at the time. There's something to be said for that.

Michael: I want to give you a quote from Sam Harris, which dovetails with why people who know about managed futures still have no interest: "Let's do our best not to mistake psychological problems for philosophical problems."

There is a lot of psychology as to why someone who knows about managed futures doesn't want to go there. What is that deep-seated issue? You and I have been at this for decades. We know what the deal is. When you take the riskier investment—not risky comparatively, but if you add something in with a different return stream to the stocks and bonds portfolio—you get something that's cool. The math is quite simple. It's clever. It's interesting. It's neat. But man, people have some real psychological hang-ups with it, don't they?

Our industry is full of people who don't want to take career risk.

Eric: Yeah, it's amazing. That's one of my favorite topics. Cognitive psychology is so crucially important in our business. But I feel like participants approach it in the wrong way. They naturally fall into an adversarial posture and start preaching to people, which can be effective if you want a lot of hits on your Twitter feed, but when you're managing other people's money, it's not the greatest way to forge a relationship with them.

I've been forced to take a different approach. I say forced, but it's not hard for me to take a different approach because I'm not a conflict guy. There's a lot to unpack there. Let's try to keep this simple and focus on the parts that matter. A big chunk of the resistance is social in nature, meaning that our industry is full of risk-averse people who don't want to take career risk. There are norms out there. It's completely acceptable to put up to 60% or 70% of people's money in stocks. You don't need to justify anything.

Bonds are completely socially acceptable as well. They can be uncorrelated with stocks all day, every day, or they can become correlated. You're never going to get in trouble for owning risk-free or investment-grade bonds. They get a free pass. I could create something that looks almost identical to bonds, but if it's not bonds, you're going to have trouble as soon as it's down in a year when the stock market's up. That is just pure social and political pressure of managing money for other people—you have to overcome that fear of deviating from the benchmark.

Equally as interesting, though, is the counterintuitive nature of how things affect portfolio returns. Portfolio math is one of the most misunderstood things in the world. Let's say I created something that's volatile, doesn't look great on a standalone basis, but when you add it into a stock-heavy portfolio, boy, does it change everything. It creates a stable, balanced compounding machine that's inoculated to most different market environments. It has you prepared for inflation, deflation, market crashes, all kinds of stuff. And you'd think, "Well, everyone's going to want this. This is going to be awesome."

You have to overcome that fear of deviating from the benchmark.

You see this in some of the tail-risk hedging products that are starting to become a little bit popular out there, but good luck trying to get people to buy it and be happy with it. Why? Because they don't evaluate it based upon its contribution to the portfolio over a long period of time. Instead, they carve it out and they evaluate it on a standalone basis. This maximizes the social and the political stuff we talked about. They don't understand that's the wrong way to evaluate this. It's an ingredient in a dish. You don't want to eat a mouthful of cinnamon because that's not so great. But if you add it to the dish, maybe it makes the dish great.

Michael: If I look at that little firm down there in Stuart, Florida with the 46-year track record, as a standalone, the DUNN return is always something that's quite interesting to look at. You make a wise point that not only do people miss the idea of adding it in, and they want to judge it as a standalone, but, on the flip side, if one is objectively looking at data, one can find data that says, as a standalone, it's viable.

Eric: That's a good case. Those are smart guys, and they're purists, meaning that they believe in what they do and they don't want to dilute it. Those guys would never do what I'm doing, which is to mix managed futures with other asset classes, and I respect that. But they're in a position to do that for a living. Those guys are probably independently wealthy. They've been incredibly successful over the long term. I look at it a little differently and say, my job is to meet an unmet need in the marketplace. And when advisors say to me, "I want a Sharpe ratio of 3, no down year," stuff like that—when they get reasonable and start talking about things that are realistic—it's not that hard.

What they want is something that doesn't fall too far behind traditional investments during runaway bull markets, but can still hold up pretty well in hostile market environments. And that is just screaming at me: what they want is managed futures mixed with stocks intelligently. They want reasonable fees. They want reasonable taxes. And what they want is what I do with my own money. That's how I invest. I respect the people who want to be purists. I'm doing something a little different. There's room for all of us.

Michael: You've been involved in this for 20-plus years, you're the head of the firm, you're a socially engaging guy. But at the heart is a guy who knows systems, data, and code. You've been in the bowels of the beast for a long time. How much time and effort have you spent at the nitty gritty level of testing, putting together, comparing, contrasting, and working on systems?

Eric: A long time. And I have a love/hate relationship with it. I would say my first exposure to system design was 1997, in college. I've always been a data guy. I studied meteorology and science before switching to finance. I love dynamic, complex systems where the rule of survival is understanding unintended consequences and non-linear relationships, and how you can remove one species from an ecosystem and crash the whole ecosystem, and how that's counterintuitive. It was a natural fit for me to come into the capital markets, because I think they're the ultimate non-linear complex system, fraught with unintended consequences and misunderstanding.

Early in college, when I switched from the natural sciences over to finance, I immediately gravitated toward data: database design, data collection, data cleaning, and data modeling. That was a humbling experience. The first mechanical system that I ever designed bought 52-week lows and sold 52-week highs—the opposite of trend following—and the back test was absolutely amazing. My ego ran wild. I was already pricing my own private island. I thought I was going to make a fortune. Now, part of that class was to run your mechanical trading system for a semester, and that factored into your grade. When I ran it, it did nothing but lose money. I thought, wow, am I the most unlucky guy on the planet? What's happening here? But here's the thing. When I reran the back test, it kept making money. So, the back test is telling me it's making money, but in real life, with my paper trading account, it's actually losing money. That's not failure to me, that's an opportunity to learn something very important.

It took me a few days to go through all the accounting and the trade signals, and I realized this is what they call survivorship bias. I call it postdictive error as well. In real life, you're buying stocks, they're going to zero. They're on their way to bankruptcy. But as soon as they get de-listed, they disappear from the database. They don't show up in your back test anymore. And likewise, when you're shorting stocks that are getting bought out in real life, losing tons of money as they go higher and higher, as soon as they get bought out, they get de-listed and they disappear from the database. So, at any point in time, if you grab a database and you run a bunch of back tests on it, you're only seeing about half the stocks because the other half get de-listed, either from bankruptcy or buyouts.

Well, what do those two categories have in common? Trends. Stocks that are going bankrupt trend lower and lower and lower, and stocks that are getting bought out tend to trend higher and get bought out at an all-time high. You're missing that dispersion—you're missing the tails from the database, unless you know what you're doing, and you do all the grinding hard work to collect all the corporate actions, all the de-listed stocks. It's expensive, it's time-consuming, no one wants to do it. But if you want to model history as it actually unfolded through time, you have to do that kind of work. That's a skillset you have to have as a systems guy. It's not rewarding, no one ever wants to talk about it, and it's certainly not going to show up in your marketing materials, but you have to do it if you're going to have a chance.

Michael: I can relate to that in a different way. I recall, perhaps in the early '90s, seeing the managed futures trend following data from different traders, unaffiliated with each other. It didn't seem terribly complicated to me, but I was unable to find, at that time, research, data or other people's opinions that verified what I was seeing in the data. And what I was seeing was interesting. I've got 10 or 15 traders here, they're all unaffiliated, and they're all making and losing comparable amounts of money in the same months. I'm relating this to what you're saying about when you get into whatever data set you're looking at, and then that aha moment happens, and you say, "Hold on. Why is the rest of the world not talking about this?"

Eric: I'm not sure why it doesn't get more attention. I've blogged about it, written papers about it, and I seem to get a lot of positive feedback, but it's from a small group of people with interests similar to my own. In the grand scheme of things, I think it's too boring, and it's too much homework for most investors. It's been 20 years and I've learned something new and important every year. But it's a full-time workload, and I happen to be interested in this stuff.

I do not begrudge the other people in this world who have full lives. They're running companies, they have families, they're buying real estate, they're doing stuff. There's no way they could ever carve out enough time to drill down into the guts of the data and understand these truisms. They can listen, and I try to do a good job of breaking it down into the four or five important things, and I've had some success with that. But we can't expect people to wait 10, 15, 20 years to pull it all together and become as comfortable as you and I are with these concepts.

Michael: Maybe, if we look back, we were too young and too early. It takes a long time when you have a big system which is a big career risk, and a lot of folks make money doing something entirely different. There's a lot of fees to be paid for putting people into bad buy and hold mutual funds, right?

Eric: It's a buzz saw; it's an old and big industry. Breaking in and doing something different forces everyone in that ecosystem to alter their behavior a little bit. It's not the most welcoming experience to launch an alternative investment in the ETF world or the mutual fund world. But that's where there's room. There's an unmet need in that world. I don't feel like there's an unmet need in the CTA or the hedge fund world, because there's already a lot of good product over there.

You have to figure out a way to do it—but you're right, you're rocking the boat for some people, so you have to be real nice because you can't pay them. With the fiduciary rule and all that stuff, the ability to pay people has gone away. So, there's a lot of disruption and changes afoot right now that make it important to be nimble, open-minded, and to pivot when necessary.

Michael: Let's speak to diversification. Let's say you are talking to a non-advisor audience about the size of your firm—it's not a huge number of people—and you start to talk about increased diversification. Everyone in the audience, they've got stocks and bonds, and they're thinking this guy's studying the fundamentals and whatnot.

But then you start to talk about your ability to trade commodities and currencies, across different geographic areas. And people start to think, well, hold on, how does this guy have the skill or the knowledge to trade all of these different types of instruments and markets across the globe? Has he got a secret room full of great minds that can tell him where the oil tankers are on the high seas? How is he pulling this off?

Eric: I've come across this several times in the past. When people find out that we're trading 60, 70, or 80 different global futures markets, one of the first things they ask is, "Who's in charge of cattle? Who's in charge of soybeans? And who analyzes corn?" They believe that you need some sort of a fundamental opinion on these things in order to participate in them. I've tried different approaches at answering that in the past, and the most successful one was, again, invert the whole conversation and show them the results of a systematic rules-based approach to participating in all these different markets first, and then work backwards from that.

Michael: Reverse engineer it with them.

Instead of making excuses as to why you don't have 70 staff members running different desks, instead of saying, "You don't need to know the fundamentals in order to make money in these markets," you simply show them what it looks like if you have a rules-based process that is standardized and applied equally across all your different markets. That's a big eye-opener for people.

Naturally they're skeptical about it, because what goes through their mind is, "How much better would it be if you were an expert in corn, and if you did have an expert in wheat, and you did have an expert in silver?" To that, I respond, "Is the S&P 500 an expert in any sector or any individual company?" No. The Russell 3000? No. Do those things beat virtually all active managers? Yes. Why is that?

And then we get into a discussion and they start to realize that those glossy marketing decks that they get from old-school mutual funds about all the CFAs studying all the fundamentals... maybe that's not worth much. And you'll find a pretty receptive audience after you go down both of those roads. It doesn't come up that much anymore, I think because managed features has actually started to become an asset class for people. Whereas 10 years ago, when I first started penetrating the mutual fund market, people didn't even know what managed futures was.

Michael: Let me get deep on you for a second. I want to quote a Zen proverb. I follow a couple of Zen feeds on Twitter, and five out of 10 quotations seem to be specifically written for managed futures trend following. Here's one: "High understanding comes from not understanding at all."

Eric: Can you elaborate on that? What does it mean to you?

Michael: It gets right to the fundamentals. The fundamentals go on forever, there could be innumerable data sets. Once you admit that you don't understand the fundamentals, what's left? What other ways can we look at this scenario and come to a higher-level understanding? What's interesting? What could possibly be useful?

Eric: I agree with you. But the way I would try to get somebody to see the wisdom in that...

Michael: You wouldn't give them Zen proverbs?

Eric: No, I like them. And my favorite book is *Aesop's Fables*. I think most of those are applicable to managed features trend following. Same thing, right?

This is an important point. It's hard to overcome the natural inclination of people that more information is better, that you have to do your homework, that you got to know your stuff. What you're saying is, how do I get them to accept that's mostly noise, and if you're a human being, you're probably going to use all that information incorrectly and screw the trade up, or screw the investment up anyways.

I tend to try to give people examples. I like to use sports analogies quite a bit. I would ask them a question like, "If the Seahawks were playing the Cardinals, who do you think would win that game?" Let's say it's a year when the Seahawks are a much better team than the Cardinals, which is most years. People would say, "Oh, clearly, the Seahawks." And I'd say, "Okay, all right. What if the line was four and a half points, though?" Then they would have to think about it some more. They're like, "Well, hold on, wait a minute."

And where do they go? They go immediately to the fundamentals, and they start talking about the players, and this guy is coming back from injury, yada, yada, yada. They go through all that stuff. And then I tell them, "Don't you think that's all already priced into the line? Don't you think that the collective wisdom of all the participants, the line makers, bookies, Vegas, Fox Sports, and all those people, have probably done a better job than you at setting the line? What if it went to a five and a half? Or what if it went to seven and a half?" Then they would say, "Well, something clearly changed." And I say, "You didn't know what that change was going to be, but you trust the line. You think it's probably fair."

Now they're starting to wrap their head around what we call a discounting mechanism. When a discounting mechanism runs away from you, it doesn't care how good a job you do analyzing the fundamentals. It's factoring them in, in real time, with real money, in real life. And, unless you're better than the collective wisdom of everyone else, you got to overcome taxes, transaction cost, the overhead of doing all the research and whatnot. Unless you're a lot better, the fundamental analysis is probably not going to help you much.

When I explain it to people like that, they grudgingly say, "That makes a lot of sense. I can see that." Now, it's still leaving a hole in their knowledge base. Well, if you can't rely on that, what do you do? That's a bigger topic.

Michael: The biggest sports players in Vegas that are running sports funds, they might give out this aura that they're oracles that can look into the ball, but behind the scenes they've got it all coded, and it's a quant system, not too much different than what you do.

Eric: Let me tell you a brief story. I'm such a data nerd. I used to have access to the sports databases. I don't gamble, though.

I downloaded all the statistics from basketball and baseball, and I put them into a database, then I created a simple trend following system on futures, and I recorded the trades. I plotted this in accumulated probability distribution, and I put them side by side by side. I asked people to tell me which one's baseball. I used pitchers, batting average, on base percentage, power hitting. And then on basketball I did rebounds, steals, a whole bunch of different stuff, and by player, by team, and then over time. Nobody could differentiate between them. Fat tails, streaks, runs, trends, you name it. They couldn't tell the difference. I couldn't tell the difference. That's how competition creates tails, runs, and trends. It's a fact of life.

Michael: I've never gambled, so you've got one up on me. Something that intrigued me though is to take the gorilla role in the team structure for blackjack. An MIT blackjack team leader, who I interviewed for Trend Following, told me about this. The gorilla role is the guy that's not a part of the whole thing, but bets heavy when the team has got the odds on their side. He wanted me to see how the process went down. I want to try that at some point in time.

Eric: There's a lot of parallels between gambling, sports betting, and systematic trading, but there's one big difference that means the world to me. One's accretive to the economy and society, and one's parasitic. I'm not passing judgment; I'm saying that this is important to me. Trading futures is a way to express an opinion, set up an asymmetric bet, and provide liquidity to commercial hedgers in their time of need. And in return, theoretically, in my mind, you're entitled to a sustainable risk premium for doing that. And if they lose on the trade to you, you win, and they win as well because that trade that they put on is heavily negatively correlated to some risk on their balance sheet that they were trying to get rid of, which gave them the confidence to use leverage in their business, or expand their business, or similar. That's a symbiotic, mutualistic relationship between trend followers and hedgers. That's why it persists over time and why it's worked for 50 years.

Michael: You're a nice guy to not pass judgment. I can think of all the times I was in Vegas casinos, eating or having fun, not gambling, but seeing all those old folks sitting at those slot machines, so sad, blowing their time and money. Or I can think of having an interview years ago with a young man outside the lottery offices in Richmond, Virginia, with cameras on him. He was a wide-eyed guy, worked for the government. And he actually told me with a straight face that he played the lottery because this was a useful strategy for his retirement. And he was serious. He thought the math was on his side, that if he kept playing the lottery, he could get to retirement.

In that way, gambling is insidious. I know you believe that; you didn't want to go there. I'm libertarian about this. If people want to play the lottery, fine. If they want to do gambling, fine. I'm a little less happy about the fact that the government gets people addicted to the lottery. If people want to go to Vegas of their own free will and have fun, that's quite different, in my opinion.

> There's a symbiotic, mutualistic relationship between trend followers and hedgers.

Eric: I'm with you on that. I don't approve of it. In fact, back when I was a teacher in the late '90s, I taught business math and introduction to computer science. And in both classes, the first lesson that I taught my students was gambler's fallacy. That guy with the lottery tickets probably thought by playing the same numbers over and over, eventually he had to be right. That's gambler's fallacy. There are ways to mix concepts together and educate in two ways at the same time.

Michael: Many people, when they think investments, they think about something consistent this year, this market. They build in these expectations that something will happen. Whereas when you look at the managed futures side of your business, you don't know what's going to be the result for the given year. You can't predict which markets will give you a gain or loss. How do you explain that to people?

Eric: I have a couple of different approaches. One, I'm candid with people about that. I like to use metaphors and analogies to drive the point home. I have the venture capital analogy where I say, look, I lived in Silicon Valley for eight years. I know people who work there. I have a pretty good understanding of how the venture capital, at least the payoff structure, works. And if you talk to these guys off the record, they have no idea which of the 50 startups they're investing in is going to work out. They're making the bet that one or two of them are going to be hundred baggers, and the rest of them, you're going to lose every penny you put into them. And that's what the data says consistently happens. A tiny minority are responsible for all the gains. You have to hold strong with that minority when they're working out, and limit your losses on the other ones that don't work out. If the guys are being honest with you, they'll tell you that's how it works.

A sports analogy I like to use is the NFL draft. How many times has your favorite team picked someone in the first round, second round, third round, that turned out to be a bust? If you evaluate every NFL draft pick that has ever been placed, I think the highest value is the late second round, early third round. Because the first-round guys, you're paying them a ton of money. But on price performance, the overwhelming majority of value comes out in the late second, early third round. That's somewhat counterintuitive, but when you draft all these guys, you have no clue which one of them is going to turn into a superstar and which ones aren't. The data says random selections, based upon the metrics, are probably more effective than the intuition that most of these GMs and coaches put into drafting, with the exception of the Seahawks. Those guys have done something—they've rocked the boat a bit with their drafts. I'm not sure if it's luck or skill.

Michael: Random selections. That can cause people to spin. But it's so cool when you bring the analogy to venture capital, Silicon Valley, and sports. Okay, venture capital—that's easy to understand. There were a zillion search engines, Google won. People can grasp that. They can get your point about the draft—that makes sense. So, if you take that mindset and you say, "Hey, there's a lot of markets to be traded out there. What if you take that thinking and bring it over here to Mr. Market?"

Eric: What I tell people is that we believe in our process. It is somewhat like venture capital. We don't know if soybeans are going to have a supply demand disruption and soar or tank. We don't know if silver's going to be a big winner, or German bonds. We don't know ahead of time. But we do believe in our process, and our process is to buy breakouts, short sell breakdowns, budget our risk for that particular trade, contingent upon what's going on in the portfolio, and then have the discipline to cut it if it turns into a loss, and wash, rinse, repeat. Keep repeating that over and over and over again.

Most people get it, and they think, "I'd like to see that work for a period of time." And then they like to look at the performance attribution and see 80% of your gains comes from 20% of your trades. They say, "Wow, it'd be great if you could identify that 20% in advance."

And I say, "Yeah, it would be great. But then I would have all the money in the world. So, obviously, that's not realistic." I explain to them that the S&P 500 is a big, dumb trend following system. It's super slow-moving, tax-efficient, and transaction cost-efficient, but the bigger the company gets, the higher the weighting. If a company starts trending down, it gets rebalanced to a lower rating and eventually kicked out. If you believe in the stock market, which most people define as the S&P 500 or the Russell 3000, you already believe in a trend following system.

Michael: Let's talk big picture. Has anything changed in the last 20 years? The whole point of what we're talking about is that you and I don't have a crystal ball, but structurally, has the Fed taken actions? Have there been government actions? Has there been a new bias? Has there been a psychological breakdown? Is something different at this point in history? Are we facing a change? Or is it still how it always has been, this putting yourself in a position to benefit when the new opportunities or the black swans swim in?

Eric: I'd love to be able to say, "No, nothing's changed. We're going to keep doing what we're doing." But that's not true. The current interest rate levels are a game-changer relative to anything that we've seen in modern history. I recently did a project for a client where I did a Monte Carlo simulation of pretty much all the possible future paths that interest rates could take. And I showed what the corresponding returns would be for different kinds of bonds. The idea was to illustrate all the different permutations, because people can visualize interest rates are going to soar, or interest rates are going to go negative, or interest rates are going to go sideways, or everything in between. But what they don't know is, what's a likely return for my bond portfolio? A lot of the money in the United States and the world is invested in these bonds. The risk management for most traditional portfolios is a 30%, 40%, 50% allocation to bonds.

It was interesting to look at the results of the simulations, because they're bad. Few of them include positive rates of return going forward. It's not that hard to see why. With the yields right now, I think it's maybe 70 basis points on the U.S. 10-year treasury. Let's use that as a proxy for the whole bond market. Historically, almost all of your return from investing in bonds comes from the yield component. The capital gains can seem meaningful at times, but over the long term they average out to about zero. In fact, you can use the current yield as a pretty accurate predictor of what you're going to get as an annualized compounded return for the 10-year bond if you hold it for 10 years, and you roll it.

Then, if you factor in a typical advisory fee of 1%, you have a pretty significant negative expected return on the bonds. And then, if you factor in inflation, even if you use half the historical rate, so you only put inflation in there at maybe 1.5%, you're looking at -3% to -5% annualized returns. That's the median result from all these different Monte Carlo simulations. Then I decided to isolate the permutations that actually made money. And it was less than 3% of the permutations—the outcomes—actually had investors making a positive, real rate of return over the next 10 years in almost all investment-grade bonds, including Treasuries. That's a big deal. I can't go back in history and see a time where that was our reality. And like I said, that's a huge chunk of the money out there.

Here's the other thing. People have become accustomed to bonds being an effective hedge. Every time the stock market goes down meaningfully, they expect their risk-free government bonds to rally. We're starting to see that wane. It's becoming less and less true over time. And most people are too young to realize that bonds were positively correlated with stocks prior to the 1990s, not negatively correlated. They were a decent hedge, but they weren't great. And I'm starting to see the correlations between bonds and stocks creep up. Every quarter, it gets a little bit higher. You combine those two things together, and you have the fuel for an epic disaster, where people are going to get results that are so far outside of what they're expecting that I foresee fireworks on the horizon.

This is part of my motivation for what I'm doing, because if you can't trust bonds, what else is there that's an effective diversifier to equities? It's pretty slim pickings. Some people can make a case for gold, and it's been reasonably effective as a diversifier, but not always. Sometimes it goes straight down with stocks. MLPs are somewhat uncorrelated with stocks, but not the greatest diversifier, at least not during hostile market conditions. Managed futures has been the best diversifier, from my perspective. Over the last 50 years it's been even more effective than bonds. And I don't see managed futures being hamstrung the way bonds are right now. What I'm saying is that people should be more enthusiastic about managed futures right now than they've ever been, because it has the real potential of solving this terrible problem that no one seems to be taking seriously.

> **People should be more enthusiastic about managed futures right now than they've ever been.**

Michael: It takes me back to 1997, 1998, talking with my CPA, first getting businesses going. I was a young guy, with not a lot of wealth at that moment in time. And he said, "Mike, it's real simple. Get $2m free and clear in the bank at 6% interest, and you're set." That was the 1998 logic. And here we are in 2020 and that's like some kind of Wizard of Oz fantasy. It is not even imaginable.

Another issue in what you're bringing up is that as people get older, they no longer have something that looks simple, like bonds, that gives them some cash in the bank each month to pay the rent or whatever. We've taken that dog bowl away, and now the choice is, you got to chase something that has a little more risk, or you're not going to eat, so to speak. As you laid out with your Monte Carlo simulation, the bond thing's gone.

Eric: Yeah, it's gone. But still, it's an uphill battle to explain that to people when you go left to right. Like I said before, I tend to go right to left, so instead of talking about managed futures and the problem it solves, I start from a different perspective, and I talk about all-weather investing and why I like it. I like being prepared. And I like something that is stable, not balanced. There's a big difference between stability and balance. Stability is the ability to maintain balance when things change. Balance is a current state. Someone doing a handstand is currently balanced. Are they stable? Not necessarily. When you talk about all-weather investing, you talk about having currencies and commodities in your portfolio, in addition to stocks and bonds, because that's what managed futures is. It's big, sustained trends in those four different asset classes.

Source those risk premiums in those other two big, deep, liquid capital markets. There are big trends in currencies, and they've been there for 50 years. Commodities is another symmetrical market where you can make money being short, you can make money being long, you can lose money too. But I think it belongs in the portfolio. There's no reason that it can't be an excellent diversifier.

You start with that all-weather approach, and you talk about why you do it with your own money, and you show what it looks like historically. Case in point, there are some successful firms out there that follow an all-weather approach. Regular, everyday investors can do it too. You don't have to cram it all into stocks and bonds. Now, most people are still going to do that, and I'm okay with that. But there are other options.

Michael: Congratulations on the setup and the start of the new firm. And congratulations on getting one of my most favorite interviewees on Trend Following, Tom Basso, to serve as your chairman.

Eric: I've known Tom for over 20 years. He's a great guy. He ran a great CTA. He knows what he's doing, and he's a great addition to the firm. I've learned so much from him over the last 20 years.

I don't know if I ever told you the story, but I applied for a job at his firm in 1999. He sent me a rejection letter, and his president at the time, separately sent me a rejection letter. And these guys put so much time and effort into their letters. Multiple paragraphs, totally coherent, going through all the reasons that you want to avoid building trading systems, focusing on entries, indicators, all that stuff. These guys made an investment in me—it was the greatest let-down I'd ever had. I took that to heart and I learned a lot from those guys. Tom didn't even remember doing it when I moved out to Arizona and ended up meeting him. So, yeah, I'm thrilled to have him on the team. He knows his stuff, he's got more experience than me, he did it for a long time. He ran a big CTA back in the '80s, and he's been a fantastic resource for me.

Michael: He's timeless. And he seems to have gotten a second life here with social media, in the sense that so many people are interested and want his insights. It's fantastic that you guys are getting a chance to collaborate and pull off the new firm.

Eric: The guy doesn't age—he looks like he's 40 years old. He's active, plays golf, travels the world. He's got a great lifestyle. I hope that my life can be more like his in the future.

Michael: Is there anything that we have not talked about that is near and dear to you? Maybe not even directly related to the firm, anything that's getting you?

Eric: One thing that's been on my mind is that there's so much good stuff hidden in plain sight. With social media, anxiety, Covid, unemployment, social security, politics, all these issues, I feel that people are overlooking the good stuff that's hidden in plain sight, more than they have in the past.

I'm hoping that this is only an episode in our existence, and we can move past it. All we can do is take the hand that we're dealt, play it to the best of our ability, and trade the right side of the chart. We have to move forward and deal with uncertainty. I'm a little bit of a cynical guy, but whether I'm talking with liberal people, conservative people, there's still a ton of good out there, and it's hidden in plain sight. And it's mildly depressing to see what we've deteriorated to and I'm hoping that episode passes. There's some parallels between that and what you and I do for a living.

Michael: There's an angel investor you might be familiar with—Naval Ravikant. I saw a quote of his the other day on Twitter: "The goal of media is to make every problem your problem." That is getting at what you're talking about. What you're saying is, turn that stuff off, it's all propaganda. And then you start to look around, go do your own investigation, do your own art. You're going to find something a lot more interesting for your life than taking the pre-programmed oatmeal they throw at you every day.

Eric: Information is not wisdom. Not all information is useful. And social media is, in my opinion, junk food for the mind, to a large degree. Now, some people use it for good, but it is bringing out the worst in people.

Michael: I use it as a blog. I don't care too much what other people have to say. I might look at some comments here and there. If they're useful, then I learn something. But generally, it's my public diary. Whatever I'm interested in, I put it out there, that's what an author does. But a lot of people don't look at it as a way to share information or insights, they see it as this insane back and forth. And that's where it's dangerous.

> Information is not wisdom. Not all information is useful.

Eric: I liken it to driving on the freeway. There's a few jerks on the freeway. Most people are just trying to get home, or trying to get to work. But it builds all this anxiety and brings out the worst in people, and it only takes a few to screw it up for everyone else. We should be aware of that.

CHAPTER 8

DONALD WIECZOREK

Trend Following
on Steroids

D ONALD WIECZOREK is the Founder and President of Purple Valley Capital, Inc (PVC). He started his career in finance at JPMorgan as a summer analyst in their Equity Capital Markets Group while still an undergraduate at Williams College. Upon graduating in 2008, Don officially launched PVC and began managing client capital professionally using his systematic risk management strategy. Don is responsible for implementing PVC's trading strategy, client service, and setting the strategic direction of the firm.

Michael Note

Donald Wieczorek might not be a well-known name in the trend following world, but he swings for the fences. He has absolutely the kind of track record you would have seen coming out of the 1970s and 1980s; the kind of track record that made Bill Dunn, John W. Henry, and Rich Dennis famous. What Don has been doing (2019 to 2022) in the trend following space is like Babe Ruth on steroids.

Michael Covel: I've been looking at your track record since we first talked in 2014. That was a great year for you—87%, right? But after 2014, you took a steep drawdown. And I kept thinking to myself: Don is laying it all out there on the line. He is completely sticking to his system. He's high-risk, high-reward. He's gutting it out. And then here comes 2020 and here comes the Don train, bringing up the rear and lapping everybody.

Donald Wieczorek: It's been a wild few years, for sure. Because 2014, when we last spoke, I had a good couple of years there and trends were around and a lot of futures markets were moving nicely, just before I stepped into a five-year drawdown, from 2015 to end of 2019. A 70% drop from the prior peak in 2014.

That was difficult. There were no trends to be found. There wasn't a lot of inflation, there wasn't deflation, there wasn't a lot of economic growth or massive recession, there weren't a lot of catalysts for large trends.

Michael: Take a step back, though. You are playing this game at a slightly higher level in terms of risk and reward than most traditional trend followers?

Donald: I run an aggressive, high-octane, old-school trend following strategy.

Michael: Let me tell people how aggressive and how high-octane that is. Don's 2020 performance—drum roll please—is 193%. Actually 193.2%. You're not running a billion-dollar fund, right, but that is still a number. And back in the '70s, there were a lot of guys who cut their teeth on that exact same type of otherworldly performance. Maybe younger generations are starting to say, "Don's 193% looks like nothing compared to Bitcoin…"

You start to come into 2020 January, and Covid is already hitting in Asia. And then boom, the hammer drops in the markets. Before people knew what was going on, you were up 17% in February. Before everybody else in America was losing their marbles in March, you already knew something was up in February in terms of the markets. Can you paint that picture? It's almost like the birds that can detect an earthquake and they start flying. Trend following detects something early.

Donald: Right. Markets are a little bit of a canary in a coal mine. Trend following trading signals get me into positions when markets start trending, well before the masses recognize that a massive trend is happening. In February, equity markets started to roll over a little bit, bonds started to creep higher, there was some stress in markets, which most people look at and think, "Oh, ordinary correction, no big deal. Let's buy the dip. And prior trends will continue." Whereas my strategy took these entries and shorted crude oil, for example. A lot of these markets were reversing trends where we started initiating positions and did well in February. And then March is when it happens. That's when equities started collapsing and here in America, we started closing down economies.

Michael: March 2020 was your biggest month ever?

Donald: Correct.

Michael: You made 56.5%. It's fun to say these numbers.

Donald: After five years of drawdown, I was ecstatic. Just rewind four or five months, and I'm talking to other trend followers saying, "I don't know when the next trends are going to come. It's been five years of no trends and I don't know where they're coming from. I don't know when it's going to happen." With five years of drawdown, that's 2,000 days of me waking up saying, "We're still in a drawdown. I don't know when the next good environment is going to come."

Michael: Again, though, when you say drawdown, I want to be clear, because I've seen some other track records that you are at the tip, so to speak—you're in the car and you're driving fast.

Donald: Right. With risk controls.

Michael: Of course. You're not a riverboat gambler. You picked this game, you knew what your risk controls were from the beginning, you modeled yourself after some of these classic guys. I wrote the number down while we were talking, I was thinking, okay, what was DUNN's max, right down the road from you in Stuart, Florida: 67%?

Donald: Correct. And a similar four or five-year drawdown or so—it happens in trend following and I run aggressive. Sure, it's like driving a sports car, but I'm still only going 15 or 20 miles an hour. I'm 70–80% cash most of the time. I'm only using 20–30% of my margin to trade. That goes to show how much firepower futures trading gives you and unfortunately why so many people blow up and can't last more than a year.

Michael: Your assets have not changed dramatically since we spoke last—you're still trading for friends and family, maybe a few pros jumped on board. Have people started to talk to you a little bit different now that you've navigated 2020?

Donald: I'm $7–8m now, which is great relative to the small amount I started with in college when I launched it after graduating.

Michael: $100,000?

Donald: Right. I can make a job out of it now.

Michael: That wasn't a knock, I was putting things in perspective. Most people never get to be the size of David Harding. People like the idea of being you, because you get to do your own thing. I'm guessing you see the family a lot and you're not checking into an office that you have to drive your car to.

Donald: Right. I remember Ed Seykota once saying when people ask him how to become a trend follower, how to run a big fund, "Take out a blank sheet of paper and write down what you want. Be honest with yourself because you may actually achieve it." That's what I was. I was honest from the beginning and so I run a fund or a strategy for my friends, family, and others who believe in it and want to stick with me. But I had limited interest in huge institutional investors who by the nature of their job can't invest in a strategy that's going to have multi-year drawdowns like me. And that's why I'm still here and didn't close down like a lot of funds.

> I'm only using 20–30% of my margin to trade.

Michael: You didn't take the wrong kind of money, meaning the money wasn't going to run away from you the moment something happened.

Donald: Right. You mentioned David Harding—a couple of years ago he was saying it's tough to be in those shoes when you have a lot of institutional investors. A lot of guys had to change their strategy and come out and say, "Trend following's dead. We don't think trends are coming back. We need to change things, add more equities, get away from trend following." There's a lot of managers that had to do that because they had the pressure from big institutional investors. I was lucky that my assets had changed a whole lot. I was trying to stay alive.

> I'm supposed to go into drawdowns.

Michael: You did that. You're alive. That's why we're talking, because it's a fun story. You passed the threshold.

Donald: But it's hard.

Michael: What did you do during the middle of this thing? Who were you talking to? Was there any kind of mentoring or was it simply Don, in Jacksonville, sticking to your knitting?

Donald: I would read a good amount. I'd go back to your books, to Ed Seykota's Trading Tribe website. I try to look at what other successful trend followers have done and how they get through these drawdowns. I remind myself that negative stretches happen, and there's no need to change. And that's what's hard. It's unlike golf—if you miss a bunch of cuts and you're struggling, you should start trying to make some changes sometimes, trying to get better, because your goal is to make a cut every weekend and try and win tournaments. But in trend following you can't. You have to fight that urge to change things. By definition, I'm supposed to go into drawdowns. I'm supposed to have tough patches. I'm not supposed to change things.

The main thing I kept reminding myself in talking and sharing with my investors and clients was that, yes, we're in a tough stretch. I understand why there's simply no trends. What I want is to see this through and see

Risk is the chance you're going to lose your money—volatility is the variance around an expected return.

how I do in a good environment, because if I perform poorly in a good environment, then I'll start rethinking things.

Michael: We're watching this situation where the United States Federal Reserve has been talking about helicopter money forever. It's no longer helicopter money, they've got armies of 747s now. The printing machines are in the air, dropping the money. The modern monetary theorists actually think this all works out in the wash, so to speak. But I think this is what's going on: if the US can essentially say, "We're going to do whatever the hell we want to do and we're going to debase the dollar anytime we as a country get into trouble and the rest of the world is going to have to suck on it," eventually that strategy might not work. And if that happens, based on your 2020 performance, you might be the first trend following trader to have over 1,000%.

Donald: If I was today trying to create any kind of investment strategy for the next five to 10 years, I would create a trend following commodity futures strategy. I do think the next five to 10 years will be wonderful for these sorts of strategies because it's almost like bubble economics. There's going to be massive moves and trends almost everywhere. And we're seeing it express itself in a lot of areas now, whether it's Bitcoin, GameStop, or whatever. The Fed incentivized people to go reach for yield by keeping interest rates so low.

Michael: Bitcoin is a big reach for yield, that's for sure. People are getting rewarded by it. For younger generations growing up with Bitcoin volatility and Bitcoin gains, your track record and your performance is going to be a lot more palatable than it would be for the baby boomers, who are sitting around praying for their half-percent yields.

Donald: I agree. Most of my investors are younger and more risk tolerant. And I always pitch my strategy as a diversifier anyway—it should be a small part of people's portfolios if they have stocks and bonds already. Volatility doesn't bother me. I think of volatility as different than risk in the sense that risk is the chance you're going to lose your money, where volatility is the variance around an expected return. With volatility, I need it to jump higher, like an elevator that needs to go up and down to reach a higher floor, whereas risk is how well that elevator is made, how strong are the cables, what's the risk of it crashing and breaking? If the elevator is well made, volatility doesn't bother me.

Michael: If I'm looking at your stats correctly from your inception in 2008 until end of February 2021, your cumulative return is 592%, against the S&P cumulative return of 291%. You're coming close to doubling the S&P in this window of nearly a decade, so why would people only give you a small percentage? I think everyone's got trained to say, "Well, if you got 100% of your portfolio, only give us 5%." But the reality is, if I'm reading your numbers right, somebody would have made a lot more money with you than the S&P for the last decade—is that fair?

Donald: That is fair, but I would have given them a couple of stomach ulcers, I imagine.

Michael: The S&P also had a major meltdown in 2008, but it hasn't yet had its big drawdown in the last decade. We're on borrowed time. What is your performance going to look like when the S&P finally does have its next 50% typical drawdown? We're not making predictions here, but you and I know generally what happens to trend following traders when stocks take a hiccup and drop 50%, 60%, 70%.

Donald: Right. A lot of new trends are created and trend followers can create crisis alpha. We have a good historical ability to do that.

Michael: Stay hypothetical with me for a second. So, here you are at a cumulative 600% compared to S&P's cumulative 300%. If the S&P drops 50% and you go up another 100% or something, would you still be telling people that you only got a small piece of their capital?

Donald: When you blend the two, that's what's beautiful. You get something better. It goes back to my stomach ulcer comment. As good as my performance has been now, looking back at it, I still had investors take out at the bottom saying, "I can't stomach it anymore."

Michael: Are you friends or associates still with any of the people that took money out at the bottom?

Donald: I am. They check in once in a while. They're good buddies; it's purely a stomach thing. They get the monthly updates and they respond, saying, "Wow, that's awesome to see you coming back."

Michael: Even after they took out at the bottom?

Donald: Right. It's a pain threshold. That's all it is. The drawdown was worse than I ever imagined.

Michael: Have they said anything pressing to you, like how they feel now to watch almost a full decade cycle of your system in action?

Donald: What's interesting is now they say, "Is it too late?" Have they missed it—is it too late to get back in?

Michael: After you've made 200%-plus in two years.

Donald: That's what makes me realize I need to stick to it. I see what makes it work. Knowing that the psychological elements exist in the marketplace is what kept me going the last four or five years during the drawdown. And it has to work again, there have to be trends again, because these psychological matters exist in markets and always will. Those same books that were written 150 years ago, like *Reminiscences of a Stock Operator*, all those truisms still apply.

What I kept returning to during the depths of the drawdowns is that there will be trends again. To be honest, the clients that do the best are the ones that almost forget about it. They put in from the beginning and they forget about it and they check in once in a while and that's it.

Michael: Everyone is upset now they ditched you at the bottom, huh?

Donald: It's hard. I would email people and try and get them in bed, but who wants to put money into somebody who looks like they're almost circling the drain?

Michael: We have a name change at Purple Valley. It's now, "Circling the Drain."

Donald: Some of the biggest names in trend following were saying, "Trends may be done. This is a new era. The Federal Reserve is not going to allow trends to happen."

Michael: I'm sure some people will think, after they look at your track record, "Oh, I want to participate," and they'll be the wrong person. They will not get it because they're only going to see the last two years. How do you filter for people? Because essentially you're having to filter a personal psychology.

Donald: I try to explain and set the expectations. Where I run into trouble is when people have incorrect expectations, thinking this performance is going to last forever, and I'm going to make money every year. I try and set the expectations that, no, there's going to be drawdowns, and they're going to be deep. I am aggressive, and you have to try to stay invested in these sorts of strategies for a minimum of at least five years to realize the potential. What's hard is trying to get them to understand those drawdowns. You can't look back at the track record like you and I are doing now and say, "Oh yeah, it was three or four years. No big deal. Look, he got out of it." Living through that is so different than looking back on it now.

Michael: When you look at what's going on with Bitcoin, how many of these big Bitcoin drawdowns have there been in the last seven or eight years? A lot. They use the acronym HODL—hold on for dear life. It's interesting that with Bitcoin, they don't say the things that you're saying. They're say, "Hey man, you only live once. Let's go for it." I know that's somewhat because of the regulatory environment, it's how you have to talk in that space, and maybe even somewhat related to baby boomers.

Donald: Right. And that anti-establishment, anti-Wall Street kind of mentality. Trend following is a little bit anti-establishment, anti-Wall Street, also. We're not predicting anything. We're not reading the news.

We're not trying to do anything fancy or special. That sort of mentality can do well as a client for trend following. It meshes well.

Michael: You can lament to me, you can say it's a steep drawdown and all this other stuff. But when you look at the track record, there it is. The risks and rewards are right there on the piece of paper. A lot of people are going to say, "Well, damn, if I would've had that guy for the last 10 years, he's twice as nice as the S&P."

Donald: I'm proud of having stuck through it. That was my third drawdown and I've had four or five good runs to the upside. I'm proud that nobody can ever take that away from me. I can always look at those numbers. They're audited, established, and real money.

Michael: Do you feel a little bit invincible now you've walked to the edge of the abyss?

Donald: I feel a lot more confident trading now than I did when I first started, I'll tell you that.

Michael: No one else in the world, that I know of, has a trend following track record that looks as aggressive as yours up and down. Your track record looks exactly like all of the legendary traders who started in the '70s. I tell people all the time to check out the old track records of trend following traders. You can learn a lot.

Donald: That's what I'm excited about. That's what I tried to create. I've read a lot about those traders and I've tried to create a strategy that would perform similarly, given the '70s were a fantastic environment. And I think we may be on the precipice of another inflationary environment similar to that, which is why I'm super excited about the next five to 10 years. I'm proud of being able to look at my strategy and say, sure, there's some tough drawdowns there, but that's to be expected if there's no trends.

Michael: I got to get you to stop talking about drawdowns. You made 193% in 2020. At the end of February 2021, you're up 44% and you're talking about drawdowns?

Donald: I sit on my hands during those periods. The good times take care of themselves. This is the last thing I'll say about drawdowns. That's the hard part. That's what takes the energy, mental capacity, and discipline. The good trend environments like we're in now are the simple part.

Michael: You say we might be on the precipice of an inflationary environment. That makes a lot of sense, if anyone understands what's going on with the economics out there. However, I want you to be clear that your opinion does not enter into the performance that we've been talking about—meaning you've got this independent opinion, but it's not somewhere in the gears and levers of your trading system.

Donald: Correct. I can have a lot of opinions about certain markets, but they're totally independent of the trends I'm capturing. For example, Bitcoin. The strategy's been long Bitcoin futures and it's done well, but who knows? In my personal opinion, I may hate Bitcoin. I may think it's terrible, a bubble, and it will collapse today. My personal opinions do not factor at all into trend following. They're interesting and fun to discuss with people. But as I get older and more experienced in this, I read less, I have fewer opinions. I just want to capture trends for people.

Michael: When did you decide to add Bitcoin to your portfolio mix?

Donald: I added Bitcoin futures when the CME brought them out about a year and a half ago, and I added other futures when they came out about a month and a half ago. I like the market in the sense that it adds diversification to the other commodity markets that I trade. And I do think Bitcoin futures has the potential to go down as one of the biggest bubbles in history. It has amazing properties.

> **The good trend environments are the simple part.**

Michael: You've been long Bitcoin inside your trend following portfolio structure. As you say, it could be a massive bubble. Remind people how your strategy would play out if Bitcoin starts to go in the other direction.

Donald: The bubble doesn't scare me as a trend follower. Trend following is all about trying to capture big moves or bubbles. As George Soros says, bubbles are one of the best ways to make the most amount of money. We want to be in bubbles; we want to try and capture big. As Bitcoin goes up, we'll be long. We try to be long term enough such that these recent corrections over the last couple of months don't knock us out, because you never want to lose your position in a bull market. By any definition, Bitcoin is in a bull market. There's only one correct position to have right now in Bitcoin and that is to be long. We'll be long until my strategy says the move's over, at least intermittently. We'll get knocked out after it turns, for example, for a couple of months, at which point the next move may be short and then we'll be able to ride that move lower.

My personal opinions do not factor at all into trend following.

I don't like being short markets because from a math perspective, the risk-reward isn't as great as being long. The profit potential isn't as much, as collapses can happen a lot faster than moves up to the upside.

Michael: What is your pick of three of your favorite legendary names—people who have inspired or influenced you.

Donald: First and foremost, Ed Seykota, who did trade aggressively through the '70s, with a record, I think, averaging 100% a year for 10 years or something ridiculous. Super wise trader who still answers questions on his website. And I learn something every time I go to it. Then one of his disciples, David Drews, a trend follower out of Hawaii, who's an emergency medicine physician turned trader.

Michael: Have you had a chance to meet either of them?

Donald: I spoke to both of them briefly on the phone years and years ago. I remember when David Drews called me. I was on East Coast time and he called me from Hawaii at 11:00 p.m. and I jumped out of bed. And my wife asked, "Why are you jumping out of bed?" I said, "Oh, Dr. Drews is calling. He's actually returning my phone call." I'd emailed him. And this is when I was new. I was trying to pick the brains of some traders. Since then, not a lot. We all beat our own drum. We all found strategies that we created ourselves and we stick to. I'll email them every so often to say, how are you doing, good to see everybody's still trading and congratulations on a good year, things like that. But not so much picking their brains for advice anymore. It's more about sticking to our own systems.

Michael: I think you were saying number three was Bill Dunn.

Donald: Correct, because he runs a slightly longer-term strategy, using moving averages I believe, and his drawdowns also are deep. He runs an aggressive strategy and he's bigger in terms of assets. I think he does a good job with marketing and growing the business side of it. That's something I admire about his fund.

> Trend following is all about trying to capture big moves.

As a fourth, I'll throw in Salem Abraham. He was instrumental initially when I was first starting. I was trying to read and learn about his strategy and his fund. He's an example of somebody who I think has switched more into equities now because trend following wasn't working so well and now he's blended it with a lot more equities. So, there's been some movement there. David Harding has also done some movement away from trend following.

Michael: And they train all trend following traders to lament the worst of everything. Some people might be listening and thinking, that guy Don, he sounds unhappy about some of his performance. It's not good. He's having a hard time.

Donald: I'm trying to keep my regulators happy. I have to be balanced.

Michael: I don't fall under the purview of those guys.

Donald: Yeah, I understand. Past performance is not indicative of future performance. Don't get me wrong. I can't be more excited about the next five to 10 years. I think what the Fed has done, like you said, spraying money around, only ends in one of two ways: debt crisis or massive inflation. The inflation is much more palatable from a political perspective.

Michael: It is a great educational lesson, especially for budding traders, to go look at Purple Valley, Inc.'s track record, because if people can actually figure out what you've done, they've learned something. It's going to take a little bit of time, but if somebody says, "Gosh, I want to reverse engineer that guy, Don," that'd be a worthy homework assignment, wouldn't it?

Donald: Sure. Your book on the Turtles (*The Complete TurtleTrader*) is a good place to start too. That's where I started back in the day, trying to develop a long-term trend following strategy across futures. A lot of trend followers' performances will be correlated; they are mostly a function of our exit points and how long term we are. In good times, we're all catching the same trends. And the same things are moving: Bitcoin's moving, the grains are moving now, everybody's short bonds right now. I tend to be more, I guess, medium term relative to, say, DUNN Capital. And then I'm more aggressive. I'll risk about 1% per trade.

Michael: Is there a side of you that gets concerned about saying things? Even things that are factually true. Your track record is factually true, it's on record with the government, but sometimes the government doesn't want you to talk about it. Have you been trained to feel some angst when you talk to someone like me?

Donald: A little bit, but I've gotten used to it over the years. It does make it hard from a business perspective to try and raise money. I also have to think about what I can post online, or what I can say, or what I can do in that regard. It doesn't affect me that much because I don't love doing that anyway. I'm not a big marketer. I'm not big on the business side. I like the math, I like the trading, and I like creating a track record. And then I let that speak for itself. When I talk about it, I need to be a little careful. Though I like talking about it, because it's interesting. Trend following is a phenomenal process of trying to capture trends. I like commodities and futures trend following because it gives me access to a wide range of markets.

> I like the math, I like the trading, and I like creating a track record.

Ever since I was a little kid, I always wanted to be in whatever's moving, whatever's hot, whatever's making new highs or new lows. By definition, we are in those things. If you pick up the paper today and see some things hitting new highs or new lows, you can rest assured that my strategy is in that. I think that's neat.

Michael: Let me give people a quick rundown. This could be dated by 30 days or so since your last report, but it gives people an idea. Long Aussie dollar, long Bitcoin, long British pound, long corn, long cotton, long crude oil, long heating oil, long live cattle, long NASDAQ, long New Zealand dollar, long Nikkei, long gas, long S&P, long soybeans, long soybean oil, long sugar, short bonds, short Euro dollar, short palladium, short US dollar. That gives people an idea of your strategy, the types of market that you can be in, and the combination of long and short.

Donald: Right. I mean there's some environments now where we'll be long more than short. But back in March 2020 when Covid was hitting, you can almost flip all those. They were short a lot and then long US dollar long bonds. It's a nice diverse group of markets. I like that. At any given time, there's usually a couple of things that are moving. Right now, there's a lot. And that's why you can put up years like this.

Michael: Are you in all of the markets I reeled off either longer or short at all times?

Donald: No. I monitor about 40 to 50 different commodity futures markets. And at any one time I'm in anywhere between 10 to 20 of them. Those you listed are the ones I was in at the end of February 2021. A few changes have been made, but I'm only in whatever's moving, which is usually about a third or a half of the available markets. They're not all trending at this one time and I don't want to be in the ones that aren't moving. Some guys like to have either a long or a short in all the different markets. That kind of dampens their volatility in their returns. I like to be in the ones that are moving a lot.

Michael: I brought up the idea of how your clients felt when they got out at the bottom and then saw everything zoom back up. You must have a handful of folks, at least, who have been in for the full ride. They must think you're a rockstar.

Donald: They like it. And a lot of them are friends, so they're more proud of me that I didn't quit, or they're excited to be a part of it. And they like the story. They like having access to the markets and they like that we're up a lot.

It's almost like trend following in itself within my own client base. I'm left now with a batch of good, winning clients. The clients that I wasn't a good fit for weeded themselves out. It was interesting to see when people took out. There were some that took out right at the bottom, others once they got back to break-even. And then there's others that have now captured a lot of the upside after that. It's similar to how markets in general work and the dynamics of why people lose consistently, why people win, and how I created the trending following strategy to begin with.

The upside is there if you have the patience and discipline.

Michael: Is your filtering process for clients like what you've done in this conversation, where you talk about the drawdowns and how much pain there is? You can't sleep for five years, can't use the bathroom, can't eat, and you've lost 50 pounds—is that what you tell all new clients?

Donald: Right. And then if they still want to talk to me after that, they've made it through the pain part.

Michael: You are literally trying to scare people away from being your client? Is that a fair assessment?

Donald: It must come across that way. I've never looked at it that way, but I don't think you're wrong. I try and be as honest as I can about it.

Michael: "Don't be my client because you might have a chance to do twice as good as the S&P over the next decade like I've done over the prior decade. Do not become my client." Let's get a tagline for your business, "I might beat the S&P again by double. Do not become my client."

Donald: The upside is there if you have the patience and discipline. I find it easier for myself because I created the thing and I can see it working every day. I don't feel bad for clients, but it's harder for them to stick to something that they didn't create, and don't see day to day. They may not understand as much as you or I do about trend following.

Michael: There's so much educational potential in your track record. It's worth studying. The interesting thing is that you have taken a drawdown and had the full cycle over a decade. And in that same window, the S&P has not taken a hit. You have blown past the S&P, taken the drawdown, and the S&P is on the most elevated position in the history of America. If you look at what happens when the S&P does have its big meltdowns, trend following does exceptionally well because all the other markets start rocking and rolling. What you have done here in the last couple years on trend following could just be the beginning if the S&P is ever allowed to come back to earth. Again, we're theorizing here. Who knows—the Fed might keep it elevated forever and bring the dollar down to zero to match interest rates.

> We don't just do well when stocks do poorly; we can still do well when stocks do well.

Donald: I think you're onto something. Again, that's why I'm so excited about the next five to 10 years because we could potentially be in an environment where equities get hammered, and also bonds. Remember, bonds have been in a bull market since the '70s when rates were so high, then have fallen for three decades.

Michael: Maybe baby boomers, as they age, are going to say, "You know what, we're tired of being at the equities casino. Can we have interest income again?"

Donald: Right. The 60:40 stock-bond portfolio is going to come under pressure. In fact, it already is. If we get an environment of stagflation, for example, where equities and bonds get hit at the same time and all of a sudden we get inflation where commodities start ripping.

That's why I'm super bullish on trend following commodities for the next 5, 10, 20 years. It could be incredible money moving into these assets. Money has been flowing into equities because the Fed has incentivized that to happen. And all that money, trillions of dollars, has to flood somewhere else. It's finding a home in commodities, Bitcoin, and housing.

Michael: Everyone's seen *The Big Short* with Christian Bale playing Michael Burry. Everyone knows what the story was up until 2008, but apparently no one thinks anything else has happened after 2008. Well guess what, kids, there's been a lot of hanky-panky since 2008 and when the bill comes due, they're going to make *The Big Short Part 2*.

Donald: Exactly. It happens every 10 or 15 years, like clockwork. People have short memories. There's day trading speculation going on now where everybody's making money. Like Buffett says, the tide will go out at some point and you'll see who's swimming naked. And hopefully trend followers will be there to capture the big moves when they happen.

Getting back to your last point about how during the last 10 years I was able to do well even with the S&P doing well, I think there's a little bit of a misapprehension in trend following that we only can do well when there are market crises. Yes, we can tend to do well during market crises because big trends happen, but we can do well even when stocks go up. What's interesting is we're totally uncorrelated—we're not perfectly inversely correlated. We don't just do well when stocks do poorly and vice versa. We can still do well when stocks do well. That's lost a lot in the managed futures space.

> Cut losers, ride winners, and use a statistical system.

Michael: I almost had an aneurism there when you used the term managed futures. Why do a lot of people not want to use the term trend following? We need other terms: time series analysis, momentum, and managed futures—anything to get away from the core term that everyone knows called trend following.

Donald: Cut losers, ride winners. Just a statistical system. That's it.

Michael: Are there any other influences or things that you like to read, such as psychology? What drives you, or keeps you balanced?

Donald: It's not so much the reading anymore. I did a lot of reading initially. Now it's about keeping balanced in a whole life perspective. I've got two young boys now, I'm married. I run around chasing the kids a lot, which keeps my mind off staring at markets going up and down every day. It's random in the short run and you can waste a lot of energy trying to watch markets all day long, thinking you can do stuff. But a lot of people do and they get into trouble, especially during the drawdowns when they feel like they need to be making changes and tweaking things.

I try to go out fishing and golfing quite a bit. I like fishing because it's similar to trading, in that I can't control where the fish are or if they're going to bite. I need to be in the river. If you want to be a productive fisher, like trend following, you got to be there every day and put yourself out there. When the conditions are right and the fish are there, you can capture some big ones.

Trend following, for example, is like blue fin tuna fishing, where you catch a couple of big ones every year and that'll make your whole year. This isn't like bass fishing or blue gill fishing, where you're catching a lot of little fish all day long and you're making money every day. This is where you may not capture something for several days, weeks, or months at a time, but when you do, it's huge. What's so fascinating about markets is you can get these big, big outlier, fat-tail type moves. I need to be around and stay alive and have all my hooks in the water to catch those big ones when they happen.

So, for me, it's fishing, being outdoors, and staying grounded, and talking once in a while to some other trend followers. Again, not as much as I used to, because I have the confidence now. I've been through so many cycles that there's nothing that anybody can tell me that's going to change anything anymore. I have my system, or like Ed Seykota says so poignantly, "The system is made up of two things. It's the actual trading system and then your ability to stick to it." And those two things have been stress-tested the last 12 years, to the point where I now feel good about it. There's little that markets or the world economy can throw at me now where I'd feel uncomfortable. I've already gone through those. I feel comfortable and now it's about trying to relay that confidence and comfortableness to my clients and making sure they feel similarly so we can stay on this ride forever.

Michael: You were talking about not being glued to the screen all day. Sometimes I see pictures online of people at their trading station and there'll be six screens on their desk. And they're talking about their discretionary trading and I'm thinking, you're a human being, you have two eyeballs, and you've got a desk in front of you that has six 27-inch screens. And you're supposedly discretionary trading all of this. At what point in time in that story does one call bullshit?

Donald: It sells. It looks sexy, cool, and fun. And that's what a lot of day trading is. It's an addiction; it's feeding the part of the brain that gets the highs and the lows. I'll be honest, trend following and trading was more exciting when I first started because of that. I mean, it's exciting trading up and down, watching the values go up and down. But after years and years of doing it, good trading is boring trading. And that's why I don't talk about it much anymore. People will ask me what I think about the markets, where I think they're going, and I say, "I don't know." I can tell you where I'm positioned—you read off my positions. That's it. Those are my views right now, as I'm long those things, I'm short other things, because those are the trends. Next month if we talk again, it'll be a little different. There's not a whole lot else to it.

> **Good trading is boring trading.**

Michael: I love looking at the track record. You look at this decade-plus, month-by-month performance, and it tells you a story. Even if someone knows little about the markets, they can see your track record for March 2020 at 56.5% and they know March 2020 was when Covid hit. And then the light bulb sparks: "Hold on, how did he make so much money during Covid? I thought everybody got killed." Then another light bulb sparks.

I remember looking at early 1995 and deducing that John W. Henry was opposite Barings bank. There's deep educational value when you can see a track record and match it up with what's going on in the real world.

And in a closet somewhere, I have an original paper disclosure document of John W. Henry from his first month with $16,000 in the account.

Donald: And John W. Henry bought the Red Sox a few decades later.

Michael: If you end up buying the Red Sox in the future, you better at least get me some good seats.

CHAPTER 9

ROBERT CARVER

PART 1
Trading, Fast and Slow

R OBERT CARVER is an independent systematic futures trader and
investor, writer, and research consultant. He is currently a visiting
lecturer at Queen Mary University of London. Robert trades and invests
with his own money using the methods you can find in his books. Until 2013
he worked for AHL, a large systematic hedge fund and part of the Man
Group, where he was responsible for the creation of AHL's fundamental
global macro strategy. He is the author of *Systematic Trading: A unique
new method for designing trading and investing systems*, *Leveraged Trading:
A professional approach to trading FX, stocks on margin, CFDs, spread bets
and futures for all traders*, and *Smart Portfolios: A practical guide to building
and maintaining intelligent investment portfolios*.

Michael Note

Robert Carver is based in London. He was formerly with
Barclays Bank and AHL, the famed trend following manager
founded by Mike Adams, David Harding, and Martin Lueck.
Whether you're new or experienced, Robert illuminates
the most important systems trading issues. There are no
secrets. There is no black box. There is no magic. But there
is common sense.

Michael Covel: What understanding did you have of money and markets before the word "system" came into your life? How did it all happen?

Robert Carver: It was pretty early on in my financial career, actually. I did a few things early on in my life, which I never continued with, and at the age of 24 I decided to go back to school to get my university degree. In my final year of university I did an internship with a quantitative trading firm called AHL. That was the first time I began thinking about trading in a systematic way. It was before I'd worked in an investment bank or traded my own money or done any of those things that other people may have done earlier in their lives. So, systematic trading has been a part of my thinking from a relatively early age, late 20s, and in terms of my investment career, almost day zero.

> I've never thought about finance any way apart from systematic.

Michael: At what point in time were you at AHL?

Robert: The internship was in the summer of 2001. Then I went back to school to finish my final year. I worked for an investment bank for a couple of years, so did what I like to call discretionary trading, then developed my quantitative skills working in an economic research center. Then I went back to AHL in 2006 and stayed until 2013, which obviously were pretty exciting and pretty scary years to be working in finance.

Michael: Before we go into the 2008 crisis, I'd like to dig a little deeper on system. When you first went to AHL, as part of your university program, what did you understand? Was there a particular person or a particular event where the system was put across your desk, so to speak, and you had a light bulb moment, or was it gradual?

Robert: I would say it was gradual. I've never thought about finance in any way apart from systematic. One of the reasons I found it difficult in the investment bank environment was because the trading we were doing seemed to be based on hunches or seat-of-the-pants stuff. I'm the kind of person who's comfortable with numbers, with a formal way of doing things, with using an algorithm to decide what your thought process should be.

Michael: I want to read something from the start of your book, *Systematic Trading*, where you're quoting Daniel Kahneman. It's a great quote to set the tone for our conversation today:

> In every case, the accuracy of experts was matched or exceeded by a simple algorithm. Why are experts inferior at algorithms? One reason is that experts try to be clever, think outside the box and consider complex combinations of features in making their predictions. Complexity may work in the odd case, but more often than not, it reduces validity.

That is such a perfect way to sum up the direction that you like to go.

Robert: Yeah, absolutely. If I have one overriding message, it's that most people are not as good at trading as they think they are. Ironically, it's the people who think of themselves as experts, who have a lot of knowledge and a lot of experience and who spend a lot of time trading, who are more likely to be overconfident and overestimate their ability.

Most people are not as good at trading as they think they are.

People rarely evaluate themselves critically and properly work out how well they've done in their discretionary trading activity, and they don't look at statistics properly to examine whether they genuinely are doing much better than a system. A lot of people out there are fooling themselves and they would do a lot better with a simple system.

Don't get me wrong. There are some incredibly good traders out there, but they make up a small fraction of the population of people who are involved in finance. And for the vast majority of what I think of as ordinary people—and I include myself in that—using a system is definitely the way to go.

Michael: How do you define a trading system in the investing world?

Robert: A system must be objective. It must be repeatable. It must be transferable. A lot of people, particularly from what I call the older tradition of pattern matching in technical analysis, look at charts and see patterns, and they claim to be systems traders, because it's only when they see these patterns that they will actually trade. The problem is, if you ask them to write down an objective rule that can be formalized and turned into a computer algorithm, or even just written down sufficiently well that someone else without any experience could identify these same patterns, they seem unable to do it.

That suggests that what they're doing isn't systematic. They're not throwing darts at a dartboard, but it's not completely objective. It's not transferable to another person. And it may not even be repeatable by the same person. They may see slightly different patterns on different days and say, "Oh yeah, that's a buy. That's a sell," but they're not applying a completely objective rule that you could formalize in an algorithm and therefore get the same results every time.

If you're not going to get the same results with a different person using your system, if you're not going to get the same results yourself when you use it every time, on different days, then you're not a systems trader, in my opinion.

Michael: Someone emailed me the other day about a price action-based system. And the follow-up question was, "But I need to use charts, right?" Here they were, going down the right path, but there was still this pull to the law of chart reading. It's a definite confusion point, trying to get people to understand your objective systematic way.

Robert: Part of the problem is the illusion of overconfidence. There's this view that you need to be an expert to do a good job. If you can write down what you're doing so that it's perhaps two or three lines of code, or two or three simple steps, or a spreadsheet with half a dozen columns, then there's the view that that can't possibly be any good, because it's too simple. It doesn't have enough expertise in it. It's not something that you need 10 or 20 years of staring at charts to be able to do. And so there's this view that people have, that it can't possibly be any good, it can't possibly work. And the more complicated and subjective the patterns are, the better, because logically you're going to be one of a small number of

A system must
be objective.
It must be
repeatable.
It must be
transferable.

people who can actually do this, and therefore you're more likely to make more money. It's not a view I sign up to at all.

Michael: Why do you think those skeptics don't find themselves eventually looking for evidence? There's no guarantee that past performance is going to dictate the future, but it is quite interesting to look at the month-by-month performance of some of the systematic traders over the decades and glean something from that.

Robert: Most people aren't able to judge what is good evidence and what is bad evidence. Most people don't have an intuitive understanding of concepts of statistical significance. If you were to ask what constitutes a track record that's long enough to make a judgment and assign a probability, say 95%, that this isn't a fluke, most people will massively underestimate the amount of time and the amount of data you need to actually make that judgment in practice, unless the trader is highly skilled or the trading system is incredibly good. Unless you're in the high-frequency realm, you do need an awful lot of history to make that judgment on skill versus luck. I'm talking about multiple decades of history.

> Most people don't have an intuitive understanding of concepts of statistical significance.

When I analyze trading systems, I've normally got about enough data to make a judgment that a particular system was at least as profitable in the past. But an individual trader, unless they've been in the game for an awful long time and their trading style hasn't changed so they can use all of their data, is unlikely to be in a position to actually say, "I'm not lucky. I am actually good."

So, most people confuse luck with skill. This is a problem because even if you were throwing darts at a dartboard, or even if there were no value in these charts at all, you've got a pretty good chance of managing to make some money in the first couple of years of trading. It's going to be hard to step back from that and say, "Well, actually, I'm doing something that isn't going to add any value," because you're not going to have enough evidence one way or the other.

People's natural tendency is to view themselves as being much better traders than they've been, and to ascribe the fact that they've made some money for a couple of years to skill in reading the charts.

Michael: Let's break apart systematic trading across the different time frames. Let's say high-frequency trading is at one extreme and a slow form of trend following on the other. Both of these strategies can be made systematic, but they're quite different. That difference is often lost to many investors, isn't it?

Robert: Absolutely. If you tell people that you are a systematic trader, most assume you are what is often called an algorithmic trader, which means you're much in the short time period, the extreme of the high-frequency traders who are holding positions for tiny, tiny fractions of a second. It is quite hard to get across that you need a completely different mindset to trade systematically in these different areas.

Take some famous people, like David Harding, who runs Winton but was also one of the co-founders of AHL; or Robert Defares, who runs IMC, which is a Dutch high-frequency trading firm. Both smart, successful guys—both dollar billionaires who've done pretty well in their chosen field. But if you were to swap them around and get them to run each other's strategies, I think they would struggle, because they are completely different worlds.

I have almost no conception of what the high-frequency guys do. They use techniques that would make no sense at all in the low-frequency world, because they have a lot more statistical data to look at. In low-frequency trend following, such as tactical asset allocation models, you don't have as much data and you need to have a much better handle on running strategies that make economic or intuitive sense, rather than being a set of weird nominal patterns that appear in some short-term data.

Michael: Even though they might be completely lost if they switched places, the commonalities go back to Kahneman's work, don't they? This goes right to human behavior. We're not exactly rational beings, and there's some common-sense reasons for sticking to a system that works, whether it's high-frequency or trend following.

Robert: Exactly. It's definitely the case that the most successful systematic traders are those that are running systems that make some kind of sense. The higher-frequency approach makes sense because you're essentially being paid to provide liquidity in the markets, whether that be implicitly through the bid-ask spread, or whether through rebates and the U.S. equity markets. As for the slower approach, there's all kinds of theories as to why trend following has worked in the past, and I personally believe will work in the future. One of my favorites is a behavioral finance theory called prospect theory, developed by Kahneman as co-author, which essentially relates to the way that people realize gains and losses differently. It's a neat little theory that explains why people struggle to invest in trend following strategies, and therefore why those are profitable to computers that don't suffer from these emotional thoughts.

The second aspect that people at both ends of the spectrum share is they stick to their systems. They believe in them. In a high-frequency world, you don't have much choice—you're trading so quickly that, as a human being, you can't step in and meddle with what the system's doing. It has to run fully automatically. Whereas for a slower systematic trader, it's more tempting to meddle with the system, to change parameters, or override it in certain situations. That's more of a danger, but I do believe you'll be more successful if you can avoid the temptation of doing so.

Michael: You've got a great story in your book about leaving the hedge fund industry at one point and visiting a trading shop. Why don't you relay that story? I thought it was enlightening.

Robert: Shortly after leaving the hedge fund industry, I began discussions about consulting and managing some capital for a local proprietary trading firm. The office contained the usual mixture of grizzled ex-LIFFE traders and naive youths, all day trading a handful of futures contracts. But the boss was particularly proud of his quantitative team, which consisted of a couple of 20-somethings, toting PCs, running an off-the-shelf backtesting software package. "This guy's only been here a month, and he's already come up with 50 new trading laws that are profitable and backtested," explained the boss. "Yes, this software is amazing. It can automatically test hundreds of rules a day," added the trader. I managed to keep a straight face and reply as diplomatically as I could, "I'm sure some of them will work."

Michael: You walk into the room and there's all this excitement. "We've got the latest and greatest backtesting software. We've got some floor veterans. We've got some bright-eyed 20-something millennials. Everyone's ready to go. And my gosh, in a few minutes, we backtested a few things and, man, we figured it all out." Now, of course, in our limited time today, we can't dig into all of the elements here. But in terms of broad brushstrokes, help people to understand what you were feeling, even though you diplomatically skirted the issue.

Robert: Part of the reason why this story rings a bell with me is that I've done it myself, although not to the same degree. I think it's tempting, when you get hold of some backtesting software and you have some good ideas, to start playing with it and see what happens. So, there's a couple of things going wrong here.

The first is easy to understand, which is that essentially you're cheating—you're using a time machine. If you run a backtest over all your data and look at the results, and then decide "This model is good, I'm going to keep it," or "This model is bad, I'm not going to keep it," you're doing something that you couldn't have done in 1975, say, when your backtest begins. You would have had to run those two models together over time and gradually work out which model seemed to be doing better.

The second problem is statistical: if you test a lot of different trading strategies, even if on average they're all bad, some of them will look good for a given time period. As an example, let's suppose that you're going to be quite strict and say, "I want to see something that has a Sharpe ratio of at least 1 in the backtest before I even consider it." And you then test a hundred different rules or variations, which sounds like a lot, but that's easy to do with many of these packages. And they're not going to be a hundred completely different rules, they're going to be a hundred variations on a theme with slightly different parameters.

On average, with a hundred rules and a minimum Sharpe ratio of 1, 16 of those rules look as if they're good, even though none of them are actually profitable; it's luck that 16 of them happen to work pretty well over your backtest period. And this problem gets exponentially worse, so you have to reduce the number of rules you look at quite considerably, before you get to the point where even a bad rule's going to slip through your net, by the fact you've looked at so many different rules. The lesson here is that you've got to be strict in trying to avoid looking at all your data, and you've got to try to reduce the number of parameters.

I believe if you have an idea that you think's going to work and you try it, then one of two things will happen. Either the backtest looks bad, and it's hard then to say, "Oh, my idea was bad," particularly when you're working for somebody else and they're expecting some return on the salary they're paying you. It's tempting to spend time polishing it and changing the parameters and adding overlays and generally messing around until you manage to improve the thing so that it looks good in the backtest. You're fooling yourself.

The other alternative, which is nearly as bad, is if you have a rule that works well in the backtest, to try and improve it. All these changes might improve the performance of the backtest, but when you trade with real money you'll likely have completely destroyed the performance.

Michael: I'm curious how you felt when you walked into this firm. Were you looking at that as a data-only backtesting development? Or were you thinking they actually had some ideas? Talk about the difference between ideas and data, and the complexity behind that, because it's not necessarily an easy choice, is it?

Robert: No. These are the labels I use for the two main ways that people come up with trading systems and trading rules. "Data first" is what most people imagine you do as a systematic trader. This is becoming an increasingly common perception as things like machine learning, neural networks, and big data become fashionable. People assume that you get all your price data, drop it into some kind of giant optimizing machine, and out will pop a trading rule that will give you a good, profitable account curve in all those data points. And that data rule may not make any sense at all. It might be something as random as, if the S&P 500 is down on a Tuesday and the moon is full, then buy pork bellies on Thursday. And it may actually be a good rule, it may work. If you look at someone like Jim Simons at Renaissance Capital, he's been following these strange nonlinear trading rules for a long time and successfully, but that doesn't mean to say that his approach will work for everybody, because you need to be incredibly careful about things like statistical significance. You need to use some fairly sophisticated techniques.

The alternative, which I call "ideas first," is when you begin with an idea. It could be economically based, such as, "Central banks set interest rates according to unemployment levels and inflation. So, I'm going to build a model which will bet on interest rates rising if inflation is rising and unemployment is falling, and vice versa." Or it could be based around a behavior. So, if you think that trend following works for whatever reason, you can build a trend following model. Then once you have your idea and you build a rule that embodies it, you go ahead and test it.

The important thing is, in both cases, you have to test it and make sure that you've got something that works. But with the ideas first approach, you have the additional validation that you know why it works. I like having that extra confirmation, that extra tick. I'm much more comfortable running a model that I understand, especially if it's losing money, I can then understand it's because that particular effect isn't working at the moment. Whereas if I don't understand where the trading strategy came from, I'm not necessarily going to understand why it's losing money, and it'd be much harder for me to stick to the plan and trade that as it is.

> **I'm much more comfortable running a model that I understand.**

When I see people who are using data-first techniques and using them in a bad way, it's kind of depressing. Both approaches work. They work better in different scenarios. So, data first seems to work better for faster trading. Ideas first seems to work better for slower trading, because there's less data to work with. But generally speaking, I see much more misuse and bad system design done by people who've started with some data, and then analyzed it without thinking about what's going on in the market and what the underlying idea of their trading system is.

Michael: I want to go back in time to 2008–09. What were you seeing on the ground from your perspective that changed you? And how did that embolden you to the idea of using a system and being religious with that system?

Robert: The crisis of 2008–09 taught me that we're bad at predicting the future. There were a small number of people who saw the credit crisis coming, famously people like John Paulson, and who also managed to place bets in the market and do well out of that. But if you go back to

January 2007, you would not find a single macro-economic forecaster who would say in two years' time, the United States is going to be in a serious recession. You would not find analysts of banks and mortgage companies who would say, "You know what? In a couple of years, pretty much every institution that we're covering with our highly complex analysis is either going to be bankrupt or be rescued by the government." None of those guys had a clue. But if you look at what trading systems did over that period, they didn't try and forecast what was going to happen, they just said in mid-2008, "Well, it looks like the equity market is starting to go down. We're going to go from being long equities to flat, and then short equities and long bonds."

The crisis of 2008–09 taught me that we're bad at predicting the future.

Michael: That wasn't a gut feeling—that was the system?

Robert: Exactly, that was the system. In contrast, in early 2007 we were following the news around the mortgage-backed security markets and those Bear Stearns firms that went down in February '07, which was the first emergence of the credit crisis. I said to a colleague, who was running the systematic equity fund, "I think we're going to see massive sell-off on equities here."

I'm not trying to make myself up to be some kind of genius forecaster, because I've already said, I don't think I'm good enough to be a discretionary trader. I think few people are. Although I was right, I was also incredibly early. And the difference between me and the trading system was the trading system carried on being long equities until much later, when it saw the market turning, and then automatically reversed its positions and then did incredibly well.

So, you've got a large number of people who had no idea what was coming, and even well into the crisis were still forecasting that it was going to be 5% earnings growth in banks year-on-year. Then you had a small number of people who saw what was coming and were able to bet in such a way that they actually made money out of it. Then you had people like myself, who saw what was coming, not through any special skill necessarily, but weren't able to capitalize on it. And then you've got the trading systems that had no idea what was coming, didn't care, but adjusted their positions according to the market movements as they came.

The thing that encapsulates it is the fact that in the middle of the crisis—when AIG was going down and Lehman was going down, and Freddie Mac and Fannie Mae were in trouble—we were all sitting in our office, absolutely terrified, running around like headless chickens, going, "What are we going to do? What are we going to do? The market's in a terrible mess. The world's going to end."

If we'd been human beings making trading decisions, we would have sold everything, bought gold bars, and moved to Switzerland. But because we were running a computer system, we seriously asked ourselves, "Should we turn this thing off? Is it safe to leave it running?" And while this was happening, the computer system itself didn't know or care about us being scared, didn't know or care about all the bad news in the market, only inasmuch as it saw the price patterns and put the appropriate position on.

And 2008 was one of the best years for that fund, ever. It was a real contrast between scared, emotional humans and a computer system that had no emotions, was not scared, and carried on doing what it had always done. The market moved. It put the appropriate amount of risk on. It didn't think, "This is a scary environment." It scaled its positions according to the risk it saw in the market, and was profitable.

Michael: You lay out a good example of a systems trader sticking with it in the face of utter chaos. Is there a negative to being a staunch systems trader?

Robert: There's a couple of things. First, I do believe that there are some people who can do much better than a trading system. If you are an amazing trader who can look at price patterns and think about economic implications and forecasts, like Paulson, for example. You couldn't have made the short mortgage trade that Paulson did up to 2007 using a trading system, because you don't have that element of repeatability. The situation in 2007, where we'd had house prices reach unprecedented levels, where we had this huge bubble of mortgage-backed debt, was unprecedented. If it had happened once a year over the previous 30 years, then yes, you could have built a model to exploit that. That's the first disadvantage. As a systems trader, you're never going to be as good as the best discretionary traders. But most of us aren't going to be the best discretionary traders, so we should forget about it and stick to a system.

Secondly, there are rare occasions when you do need to intervene in your trading system. A couple of examples from my career. Once there was a coup in Thailand and we knew there was a pretty good chance it would suspend the convertibility of its currency and impose capital controls, so we quickly shut down our positions in the Thai baht. The system didn't know about this. It's not that we thought we could do a better job of forecasting what the price would do than the system; it's that we knew that trading that market would be impossible and therefore we should stop trading it as soon as possible.

The second situation was when one of our prime brokers, MF Global, got into serious trouble. And again, we knew a few days in advance that was likely to happen, so we had to get out of those positions where we were trading with them as our sole prime broker, or risk being in a situation where we'd be losing client money.

But I'm talking about two instances—I could perhaps name three or four more over a seven-year career—where it was the right thing to intervene with the system. That's how rare it should be. I'm not talking about changing the system every month according to what your perception of risk is at the moment.

Michael: You mentioned exceptional discretionary traders, like John Paulson. I can also think of Michael Burry. The way they define risk would make most systems traders pretty nervous, because for as many Paulsons and Burrys as there are, there are others who had the same idea but didn't get the timing right, or took that kind of bet and became a footnote in history. It seems like the risk for an excellent discretionary trader is much different than the systematic styles that we've been talking about.

Robert: I'm going to illustrate the problem in a couple of different ways. One is to take the view that Nassim Taleb takes in many of his books, which is, if you were starting your career as a trader, should you be discretionary or should you be systematic? If you're going to be a systematic trader, then it's reasonable to expect to earn an average of maybe 10% or 15% a year, without taking on too much risk. If you're an absolutely top-line discretionary trader, then you could multiply that number many, many times, but 99.9% of the people who go down that route will fail. The high end is better, but the average, and the dispersion, is an awful lot worse.

The second point is that it isn't a systematic versus discretionary thing—it comes down to different trading strategies and different return profiles. Paulson was doing the kind of bets where you take potentially a number of small losses for many years, and then you have huge outside returns in one or two years. Now, that's actually on the same side of the playing field as trend following, where typically maybe six out of 10 months you'll lose money, but in the four months you make money you'll make much more and it all comes out ahead. So, they're actually more alike than you might think. And that's quite distinct from—to use a technical term—a negative skew style of trading, something like FX carry, or the other side of the John Paulson trade, for example, where you're selling credit insurance every year and you get lots of small gains and you feel good—and then every few years, you have a huge loss and you get wiped out.

The way you think about risk management and the psychology of those two sides of the risk spectrum are quite different. But the Paulson method of lots of small bets, occasional large payoffs, is more similar to trend following than it is to the other side of the field where, whether you're trading systematically or discretionary, you're getting lots of small gains, which psychologically feels better, but on occasion you're going to have huge losses, so you have to build risk management into your system carefully so that those huge losses don't wipe you out.

Michael: Big question: Should you have, from your perspective, one trading rule for all markets, all instruments? You've written a book on this subject, so people can read your views in depth, but I'd like to hear you talk about it.

Robert: In general, yes. I trade my own portfolio, about 40 futures markets covering most asset classes, most countries. And the only distinction I make between them is the cost of trading that market. I trade cheap markets quicker and I trade expensive markets slower. Something like Australian interest rate futures, I trade them slowly, because they're expensive. Something like NASDAQ, I trade a little bit quicker. But the difference in fast and slow here is not that much. You're talking about, at the one extreme, maybe a two- to three-week average holding period, and then at the other extreme, perhaps a two-month holding period—so they're not that dissimilar.

On the other hand, I'd use a different set of rules to trade something completely different, for example, pairs of U.S. equities. But if you're talking about things that are fairly similar, then generally speaking there isn't much evidence to suggest that you should trade, say, British pound versus U.S. dollar currency futures differently from yen-dollar currency futures. And even different again from U.S. equity futures. You do see in the data some differences, but they never come out statistically significant.

This is a real hardening of my attitude on this subject, because if you go back five years, when I was at AHL, I would have said that there were good reasons to trade different things differently, but now I don't see the evidence for that. I think, especially as an individual investor who's doing your own research and doesn't have teams of people, you should do the simplest possible thing that makes sense, and only do something more complicated or fitted to different markets where you can find incredibly strong evidence in support. And I rarely see that evidence looking at just futures markets.

Michael: Break apart Donald Rumsfeld's favorite descriptions, the predictable risks and the unpredictable risks, the known unknowns and the unknown unknowns. I think sometimes people don't allow themselves the time to think about what he was saying, which could sound kind of quick and cute and maybe political, but there was a lot of depth behind it.

Robert: Absolutely. Risk is about unknowns. And if we knew what was going to happen next week, there would be no risk involved. But there are known unknowns and there are unknown unknowns. I would call those predictable and unpredictable risks. To predict something, you need to have some kind of model. You need the mathematical functions, and then you need to feed into them some estimates of what you think the number should be. It would be pretty simple to say, "I think that all asset returns are what a statistician would call normally distributed, and they have a particular standard deviational variance, and they have a particular correlation." What that means in practice is that you can summarize what you think will happen to asset returns with a relatively small number of variables.

You can then take things a step further and say, "I don't think this model predicts enough of the risk in the world. I want to make my model more complicated and introduce all kinds of other factors." People working in quantitative finance will come up with more and more esoteric risk models. The danger is that the more complicated your notion of the predictable risk, the less you think about the unpredictable risk—the less you think about what Nassim Taleb calls the black swans, the things that come for you completely from left field.

If we knew what was going to happen next week, there would be no risk involved.

Going back to the credit crisis, a good example is the models that were used to price mortgage securities with something called a copula, which is sufficiently complicated that the people using those models assumed that this completely embodied the world. They forgot that a model is just a model. It's a simplification of reality. It isn't reality.

My personal approach is to go to the opposite extreme and use the simplest possible risk model, and always make sure that I limit my exposure to unpredictable risk as much as I can. So, if the S&P 500 dropped 80% in one day (which has never happened) and exposed me potentially to large losses, at least I have in the back of my mind that something like that could happen. Whereas if I was using a more sophisticated risk model, the danger is I'd be thinking too much about the known unknowns, and forgetting completely about the unknown unknowns, the unpredictable part of the risk model.

PART 2
Portfolio Building

Michael: Right in the beginning of your book *Smart Portfolios* you have a couple of quotes, and I love this one from Warren Buffett: "Fund consultants like to require style boxes, such as 'long-short,' 'macro,' 'international equities.' At Berkshire, our only style box is 'smart.'"

When I read that I'm thinking, "That is a nice pithy piece of wisdom. Makes a lot of sense. Put aside all the names for a second and all the jargon, just being smart is the way to go." But then the second thought I have is, "How in the world do we define the word smart, Mr. Buffett?"

Robert: Buffett might say that smart is whatever he happens to be doing. But the point is that not everyone can be Warren Buffett. And actually, in trying to replicate what he does, you may end up doing much worse than if you did some relatively simple and straightforward things yourself.

If I look at the investment books on my shelf, at one end I've got a book that's almost entirely full of mathematical equations. You have to have an academic background to read it and the content is good, but not of much practical use to the average person on the street. At the other end, you've got books like the *Market Wizards* series that are rather easy to read, quite entertaining, but you need a little bit more substance to actually go down and start doing something sensible.

For me, smart is in the middle: you're intelligent and you know what you're doing, but you're not trying to overdo it with academic theory. You're doing stuff that you know works. You don't make things more complicated than they need to be, you keep them as simple as they can be without making them too simplistic.

Michael: A big picture point before I get into some of detail. So many people get caught up with the idea of wow, look at Warren Buffett's fantastic career. The thing is you're not going to replicate Buffett exactly. And to take it a step further, even if you have a smart portfolio, it doesn't mean your neighbor's going to have it, and it also could mean your neighbor has a smarter portfolio than you. One of the tricks here is how one puts the ego in check, to not spend one's life trying to compare to either the neighbor benchmark or the investment benchmark. If you go through life constantly comparing yourself to everyone else, that's a little bit psycho, in my humble opinion.

Robert: Coming from the hedge fund industry, we spent our lives comparing ourselves to other people and to benchmarks. You're right, it's become a bit of an obsession. I call this phenomenon "embarrassment," because if you're performing versus a benchmark and you're doing better than the benchmark, that's fine, but when you're underperforming, that's embarrassing.

It's important that people have a degree of self-knowledge and ask themselves, "How much embarrassment can I cope with?" Because, frankly, if you're the kind of person that any slight

> **Traders must recognize their tolerance for embarrassment.**

underperformance or deviation from what the market is doing will make you feel bad and tempt you to start messing around with your portfolio, then maybe you should hold a market portfolio. Maybe you should invest in a big global market cap ETF and stop worrying about your investments.

But if you're someone who doesn't mind underperforming and doesn't give a damn what anybody else thinks, that's fantastic, and you can obviously deviate your portfolio much farther away from that. Traders must recognize what their tolerance is for embarrassment, as much as you need to calibrate your tolerance for risk when constructing a portfolio.

Michael: Is there also an element of people coveting their neighbor's success; a certain jealousy involved there too? When an individual is always thinking about what the other person is doing, that's a lot of psychological energy to burn.

Robert: I agree, and it's certainly wired into our human nature that we like to compare ourselves to other people. It requires a real conscious effort not to do that, to force yourself to focus on your own life and your own goals. I'd be lying to you if I said I never compared myself to other people.

Michael: Same here. Of course.

Robert: I'm sitting here looking at my neighbor's house, and it's bigger than my house. I see that. I see that every time I walk out the door, but the secret is to not let it affect me, and for me to think about all the things in my life that I'm happy with and comfortable with.

Michael: You have set forward three big questions that all investors have to think about. Number one, what should you invest in? Number two, how much money of our limited capital goes into each of those investments? Number three, do we make changes along the way? Meaning: Do you buy and sell along the way? Do you rebalance?

That's a simple framework to look at markets and how one deploys one's capital. As we're going to find out, some of the details get a little more complicated, but that foundation's a pretty good place to start, isn't it?

Robert: Whenever people come to me for investment advice, pretty much any question they ask can be divided into one of those three categories. Should I buy Bitcoin? What should I buy? How much of my money should I put into stocks? Things look pretty bad in South Korea at the moment, should I sell? Should I make changes to my portfolio? Should I sell my South Korean stocks? These all come under those three questions you mentioned.

Michael: I think you're going to agree with me that people are always asking questions for a finite time. They want to know, "Tell me what to do *right now*." They don't seem to have any curiosity about what to do later. It's "Hey, man, can you give me a quick one that will give me instant gratification?" They get so focused on the outcome that they don't ask a smart guy like you, "Hey, man, I want your process." And if they asked you for your process, you're going to be 10 times more interested in that person and giving them all you know, versus whether they ask you for an outcome.

Robert: Again, you're right, but this absolutely does come down to human instinct. Let's take an activity at which I'm definitely not an expert, like car maintenance. My brother-in-law used to be a mechanic, so I'd go up to him at a party and say, "Hey, Simon, got a problem with my car," and I'd describe the symptom. And I'd expect him to say, "Oh, you should do X or Y," or "That sounds a real bad problem, you need to take it to the garage and get it fixed." I wouldn't expect him to start saying, "Oh, well, actually, I think the problem is that every week you need to be putting more oil in the car, and you need to be doing this, you need to be doing that, and there's a whole regime of car maintenance that you should be getting involved with to avoid this problem coming up to begin with." Instinctively, I'd be quite annoyed if he started giving me this lecture. I want a quick answer. That's a natural human instinct.

The key point here is that the amount of damage you could do to your financial wealth by not looking after your portfolio in a sensible way many times exceeds the damage you could do by not looking after your car. For most people, time and effort thinking about their portfolio will be rewarded many times over because of the benefits of compound interest over time. But most people spend much less time thinking about their portfolios than they do thinking about getting their cars fixed, which is why there's even more pressure to have this quick-fix answer.

Michael: Their thought process might be, "Why do I need to think when the U.S. equity markets are straight up for close to 10 years now?"

Robert: Exactly. We're both old enough to remember what was happening in the late '90s, when you only needed to buy any old stock with .com at the end of it and you'd make loads of money. And in fact, if you listen to any academic expert who said, "You ought to have a diversified portfolio with a spread of asset classes," relatively speaking, that would have looked like a pretty poor decision for those few crazy years when the tech stocks went to the moon.

Michael: An overriding topic—and one we all discuss once we get into the investment thinking process—is diversification. I have a sneaky suspicion that the home bias is strong, and the majority of individuals think only about their home country. And that doesn't make a lot of sense.

Robert: The world we live in today is one where capital does not respect national borders. Companies are operating across borders and consumers are buying things across borders. To be focused purely on investments in your own country doesn't make a lot of sense, but the reasons are fairly obvious.

If I pick up a newspaper, I'm going to read all about all kinds of companies in my own country, because newspapers tend to be fairly parochial in their coverage. In my case they'll mostly be companies based in the UK, perhaps a few glamorous U.S. tech stocks thrown in for good measure. When it comes to an investment portfolio, the average person will think, "Well, I want to buy a company that I understand, and that I think I know something about." The first of those statements is okay—it makes a lot of sense to stick to investments that you understand. For example, I can't see myself ever investing in Bitcoin, because no matter how many times I read about it, I don't understand why you would want to own it.

But to buy something because you think you have some information that will allow you to improve your return and to beat the market, that's where the fallacy comes in. The idea that having a more concentrated portfolio of stocks that you think you understand, and you think you can forecast the performance of, will allow you to outperform the benchmark is wrong. Sure, a few people will do it. The problem is that people aren't used to thinking about life probabilistically, or thinking about alternative scenarios. And sure, if you have a highly concentrated portfolio, then your upside is much higher than if you have a diversified portfolio, but your downside is also much higher, and your expected average performance, which is what people ought to be thinking about, is going to be less. If you can't predict the future—and generally speaking, you can't—then diversification is the best way of dealing with all the uncertainties that lie ahead.

Home bias doesn't make a lot of sense.

Michael: As I think about the human lifespan, when does one start to have assets to invest? Typically, unless there was some good fortune, it's going to start in your 30s. But this is where diversification plays such a critical role. If you think about when you're going to be dealing with money, let's say between the ages of 30 and 50, there's no way that anybody can know, during that window, when will the boom happen, and when will the downturn happen, and how many of those will happen in the period. One generation could get their home run boom in their 20s, another generation could get it in their 40s. When you talk about thinking probabilistically, it's thinking about all the contingencies that could possibly happen and realizing we can't know a damn thing, which brings us right back to diversification.

Diversification is the best way of dealing with all the uncertainties that lie ahead.

Robert: Exactly. Looking at the last 20 years, in 1997, we had the Asian crisis, in 1998 we had the Russian crisis, then we had the dot-com boom, then in 2000 it burst, then things went pretty quiet for a few years, then in 2007 things got crazy again. And even in the last 18 months there's been the Brexit vote in the UK, there's been the accession of Trump to the presidency in the United States. In six months' time, we could be in the middle of a nuclear war, the stock market could have collapsed, or it could have carried on. People need to think back and honestly say to themselves, "If I was sitting in 1997 without any of the information that's available to me now, with no hindsight bias, could I have predicted all these things?" Even Warren Buffett doesn't try and predict the future.

Michael: He's such an outlier, though, in many ways. We all love to talk about him, and he's got some great lines, and he's extremely successful. But when the world goes to hell in a handbasket in 2008, and you're Warren Buffett, and you can start buying banks, because you have all the cash. The rest of us can't really apply that with our own money.

Robert: That's true. As I said before, we shouldn't look at his mostly concentrated portfolio and say, "We can copy that." But we can look at a couple of his attitudes. He tries to buy companies that he thinks are a good value and he expects that over time he'll get a good return from. But he's not going to say, "Over the next 10 years, I expect to make this much percentage from that company." In many respects, he's got a much better calibrated idea of his limited ability to forecast than a lot of other people.

Michael: I had an email from somebody recently with a particular trading style, who was down 40% and seemed panicked. And I said, "Well, have you looked at what the elders who have come before you have done?" Buffett has a great line: "If you're in the markets and you can't afford to lose 50%, maybe you should not be in the markets." I realized my correspondent had not read that line; he had not looked at the track records of other market wizards, so he was naive in that sense.

Many people, when they start to put together a smart portfolio, say, "I want to target my return. I want to control my volatility." We're back to your line about probabilities: There's no such thing as perfection, but so many people want perfection. How many of the investing public right now would buy into Buffett's view? Would they think it's important? Would they think it's relevant? It's a minefield, isn't it?

Robert: Absolutely. You mentioned targeting risk and controlling volatility. I think one of those things is at least almost possible, and the other is much more difficult. Targeting a certain return is extremely difficult, because you do not know what's going to happen in the future. But I think you can construct your portfolio in such a way that you have a reasonable idea of what your volatility is likely to be.

The important thing is to be able to say, "I put together my portfolio, I've got a certain percentage of stocks, a certain percentage of bonds. Now if I look at history, I know there's a chance that over the next 20 years, I could lose perhaps 50%." And then to be able to say, "Yeah, okay, I'm comfortable with that, because I think I need that kind of aggressive portfolio to hopefully compound my money in the future." You should have an understanding of what your likely volatility is going to be, and what your likely downside is going to be.

> **Targeting a certain return is extremely difficult.**

And you're right, most people have extremely unrealistic expectations. What you have to say is, "It might be that I'm good. It's more likely that I'm going to be average, but if anything, I'm going to be a little conservative and assume that things don't go well. If things don't go well with this portfolio, I may end up with a 50% drawdown. That's too much. I can't cope with that. Fine, I need to dial back my volatility with the understanding I'm going to be dialing back the expected return I'll make in the future."

Many people start buying hot stocks or running some leverage trading strategy, and quickly they run into a large loss. It will happen, it's the laws of statistics. They may get lucky to begin with, or they may lose money to begin with, but at some point they'll get a large loss. And because they aren't psychologically ready for it, the first instinct is to pull the panic lever and turn the whole thing off—sell everything.

You can't remove volatility entirely without also removing risk.

And of course, that's the worst thing to do, because these kinds of strategies and ideas and concepts only work if you stick to them over time.

Michael: I know it's not an exact representation, but many people think about volatility as risk. They think, "Let me get the tiniest volatility, and then I will then magically have all of this fantastic return." They get preoccupied with reducing volatility, rather than targeting a return. But if your volatility is so low in your portfolio, I don't know where the return is supposed to come from.

Robert: In quant finance, some people call this the waterbed effect. Imagine your portfolio is a waterbed. If you sit on one edge of the waterbed, you're pushing down the risk that you're aware of, because it's right underneath you, but that risk is moving away somewhere else where you can't necessarily see it.

A good example of this is the lead-up to 2007–08. Those guys were constructing portfolios using much more sophisticated methods than we're talking about, but where the volatility was minimized—close to zero. They were comfortable with those portfolios. But all that happened was the risk had been pushed away into another place, and they actually had a massive bet on something else going on that they assumed would never happen. And then when it did happen, these portfolios went from having little risk to having huge amounts of risk. Personally, I'd rather have a portfolio where the volatility is reasonably large but all the risk is happening in front of me, there's no weird stuff lurking in the corner of the waterbed to come and bite me later.

You can't remove volatility entirely without also removing risk, and if you think you can, then you're either an idiot or perhaps, at the other extreme, you know so much mathematics that you think you can do it in theory, when in practice it's not going to happen.

Michael: You have done work on different types of return. You go down the path of making sure people understand the difference between geometric mean return and arithmetic return. Walk us through your process.

Robert: It's easiest to explain this by looking at a simple example. You've got an investment over three years. The first year you get 30%, which is great. And the second year you get 30%, which is also great. And the third year you lose 30%. Let's say you started with $100. Roughly how much money do you think you'd have after three years? So you made 30%, then 30% again, and then you lost 30%.

Michael: You're going to be worse off. Those first two 30s didn't help you.

Robert: Exactly. You will have still made some money, but not as much as you might expect. Most people, when you ask them that question, will say, "Well, I'm going to have another $30, right? Because I've made $30 in the first year, I've made a bit more than $30 in the second year because of compounding, and then I lose $30 in the third year, so I've got about $130." But actually, you've got a little bit less than $119. You've made 18%. And if you average that out over the three years, that's the same as if you'd made about 5.8% every year. The arithmetic average of 30, 30, and minus 30 is easy to work out, because the last two numbers cancel, so you've got 30% over three years, which averages out to 10% a year.

A geometric average, which is the amount of money you'd have made if you'd had constant growth in each year, comes out at 5.8%. That's pretty much almost half the arithmetic return, so there's a huge difference. The important point here is that arithmetic returns don't matter to most people. An extreme case might be that you gave all your money to Bernie Madoff and you were making 8% a year for 30 years, and then in the last year, you lose 100% because it turns out that the whole thing was a giant Ponzi scheme. If you work out the arithmetic average of 8%, 8%, 8% over 30 years, and then minus 100% at the end, it'll come out to about 6% or 7%. But you haven't made 6% or 7%, you've made nothing. If you've lost everything you've got, your geometric return is massively negative.

It's dangerous to think about arithmetic returns rather than geometric returns, because geometric returns accurately reflect what you're going to be left with at the end of your investment period. The important point here is that the more volatile an investment, the more you've got big swings, the greater the difference between an arithmetic return and a geometric return. The simple example I gave, 30, 30, minus 30, that's quite a lot of volatility. The geometric return is quite a lot less than the arithmetic return.

For stocks, which are relatively risky investments, there's going to be a relatively large gap between arithmetic and geometric returns. For bonds, which are usually safer, there's going to be a smaller gap. If you've got a huge appetite for risk and you're happy to see a lot of volatility in your portfolio, the idea is you should have all your money in stocks. But if you do the math, you find that adding a little bit of bonds to an all-stock portfolio actually keeps the geometric return constant, or even improves it slightly. So, once you start thinking in the geometric return space, you will tend to be pushed toward holding a more diversified portfolio than if you're thinking purely about arithmetic returns.

Michael: You give a three-year period example, but three years is not going to be the period that people are thinking about, generally. And how do you define swing? It's going to be different depending on what that portfolio looks like and what you're comfortable with. And then, as you go down the diversification path, you have the typical long-only investments you can make, but you also start to think about diversification in terms of strategy. It quickly opens up a Pandora's box of potential issues. The question I come back to is, how much is too much? How do we know, from your perspective, that we have reached the diversification threshold?

Robert: That depends on your appetite for risk. Let's say you start with a portfolio entirely in stocks. You need to put roughly 20% of that portfolio into a safer asset, like bonds. If you do that, your geometric return will pretty much remain unchanged, and there may be a slight increase. So, I would say that's the absolute minimum amount of diversification. If you believe in the story of geometric return, then no one should be running around with 100% invested in stocks. They should have 20% of their portfolio in assets with a lower volatility, which could be bonds, or could consist of alternative assets or strategies.

Michael: But beyond the math, there's also a practical thinking here, like saving for a rainy day. It's like the old standards.

Robert: Exactly. The nice thing about putting a little bit of safer assets into a risky portfolio is it has a fast effect on reducing your drawdown—the maximum amount of money you'd expect to be down during a 30-year investment period. It makes the worst months look that little bit better, quite quickly. You don't need a lot: 10%, 20%. Beyond that, you will actually start affecting your returns, and that will make sense if you're someone who isn't comfortable with the large swings or drawdowns of a portfolio that's 80% stocks, 20% bonds.

> No one should be running around with 100% invested in stocks.

You'll reach a point of diversification where you're giving up more return than you're happy with, for less risk that you don't need. I would say that for most people, the right asset allocation should be somewhere between 20% and 60% in bonds. It's still a pretty wide window, but it does help narrow down the problem set to a smaller area.

Michael: You've described the best path for the average investor, but what would be the best path for the investor who wants to be above average, perhaps wants to be rich? And what would be the best path for the investor trader who wants to get super rich? People generally think that it's a pure choice between those three. If you choose the super-rich direction, you've got to crank up the risk and be willing to tolerate the drawdown, but it doesn't mean you're going to get there—there's so much luck in play, there's no guarantee.

Robert: A good analogy here is buying lottery tickets. Most people are unlikely to be worth $100m starting from zero in one day, unless they buy a lottery ticket. There are no other investments, and I use the word investment here loosely, that give you that payoff profile. If you want to even have the tiniest chance of being a deca- or a centimillionaire tomorrow, then yeah, you should buy a lottery ticket. But that doesn't mean it's a good investment, because the vast majority of future possibilities is that you'll end up losing the two bucks or whatever the lottery ticket cost you. And then there's a small fraction of paths where you'll make a relatively modest amount of money.

It's the same with making risky investments, except that the numbers aren't quite as dramatic. But if you invest in an extremely concentrated portfolio, so maybe buying one or two risky tech stocks, then yes, there's an outside chance that in 30 years' time that portfolio will be worth $100m. But doing that is extremely difficult, and in most future possibilities, like that worthless lottery ticket, you'll end up with a poor return, even losing your entire investment, because risky companies have a nasty habit of going bust.

If someone wants to get rich, there is a more sensible way of doing it, which is to invest in a portfolio that has the maximum amount of diversification possible, which means putting perhaps two-thirds of your money in bonds and one-third in stocks. The reason for that particular ratio is that the bonds in your portfolio will be contributing less to the risk of the portfolio, overall. Stocks will be contributing more. If you work out the numbers, you end up with a risk contribution of about 50/50, so that's the most diversified portfolio you could have. Then you leverage that portfolio. You buy it using margin in a brokerage account, or you use futures, or you use leveraged ETFs—although of those three options, I would argue against the latter, I think it's not such a good move. If you do that, you will have a reasonable chance of becoming wealthy, but of course the downside will be much bigger than if you hadn't leveraged the portfolio. Still, that's a more sensible way of doing that kind of investment with that kind of risk than buying one or two tech stocks and crossing your fingers and hoping.

Michael: Your practical approach to trading is a contrast to the Hollywood version in *The Big Short*. Michael Burry, a brilliant man, was not acting like a typical investor. He saw this unique opportunity. Perhaps he might not have had the ability to short what he wanted to if not for some luck. He could have had the right strategy and not been able to execute it. The film shows the success of one person with one super bet, and that's fun

Good investors
should be thinking
about having a
diversified set of
opportunities on
which they have an
expectation they will
make a small profit.

to watch, but I've always been more interested in traders who've made buys and sells over many decades rather than the one-offs. Look at the VC community right now—there are plenty of venture capital investors that hit it big on Snapchat. There's a lot of luck involved in some of these one-off events, but what's so crazy is these become the headlines, the books, the things of legend. I'm not trying to criticize or take anything away from someone's success, but if we're going to be honest about it, from a mathematical standpoint, the direction you've gone in your work is much more reasonable and much more truthful.

Robert: Although, unfortunately, no one's ever going to make a film about me. And I'm not sure that anyone will necessarily make a film about Warren Buffett either, but we keep returning to him as an example. He has a process that he's repeated many times over a long period, and he's made not one decision but hundreds or even thousands, of which the vast majority turned out to be good.

The way that VC works is they had in their portfolio 50 or even 100 investments, of which one turned out to be Snapchat, and a couple maybe broke even, and all the rest disappeared. That's the economics of that business. You have to make a diversified set of investments.

Michael: That's what the main players on Sand Hill Road in Palo Alto are doing, but there are plenty of people in the modern age that are plunking down some bucks and getting lucky on their first hit, and then they're world famous.

Robert: It comes down to the old adage: Are you better off being a gambler in a casino, or are you better off running a casino? Every time someone comes into your casino and puts money down, you're essentially making a bet with them, but the odds are tilted slightly in your favor. You know that over time, you've got this vast diversified set of investments. And every now and then a big gambler comes in and puts a lot of money down on the table, which picks up your volatility, and you may end up down on that day. But over time, your expectation is that you'll be profitable.

Good investors should be thinking about having a diversified set of opportunities on which they have an expectation they will make a small profit, which will limit their upside, but will also limit their downside. Then it's a question of how much downside you think you can cope with, and you can swap that for upside by making your portfolio a little bit riskier, as long as you don't go too far.

CHAPTER 10

NICK RADGE

Consistency is the Key

NICK RADGE is the Head of Trading & Research at The Chartist (Australia). He is a professional trader, educator, and author, who has been trading since 1985. Nick has worked in the pits of the trading floor of the Sydney Futures Exchange, and international dealing desks in Sydney, London, and Singapore. His expertise lies in trading system design and technical analysis, with a particular focus on momentum investing and trend following strategies.

Michael Note

Nick has a mild-mannered, confident, and likable approach. No nonsense. If you don't like that kind of stuff, you won't like me and you won't like Nick.

Michael Covel: I have an email series that goes out, and it asks people, "What's your biggest challenge?"

I hear: "When to enter," "I need consistency," and, "I'm afraid to take losses." My first response is, "Do you even have a strategy?"

Nick Radge: That's the right question to ask. If they're looking for an entry, that's a part of the strategy. I'm also asking myself if they have a strategy.

Michael: When you hear the word "consistency," what's your first thought?

Nick: In the retail space, that immediately suggests they want to make money every hour, every day, every week, every month, every year without fail. If that's what they think professional traders do, they're going to be disappointed for a long, long time.

Consistency as a professional trader is pushing the button every hour, every day, every week, every month, every year, which I've been doing for 34 years now.

I come across people who were able to do it for two or three months. Then, they forget it for whatever reason. It's not necessarily that they're losing money, but their heart is not in it. They don't get it. They're not understanding. This is a long-term game. The only way you can have returns like DUNN Capital and Abraham Trading is by pushing the button every day, every week, every month, every year for decades.

Michael: You're talking about the consistency of waking up to Nick's plan every day, and executing it. They're talking about, "I want consistency. I want to imagine there's a tooth fairy that puts a trading nickel under my pillow every hour, every day." Right?

Nick: Sure.

Michael: I think people are generally smart, but I don't know where the idea comes from that you're sitting at your house, you don't know anything about trading, investing, or whatever, and you say to yourself, "I need to make money every day, and I need to make money every week."

Nick: I see a lot of that as well. I recently had a phone call from a guy and he says, "I want to trade for a living." I said, "Okay. How much trading experience do you have?" He said, "None." I said, "Right. Do you play golf?" He had to think about that for a second. He said, "Well, yeah, but what's your point?" I said, "Well, do you think you can be on the PGA tour competing against Tiger and all the boys by the end of the year?" He goes, "Don't be an idiot. Of course not." I said, "Well, you play golf, but you acknowledge that you can't play for a living and be on the PGA tour

Consistency as a professional trader is pushing the button every hour, every day, every week, every month, every year.

by the end of the year. On the other hand, you've never traded before, but for some unknown reason, you think you'll be able to make a living out of it by the end of the year. It doesn't compute."

Michael: There's plenty of people out there telling people they can do this. They can fulfill the exact dream and fantasy that they have, and here, I will show you how to do it. Of course, it doesn't work that way.

Nick: It's present in every industry. Australia is going through this mega property boom, and you get all those brokers out there saying the same thing. You've got this Amazon drop shipping going on. It occurs everywhere, and of course, everyone is willing to sell that knowledge for a hefty price. Trading is no different. Investing is no different.

Michael: You mentioned DUNN Capital. Why don't you put your best professor hat on and start at the elevator ground level? What is price trading to a Nick Radge?

Nick: I did a talk at the Australian Investors Association Annual Conference. I asked myself, "What the heck am I doing here, I'm the only guy who looks at price?"

The other 25 speakers and 700 delegates were all staunch fundamentalists. They use narratives. They use these home-spun motherhood statements that we hear from the Buffett investors and that kind of stuff. "You can't time the market." "Diversification is the only thing that we have." "You got to have a 60/40 portfolio."

People latch onto that and say, "Well, you got to know what you're doing." I stood up and was frowned upon because I showed them a trend following strategy for Australian stocks and made the comment that I actually had no idea what half of these companies did. It gets a giggle out of the crowd, but they probably walked out, shaking their heads and saying, "That guy is an idiot."

Michael: Do you think they listen enough to know what you mean when you flippantly say you don't know what some of these companies even are? Do they immediately think, "This guy is not that bright," or do you think some of them get what your real point is?

Nick: Like you, I've spent my whole career hammering home this trend following thing. You do definitely get that message through to people. It's like the light bulb moment. I get people come to me and say, "Gosh, I followed this big trend that's been going for nine months, and I've made so much money. I've done nothing. I've sat on my hands for nine months. What was I thinking, doing all that day trading crap, or that other stuff that I was doing?"

> I do not understand what a lot of the companies that I trade actually do.

Once they get it, they understand, but it's like any other learning process. It's difficult to tell someone what to do. They've got to get it themselves. They've got to have that light bulb moment.

It's like sitting on your psychologist's couch. You do all the talking, and the reason why you do all the talking is because that's the only way you're going to get it. You'll come to that realization, whatever it may be, by nutting it out yourself.

With this particular audience, there certainly were people that got it, and understood that I wasn't being flippant. I wasn't being smart ass.

I generally do not understand what a lot of these companies that I trade actually do, and I don't care because when I put my tax return in at the tax office, all they're after is the price I've bought and sold. They don't care about the valuation I've put on the company or the earnings per share. They don't ask those questions. All they want to know is where you buy, where you sell, and that's what it comes down to.

Michael: They've all got careers, and they've got time invested in something. That's how they make their living.

Then a guy like you walks into the room. It's like instant cognitive dissonance for the audience. "What does someone do when they've made the wrong bet?" The smart person that makes the wrong bet gets the heck out, but that's easier said than done.

Nick: Absolutely. There was a speaker there who, I understand, was kicked out of his own fund management business. He's a staunch fundamentalist, bought into a company, and the share price kept going down, and down, and down. He kept buying more, and more, and more. I believe eventually there was 50% of the fund's money in this one position, and that kept going down. He was forced out, and it ended up in all sorts of excuses. "The company misled us," "We weren't given the right information," so on and so forth.

If you plunge 50% of your money into a single position that goes pear shaped, the outcome is not going to be good. Having such conviction in a position is the wrong thing to do.

I have no conviction to any position. I don't care. It's like water off a duck's back. Okay? Move on. Next thousand trades. That's what I'd say. Next thousand trades.

Michael: It's a game. You're like a big kid playing a video game. "What are the rules? How do I have to play to stay alive? How do I have to put myself in a position to profit when something happens that I can't predict?"

Nick: It's a game of mathematical expectancy. That's all it is. Everyone plays the same game. It doesn't matter if you're Warren Buffett. It doesn't matter if you're a staunch fundamentalist value investor. It's how much you win when you win and how much you lose when you lose. The only thing you can control is how much you lose. You can put any valuation on any stock you want. You can say, "Gold is going to go to 10,000." It doesn't matter how you want to do it. The only thing you can control is how much you're willing to lose. Believe me, like we saw in the Great Financial Crisis in 2008, it only takes a bit of a knock in a few positions to do the damage to someone's portfolio. Not only their portfolio, but their long-term wealth, and more so, their psychological perspective.

> I have no conviction to any position. I don't care.

A lot of people lost so much money in 2008 that they could not step back into the market in 2009, and they missed a fantastic opportunity. Now, don't get me wrong. Personally, I lost 13% in 2008, but psychologically and even financially for that matter, I was still in a position to be able to step into the market in 2009. From memory, I made a 28% return in 2009. That's the difference right there—being able to say, "Okay, I may have lost that year, but it's not going to take me out of the game. It's not going to take me out psychologically, so I can keep playing." As you say, it's like a video game.

Michael: I don't know what the acceptance of trend trading, trend following, and price action trading is in the U.S., but I would say it's still small, relatively speaking. Now, I do find in the last six, seven, eight years, hustling around Asia here and there, that Asian audiences accept the idea of price action trading quickly. They seem to have a built-in understanding that the fundamental stories are all bullshit. Do you think Australia has a leg up on acceptance of your style?

It's how much you win when you win and how much you lose when you lose.

Nick: I would say we're worse than the U.S. I'm sure there would be a small segment of fund managers here in Australia who would use some kind of trend following/ momentum style approach, but I'd be struggling to name more than two, three, or four. You'd have a few more than that in the U.S. Admittedly, the U.S. is a significantly larger, more sophisticated market, and more open.

Michael: I know you do well with your life and your business, but what keeps you going when the acceptance is not as strong as you'd like?

Nick: I don't care. I'm not going to stand up on a chair and say, "You people are missing out here. This is the best thing since sliced bread." I can put my message out there, but I'm not going to press it. I follow what Bill Dunn said back in the day: "We're not trying to be everything to everybody. We attract like-minded people."

That's how I think about my trend following. If you don't like what I do, that's fine. It's not going to impact my life. It might change your life, but it's not going to impact mine because I'm not going to stop doing something that I've done reasonably well for 30 odd years.

I'm happy to help out people as much as I can. If they shrug their shoulders and go, "That guy is nuts," that's fine. No problems.

Michael: Take me back to a start time. What was the trigger for you where you had that light bulb go off, the eye-opening moment where you're like, "Oh, wow." Did you start with a fundamental take?

Nick: No.

Michael: Explain it to me. How do you come at this?

Nick: I remember exactly. Absolutely crystal clear. November 1985, give or take a month. I was a junior. I was 18 years of age. I had just left school. I had no idea what I wanted to do. In fact, here it is. This is what I wanted to do. You'll hear it here first, and you can confirm with my wife, Trish. She'll tell you the same thing. Nick wanted to catch a train, work in an office building, and carry a briefcase. That was my goal after I left school. I thought that was the bee's knees of success.

Michael: I was fully prepared to go do that in Manhattan as well.

Nick: I didn't care what I did so long as I caught a train, worked in a building, and carried a suitcase. Everything else was insignificant, but here's what happened. The brother-in-law of a girl I was seeing back in those early days worked for a big, blue ribbon stockbroking firm. He was the accountant and he needed someone to help push paper around, so he said, "You don't know what you want to do. Why don't you come and do this?"

So I started pushing paper around. We were all on one floor in the office and up the way was the private client desk. I wandered on up there one day and there were all the private client advisors. One guy had some chart paper. He was plotting a moving average crossover strategy with pen and paper on the Australian Index Futures. The equivalent of the E-mini S&P 500 futures. That's what he was plotting and that's what he was trading.

I took one look at that chart. I said to him, "What are you doing here?" He said, "When the red line crosses the blue, you buy, and when the red crosses back down, you sell." I could see the trends. By that afternoon, I had gone down to the local stationery store, bought some chart paper, red pen, black pen, blue pen. From that day forward, I started plotting moving average crossovers exactly as that guy was doing. It was trends right there.

Michael: What was the next step?

Nick: I went to the office manager. I said to him, "I'd like to trade futures." He was a wily old guy. He's taking a look at this 18-year-old, and he said,

"If you want to trade futures, you need to have me sign off on the ticket. You write the ticket, and then I will bring it down to the trading floor." Now, if we go back to 1985, I was earning about $12,000 a year, maybe $10,000 a year. The share price index futures back then was a hundred dollars a tick. I was playing with dynamite, and I had no idea.

Bear in mind, all I had was a 5- and 10-day moving average crossover. That was the extent of my trading strategy. No position sizing, no risk management, no nothing. I had to write a ticket, then wait to get into the manager's office so he could sign off. I couldn't even place a stop. I couldn't do anything. It was crazy stuff. That went on for a little while. I can't remember a great deal about where that went from a profitability standpoint because in the heady days prior to 1987 I got pulled into other stuff that I thought was significantly more profitable, which in the end was what blew me up in 1987.

All I had was a 5- and 10-day moving average crossover. That was the extent of my trading strategy.

Michael: That was a foundational, pivotal moment for you?

Nick: If I had stuck with that moving average crossover system, I would've been short into 1987. That's the irony. But I was young. I was stupid. I had no idea what I was doing, jumping from place to place, pot to pot.

I vowed to never make that mistake again, and touch wood, I never have. I guess the big move back into trend following was a few years later, when I came across a random talk.

It was, if you like, a reintroduction to trend following, and more important, it was my first exposure to volatility-adjusted position sizing. Up until then, I knew nothing about that kind of stuff. To hear that talk about that was like, "Wow. Yeah, I get it." That's a big part of the equation that I had not even considered.

Michael: It's rare that people are willing to say, "I was stupid." I don't hear that often. So many people are looking to save face and keep the illusion going. There's power in saying, "I was stupid," because it's Zen in a way. It's an acknowledgement to let go and move on. A lot of people would do the opposite of what you said. They would never admit they were stupid, and they keep trying to rationalize something and hang onto it. This gets into the psychology, doesn't it?

Nick: I'm on the wrong side of 50 now. I can reflect and think of all the things I've done and some things I'm not proud of. You can't change it though. All you can do is take the lesson, build experience, and keep moving forward. I took a lesson in 1987. You got to learn to lose money before you can learn to make money in my view, and I certainly did that, and I understand what went wrong and how it went wrong. There were a lot of bad things going on there with regard to leverage, and stupidity, and no position sizing. I don't have enough time to talk through all of them, it was a tsunami of all these things coming together.

Michael: You were a young guy, you were randomly exposed to a strategy, and you immediately believed in it. You don't think to yourself, "I've got a certain type of personality, I can't accept this strategy. I must go analyze my personality, and then come back to find out if this strategy fits with me."

Where is the list of the trading styles that coordinate with the personality? There is no such thing. People repeat this stuff and I wonder why. It doesn't make any sense to me. You gave a great example that you weren't trying to think whether it fit your personality or not. You looked at it and said, "True. I believe that. I'm with it."

> You got to learn to lose money before you can learn to make money.

Nick: That's an interesting statement. One could argue that I had no idea. I was a clean slate. I didn't even want to trade; I had no inclination to do so. I didn't know what people were doing. But you make a good point. All of a sudden here was something I wanted to do, where 10 minutes beforehand, I'd never even thought about it. It's not like I had a want to start trading when I started working at the stockbroking firm. I couldn't give a damn. I was only interested in carrying that briefcase on the train and working at a building. That's all I wanted, but there was a trigger there.

Michael: You're a blank slate. You see something and then boom.

Nick: But why and how? I'm not the guy to ask.

Michael: Does it have something to do with truth? That's why it gets back to the measurement of personality. You're a guy that wants to code. You're a guy that wants to look at math. Measurement of personality is subjective. There's nothing objective there.

Nick: Especially when you see my math results from high school and understand I never went to university. I'm the last guy you'd trust to code up a strategy.

Michael: My point is that with your kind of world, my kind of world, we measure things, count things, and try and figure things out. And again, personality is subjective. It's just another story. Can you validate the story? If you can't validate the story, then it's only a story.

Nick: Absolutely, it's a narrative, isn't it? Having a clean slate is one thing. But if we take someone who's in their mid-30s, or mid-40s, and has been exposed to endless Warren Buffett books like most people are, then perhaps they don't have that clean slate. Perhaps they do have an ingrained bias, rightly or wrongly.

Michael: The environment shaped their personality and to go backwards becomes difficult. The environment has taken them to a place where they might not have been if they were a clean slate?

Nick: That's my belief. I get to see that when I'm talking broadly with my clients. A lot of my clients are engineering types, for example airline pilots. They're the kind of people who need to know ahead of time that there's a structure in place.

Michael: A flight plan.

Nick: Correct. They need to know that there's backup buttons, and backup procedures, and whatever else is in place. Same with engineers. You don't randomly dig a hole in the ground somewhere and throw some concrete in there. There's a lot of stuff that goes into what needs to be done for the structural robustness of the building.

Michael: That's a lovely word, isn't it, robustness?

Nick: It's very important and it's not a narrative. That's the difference, but maybe I attract those people. Someone who's a staunch fundamentalist ain't going to pick up the phone and give me a call. Call it selection bias or survivorship bias. I'm not exposed to those that disagree with what I have to say because they don't come across my desk, unless they're trying to be a smart ass, which happens here and there. But for the most part, a lot of my clients are more technical in nature. They're engineers. They're aircraft pilots. They're programmers working IT. That kind of stuff.

Michael: When you were first exposed to the Turtle trading story? We are talking about blank slates, and they are a pretty good example of blank slates, or of the types of individuals that come to you. They were the same types of individuals that Dennis picked as well. When you had that exposure to the Turtle trading story back in the day, did you also see that as a blank slate thing? Did that hit you as, "Wow, that's pretty interesting. They were open to the learning."

Nick: It wasn't so much, "Oh, these guys started with a clean slate like me." That wasn't the thinking. It was more confirming what I was already starting to learn, that every trend starts with a breakout and trend trading is quite possibly one of the easiest ways to create a positive edge. I was getting confirmation that what I was already doing was being done by these guys, and being replicated and taught. That gave me a great deal of confidence to continue. Absolutely a big influence on my life.

Michael: Do you have any other influences that you want to mention, such as people, events, or favorite books that have shaped you?

Nick: Oh, it's a good question.

Michael: A big one I remember is Ed Seykota's famous expression, "Everybody gets what they want."

Nick: He's a big influence. Here's one thing I do on a regular basis. I go and look at the performance tables of all those guys that you talk about.

David Harding, David Druz, DUNN, Campbell, Abraham, Chesapeake (Jerry Parker). I go back and look at their monthly performance tables, especially when I'm having a bit of a rough period. These guys are pushing the button every day, every week, every month, every year for decades. By looking at their monthly performance tables, I can see, "That crap happened to him as well back then. Look, he's had that losing streak. Look, he's actually had a losing year."

It enables me to keep moving forward, knowing that these guys have trodden this path well ahead of me. The same thing happens to them. It's all part and parcel of the journey, and I don't think that's something you get in other kinds of fund management businesses. You usually get an equity curve and comparison to a benchmark, but you don't get that month-to-month split of the performance tables. I encourage my clients and students to heed what these guys have done ahead of us and understand that, hey, this is the journey that they've traveled, and they are considered very good traders. It's going to happen to you.

Michael: I have put a lot of this performance data in my books. I remember when I was doing my *TurtleTrader* book, how excited I was when somebody unexpectedly dropped on me for the first time the monthly Turtle performance data for while they were in the program, which had never been published, and I thought, "Oh my gosh, so fascinating."

But here's the negative to this. I wonder if the last 40 to 50 years will be an aberration, and the reason I say that is because if you look at the trend following space, it got started in the '70s. There are long track records established, but people get old. People go away.

Maybe in the future it becomes harder and harder to see the lesson that you're talking about, which I do believe firmly in. I wonder if there will end up being this 50- or 60-year window of performance data, and that will be it because then everything else will get secretive and disguised in the future. Maybe it'll be harder and harder to find those like-minded people who share the monthly figures.

Nick: Possible. Look at Marty Bergin. He's taken over from Bill Dunn. They're going from strength to strength. You're saying potentially, if I'm reading that or listening correctly, that maybe there's going to be a generation drop out or that's going to be it.

Michael: For example, if I look at AQR, they're managing hundreds of billions in assets. David Harding has been at $30 billion in assets for close to a decade. Many of the great names that we're talking about, even a guy like Bill Dunn probably never got to $2 billion AUM.

This is speculation. I hope I'm completely wrong that this doesn't go away, and that there will continue to be people like Bill Dunn and Marty Bergin doing what they're doing. I hope I'm completely wrong.

Nick: We're going to have to let time take its journey and see where we end up. In this day and age, there's a lot going on with regard to technology that will drive us potentially in vastly different directions to where we were back in the '60s and '70s, and maybe the early '80s, that could certainly lead to a distinct change. Saying that, trends will persist.

Michael: The strategy won't go away. The only way the strategy goes away is if the government rigs the markets to only go sideways.

Nick: It will be interesting to see who's coming up and how they take it on. Let's think of momentum. Momentum is essentially trend following. I don't want to get into the debate about diversified commodities and that kind of stuff. At the end of the day, momentum runs on the same skew that trend following does. If we look at momentum, that's now become one of the biggest academically studied factors of the market over the last 25 years. We go back into the '80s. Nobody was talking about it. It's certainly getting a lot more traction than it was even 15 years ago. That's a good thing.

Michael: Academics threw out two forms of momentum: time series momentum, which is trend following; and cross-sectional momentum, which is relative strength. I always say to people, we can find all the trend following traders, all the time series momentum. We can find that proof. It's harder to find the relative strength track records. They don't exist in the same way that the trend following track records exist.

Nick: I agree with that. You're quite right. I don't know if you remember this, but when you released *The Complete TurtleTrader*, I bought every single copy in Australia.

Michael: Other people need the book too!

Nick: You'll have to do a reprint if you haven't already. I bought every single copy and distributed that book to all my clients. I've never done that before, except for my own book. I still have my original copy of *Turtle Trader*. It's getting a little faded now.

Michael: Sometimes you stumble into things in life, and that was a stumble into for me. I read about that story, and thought, "This isn't real. This didn't happen. This is fake." Then, you get behind the scenes, and you realize…

Nick: Yeah, I bet, which is amazing. One last influence I would mention is Jerry Parker. The guy has been around a long time. He's laid-back. He gives a lot away between the lines.

Most people miss the point of what's going on between the lines. Jerry Parker is one of those guys that can put a nice, strong message, albeit between the lines that rarely people listen to. That's a significant point to make. I especially make it to my clients. Don't listen to Jerry Parker for the sake of doing so. Listen to what the guy is actually saying.

APPENDICES

1

Optionality, Stop Losses, and Running Profits

Never refuse an option when you can get it, cut short your losses, and let your profits run on.

—David Ricardo

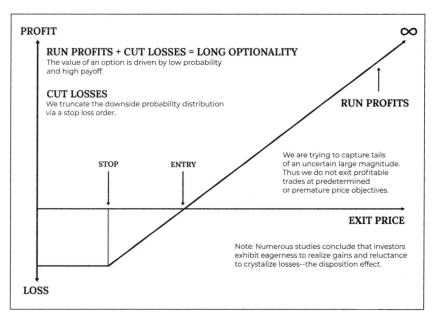

Source: Mulvaney Capital.

2

The Source of Returns Generated by Systematic Trend Following Strategies

For many investors, DUNN Capital's dollar-weighted composite track record, which covers twenty-seven years (now 45 years, as of 2022) of continuous trading, speaks for itself. The returns, which exceed a 23% per annum compound rate, net of all fees, were generated by the consistent application of mathematical models to trading and risk decisions. Over this period, many thousands of trades were undertaken. It does not take any statistical expertise to draw the inference that DUNN's results were produced by design, not luck. This "show me the money" proof is important because of its simplicity. But, it does not explain how these returns were generated or why similar results should be expected to continue.

Price trends are, by definition, price changes that occur over time. In free markets prices change because market participants react to economic events. Trend following pioneers, such as Bill Dunn, observed this fundamental fact and developed systematic methods for capturing large profits from the inevitable trends in market prices produced by economic change in a free society. Moreover, he understood that it was unnecessary to predict price trends, rather he needed mathematical filters that would ensure participation in trending markets and limit trading losses in non-trending markets. In addition, Dunn developed a robust statistical approach that dynamically and constantly managed portfolio risk, thereby controlling losses during extended periods of unfavorable (non-trending) markets.

Thus, the "raw material" of trend following returns is the free market economy and the "production process" is the disciplined application of carefully developed and tested mathematical models for trading and risk management. As long as the markets are free and the trading and risk management disciplines are not violated, the long-term returns from systematic trend following should be expected to continue.

A question that often arises when discussing the returns generated by trend following strategies is: How can returns be extracted consistently from a zero-sum game played in an efficient market? The efficient market hypothesis states that prices in liquid markets reflect all known information at every point in time. This is commonly misinterpreted to mean that nobody can make money from a zero-sum game unless there is some identifiable "inefficiency" to capitalize on. In fact, the theory in no way precludes the possibility that someone may be consistently better at interpreting the available information. In short, traders, including trend followers, may have insights into the market that others do not. It seems reasonable that some people might be smarter than others, thereby profiting from participation in a zero-sum game. But, wouldn't the "dummies" stop playing by choice or be forced to leave the game when they ran out of money? Yes, they would if it were a card game, but it is not. The zero-sum futures markets are an integral part of the world economy and large institutions rarely use them in an isolated way. Such institutions have large balance sheets and use futures to help them manage the pattern of asset returns and liability costs that determine the success of their businesses. The market's biggest loser on a short bond trade may have actually been the biggest winner as bond prices rallied because of positions held in other highly correlated cash, forward and derivative markets. Viewed from this broader perspective, the futures markets combined with related markets are not a zero-sum game.

Moreover, because the efficient market theory states that price embodies all information available at any point in time, DUNN appropriately uses price as its only model input variable. Instead of sifting through the welter of fundamental facts and opinions that constantly swirl around the markets, and then making some sort of prediction, DUNN analyzes the one piece of information that is distilled from this mass of data by market participants themselves.

To summarize, DUNN has developed statistically robust computer models using price to produce trading decisions that systematically capture large price changes over time. Equally important, DUNN dynamically models and manages the risk profile of its futures portfolios. As long as free markets exist, prices will change in response to the inevitable forces of human nature underlying all economic activity and trend followers like DUNN will be in a position to reap the rewards of their disciplined methodology.

_____

For a much more in-depth discussion about the trending behavior of futures prices read:

"Is Real-World Price a Tale Told by the Idiot of Chance?" by Paul A. Samuelson, *The Revue of Economics and Statistics* (MIT Press-1976): 120–121.

Selected Writings on Futures Markets, Vols. 1&2, Anne E. Peck, editor.

Michael Note

While this Dunn article is almost 20 years old, it's timeless education. That's why I included it.

_____

3

DUNN Capital Process Chart

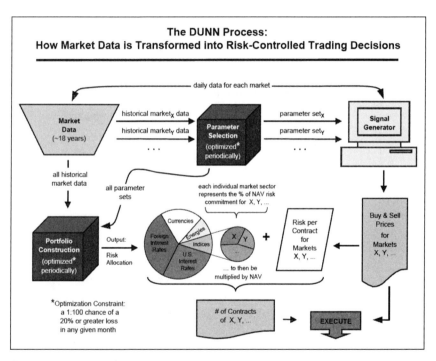

The DUNN Process:
How Market Data is Transformed into Risk-Controlled Trading Decisions

Source: Dunn Capital.

4

DUNN Capital Performance

One of the most important charts in the history of investments.

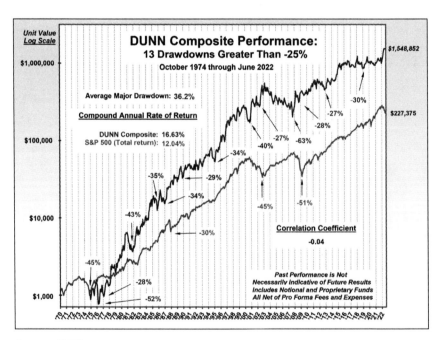

Unit Value Log Scale

DUNN Composite Performance:
13 Drawdowns Greater Than -25%
October 1974 through June 2022

$1,548,852

$1,000,000

Average Major Drawdown: 36.2%

Compound Annual Rate of Return

DUNN Composite: 16.63%
S&P 500 (Total return): 12.04%

$100,000

$227,375

-30%

-27%

-28%

-27% -63%

-40%

-34%

-35% -29%

-34%

-45% -51%

-43%

$10,000

-30%

Correlation Coefficient
-0.04

-45%

-28%

$1,000

-52%

Past Performance is Not Necessarily Indicative of Future Results
Includes Notional and Proprietary Funds
All Net of Pro Forma Fees and Expenses

Source: CFTC.

264

5 Mulvaney Capital Performance

Mulvaney Capital is run by Paul Mulvaney. Paul is featured in my "Little Book of Trading." I include this performance table for two reasons: it's great and I want you to reverse engineer it.

	JAN	FEB	MAR	APR	MAY	JUN	JUL	AUG	SEP	OCT	NOV	DEC	YEAR
2022	14.71%	6.49%	21.57%	26.45%	5.08%	-4.45%	4.90%	2.47%	9.96%	9.86%	-21.18%	1.40%	87.79%
2021	2.21%	13.98%	0.90%	8.52%	-5.44%	-0.14%	3.43%	-2.58%	-11.87%	2.41%	0.62%	19.63%	32.93%
2020	-5.58%	-6.99%	31.16%	-0.46%	-4.97%	6.92%	9.04%	29.96%	-23.00%	-12.00%	-5.39%	0.88%	18.53%
2019	-19.33%	-2.94%	10.05%	-1.89%	-7.23%	4.57%	15.55%	16.15%	-1.12%	-25.79%	15.60%	-6.35%	-21.28%
2018	12.99%	-15.33%	-6.57%	3.46%	-0.41%	-4.53%	-5.42%	2.38%	-8.08%	10.68%	-2.29%	7.93%	-4.33%
2017	-6.33%	9.23%	-7.77%	8.97%	-8.35%	27.33%	-1.01%	-13.30%	18.22%	-10.77%	-0.71%	-5.05%	1.57%
2016	5.94%	10.75%	-13.52%	-2.84%	4.13%	-6.07%	4.77%	-9.23%	6.15%	-11.05%	13.52%	-2.10%	-1.82%
2015	6.93%	-0.50%	3.84%	-7.98%	-4.47%	2.37%	2.25%	9.33%	17.69%	-1.67%	13.05%	9.05%	-0.77%
2014	-1.46%	1.36%	4.65%	2.67%	0.13%	-3.15%	-4.03%	-10.90%	2.61%	7.29%	11.58%	-1.24%	67.36%
2013	10.46%	7.39%	9.29%	9.73%	-0.90%	-18.12%	11.38%	-6.26%	-8.58%	-15.07%	-0.97%	0.76%	43.12%
2012	-3.75%	0.78%	5.21%	-1.08%	-11.82%	-7.41%	11.15%	1.59%	-4.20%	-14.14%	12.05%	-1.64%	-33.72%
2011	2.07%	9.78%	-4.62%	6.07%	-8.77%	0.53%	-12.03%	14.59%	16.46%	22.29%	-5.36%	25.30%	-5.26%
2010	-3.84%	-7.15%	-5.15%	2.02%	-1.30%	-6.81%	-0.53%	10.85%	1.32%	-7.86%	10.70%	-3.19%	34.90%
2009	1.60%	-0.03%	-3.36%	-5.51%	5.35%	8.51%	-18.78%	-6.73%	11.58%	45.49%	6.97%	5.30%	-5.90%
2008	21.65%	28.86%	-7.96%	-8.58%	4.70%	4.85%	-16.89%	-19.40%	3.92%	13.72%	-8.59%	8.47%	108.87%
2007	0.56%	-5.18%	-8.82%	2.59%	-4.27%	-6.10%	-5.20%	1.95%	1.00%	-0.13%	0.56%	1.60%	-23.14%
2006	11.09%	-2.70%	13.05%	11.46%	-4.08%	5.32%	6.62%	2.78%	13.57%	-5.64%	15.27%	8.35%	21.94%
2005	-4.28%	0.54%	2.30%	-9.28%	-6.99%	-0.73%	-0.41%	-6.21%	7.76%	0.76%	9.63%	-4.94%	32.34%
2004	4.19%	8.45%	2.37%	-11.50%	7.64%	-7.61%	-6.33%	0.07%	6.66%	15.32%	-0.27%	5.35%	-0.10%
2003	13.20%	7.22%	-12.83%	1.45%	6.75%	7.38%	5.95%	5.44%	5.13%	-7.73%	-5.08%	7.80%	29.28%
2002		–	-7.52%	1.55%									19.37%
2001	-9.62%	18.76%	13.46%	-15.25%	-0.66%	5.39%	-1.26%						6.69%
2000	-5.02%	2.52%	-8.40%	-0.27%	6.97%	1.55%	-1.25%	12.68%	-4.36%	1.96%	9.05%	8.90%	24.51%
1999		–			-0.29%	-0.14%	-2.22%	2.13%	-4.81%	-4.80%	7.01%	4.84%	1.09%

Source: USA CFTC.

265

6 Purple Valley Capital Performance

Purple Valley Capital is run by Donald Wieczorek. Again, reverse engineer this. That's your assignment.

YEAR	JAN	FEB	MAR	APR	MAY	JUN	JUL	AUG	SEP	OCT	NOV	DEC	YEAR
2022	12.80%	8.30%	12.41%	25.82%	-5.71%	-9.47%	-1.24%	-2.23%	-1.66%	-2.77%	-12.22%	-13.03%	72.78%
2021	7.86%	35.24%	19.40%	3.67%	-5.61%	-12.99%	27.16%	10.83%	-21.09%	10.62%	20.66%	51.81%	8.62%
2020	-0.69%	17.65%	56.50%	-11.45%	5.92%	2.19%	-17.34%	24.86%	-19.57%	0.37%	0.45%	10.08%	199.65%
2019	-7.79%	8.24%	-12.08%	5.09%	-22.21%	4.82%	-4.60%	14.49%	0.20%	-16.71%	12.92%	3.06%	-8.07%
2018	17.56%	-16.35%	-4.16%	-0.62%	-3.56%	-2.78%	0.68%	-0.41%	-8.35%	7.44%	3.96%	0.25%	-18.97%
2017	-6.14%	-0.70%	-2.93%	0.86%	-10.12%	-6.89%	3.01%	-12.34%	-10.60%	1.06%	2.97%	-2.02%	-11.95%
2016	-1.21%	4.33%	-16.59%	18.18%	-6.87%	-9.48%	13.30%	-0.67%	4.45%	-15.83%	10.72%	-9.26%	-30.01%
2015	19.00%	-5.65%	2.15%	-9.01%	-8.09%	11.12%	-7.44%	1.14%	33.18%	0.70%	13.47%	6.37%	-12.56%
2014	2.93%	8.82%	6.88%	1.42%	6.30%	9.50%	-7.92%	3.34%	-10.59%	-15.49%	-2.23%	0.58%	87.94%
2013	3.15%	-11.19%	-4.75%	6.92%	15.27%	-11.55%	10.54%	3.26%	-2.92%	-10.66%	-1.74%	3.42%	-23.21%
2012	-3.14%	12.48%	-1.84%	-6.34%	-17.28%	-12.14%	-0.79%	17.05%	-5.17%	-17.47%	1.48%	-0.06%	2.73%
2011	-0.61%	18.00%	-0.52%	13.64%	0.67%	5.33%	-16.07%	-1.70%	32.59%	28.39%	0.99%	23.32%	-11.17%
2010	-8.48%	-6.65%	-2.46%	-0.77%	38.24%	-13.27%	2.31%	11.66%	2.94%	-2.10%	27.26%	-21.51%	53.36%
2009	-12.07%	3.14%	-5.74%	-1.68%									15.89%
2008								10.83%	0.86%	47.09%	5.79%	-1.79%	70.81%

Source: USA CFTC.

7

The Importance of Curiosity
for Trend Followers

A top CEO recently spoke before a Harvard MBA class. A student asked, "What do I do?"

He replied, "Take the rest of the money you have not spent on tuition and do something else."

If you are curious you will figure out *why*.

However, curiosity has been lobotomized from many. Freud lamented: "What a distressing contrast between the radiant intelligence of a child and the feeble mentality of the average adult."

Today, many are waiting for an order to act.

Simple childlike curiosity with no agenda except to know—that's the real path. That is the precious commodity, the secret weapon. Kids have that wide-eyed wonderment when they take apart their first toy to figure out how it works—and so should you. As simplistic as it sounds, maintaining childlike wonder and enthusiasm keeps your mental doors open.

Curiosity is the reason I wake up to go digging in the sometimes secretive world of trend following trading.

Taking little at face value and always questioning the system is my modus operandi. With the way I am talking do you think teachers liked it when I raised my hand? Bloodhounds find things—sometimes things people want hidden.

One of the more unlikely people to have asked me, "How do you go about unearthing details?" was former U.S.S.R. President Mikhail Gorbachev.

He had been told in Russian via a translator that my career involved traders who make big money. When an introduction was made he asked in Russian through his translator: "What is it like to write about these traders?"

My brief response: "Very interesting."

He waited for the translation: "It must be difficult to get behind the scenes; how do you do it?"

With a smile I replied, "Oh, I am very good at digging."

He laughed. No translation needed. He understood my English perfectly from the start.

My education comes directly from some of the great trend traders of the last five decades. No hyperbole. However, it did not start that way.

It started while finishing grad school in London (school was a mistake, but London and travel was not). The book *Unlimited Power* by motivational speaker Anthony Robbins convinced me that getting close to great traders was the solution.

That sounded easy, but how to do it?

One part of Robbins's book smacked me upside the head.

Unlimited Power featured a story about director Steven Spielberg.

His life changed when he took a tour of Universal Studios at the age of 17. The tour didn't make it to where all the action was, so Spielberg took his own action. He sneaked off to watch the filming of a real movie. Later, he ended up meeting the head of Universal's editorial department, who expressed an interest in one of his early films.

For most people, that is where the story would have ended, but Spielberg wasn't like most. He kept pushing by meeting directors, writers, and editors—learning, observing, and developing more and more sensory acuity about what actually worked in moviemaking (excerpt: *Unlimited Power*).

That Spielberg story was the motivation I needed.

For example, I once flew to Berlin, Germany, spending thousands of dollars not in my bank account, for the chance to possibly meet and learn from a few traders at a conference—a conference where no one knew my name.

My credentials were a nametag and moxie, but that calculated gamble, that intuitive belief that I would find the unexpected, worked out enough to spend quality time with a former chairman of the CME.

Those early efforts continually allowed face-to-face access to legendary traders—enough personal contact to see that they put their pants on like everyone else and that what they were doing could be learned.

Attendance at those secluded conferences triggered my confidence and passion.

Unfortunately, we have a culture where that go figure it out attitude is not the norm. Children grow up with soccer leagues and spelling bees where everyone gets a prize.

On the playgrounds dodge ball is too traumatic.

Parents now consider musical chairs dangerously exclusionary.

Those kids will never be curious. They will end up addicted to Xanax-Ritalin sprinkled cupcakes so they can cope. Am I being a pessimistic grouch? Far from it—just describing the playing field's status quo.

What are some ways that I have learned about the right direction?:

- Bring joyful, imaginative and impassioned energy every day. Don't fake it.
- You don't need to be big to be good, you need to be smart.
- When there is no one there, insert yourself. Take over.
- Engage the world as if your life depends on it.
- Nothing is more important than transforming someone.
- Have a vision grounded in your uniqueness.
- The race winner is often curious and slightly mad.
- Dry obligation in life will figuratively kill you.
- No one will give you permission. Seize the mantle.
- If you can't solve a problem you are playing by the collective's rules.
- Hard work, sustained concentration, and drive are the so-called secrets.
- Winners understand sunk costs and opportunity costs.
- Plan to win, prepare to win, and have every right to expect to win.
- It's in your power to change your belief systems. No one is stuck Be unstuck.
- Winning is never about your limited resources, but rather always about your unlimited resourcefulness.
- By not questioning the world you always lose.

Those are not necessarily intuitive.

Society doesn't encourage and celebrate the unproven striver.

It is much safer to beat up new thought or heap scorn. Too many are encouraged to take the safe path.

This is awful and shortsighted advice.

And for those who complain they were born without a silver spoon, who think they need more money to start, who say that they were not blessed to have trend following rules in their early 20s (like the famous Turtle Traders), money cannot compensate for a lack of talent, sloth, flawed vision, or a pedestrian frame of mind.

Nothing can keep you from winning if winning is what you want.

To think otherwise suggests a lack of imagination and a failure of the optimism needed for attracting good things.

No optimism?

Stop now.

But if you have a pulse still, never forget these wise words: "The phrases gifted musician, natural athlete, and innate intelligence are genetic prisons. Abilities are not set in genetic stone. They are soft and sculptable far into adulthood. With humility, hope, and extraordinary determination, greatness is something everyone can aspire to."

And always, "Serendipity rules!"

Michael Covel

ABOUT
MICHAEL COVEL

Michael Covel searches. He digs. He goes behind the curtain to reveal a state of mind the system doesn't want you in. Characterized as essential and required reading, Michael teaches beginners to seasoned pros how to generate profits with straightforward and repeatable rules. He is best known for popularizing the counterintuitive and controversial trading strategy, trend following.

An avowed entrepreneur, Michael is the author of six books including the international bestseller, *Trend Following*, and his investigative narrative, *TurtleTrader*. Fascinated by secretive traders that have quietly generated spectacular returns for seven decades, those going against the investment orthodoxy of buy and hope, he has uncovered astonishing insights about the right way to think, develop, and execute trend following systems.

Michael's perspectives have garnered international acclaim and have earned him invitations with a host of organizations: China Asset Management, GIC Private Limited (a Singapore sovereign wealth fund), BM&F Bovespa, the Managed Funds Association, Bank of China Investment Management, the Market Technicians Association, and multiple hedge funds and mutual funds.

He also has the distinction of having interviewed seven Nobel Prize winners, including Daniel Kahneman and Harry Markowitz, and he has been featured in major media outlets, including *The Wall Street Journal*, Bloomberg, CCTV, *The Straits Times*, and Fox Business.

Michael posts on Twitter, publishes a blog, and records his podcast weekly. His consulting clients are across hedge funds, sovereign wealth funds, institutional investors, and individual traders in more than 70 countries. He splits his time between the United States and Asia.

Author's Note

If you would like to reach me directly, I can be found here:
www.trendfollowing.com/contact

My podcast can be found here:
www.trendfollowing.com/podcast

All of my books and foreign translations can be found here:
www.trendfollowing.com/translations

My training courses and trend following systems can be found here:
www.trendfollowing.com/products

To receive my free interactive trend following presentation, send a picture of your book receipt to:
receipt@trendfollowing.com.

A big thank you to my assistant Joanne Umali. She put in many long hours to help me pull all of this great content together.